CONGRESSIONAL ELECTIONS

SAGE ELECTORAL STUDIES YEARBOOK

Other volumes in this series:

1. The Future of Political Parties
   LOUIS MAISEL and PAUL M. SACKS, editors
2. Changing Campaign Techniques: Elections and Values in Contemporary Democracies
   LOUIS MAISEL, editor
3. The Impact of the Electoral Process
   LOUIS MAISEL and JOSEPH COOPER, editors
4. Political Parties: Development and Decay
   LOUIS MAISEL and JOSEPH COOPER, editors
5. Political Finance
   HERBERT E. ALEXANDER, editor
6. Congressional Elections
   LOUIS SANDY MAISEL and JOSEPH COOPER, editors

SAGE ELECTORAL STUDIES YEARBOOK
VOLUME 6

Congressional Elections

edited by
LOUIS SANDY MAISEL
and
JOSEPH COOPER

SAGE PUBLICATIONS Beverly Hills London

For information address:

SAGE Publications, Inc.
275 South Beverly Drive
Beverly Hills, California 90212

SAGE Publications Ltd
28 Banner Street
London EC1Y 8QE, England

Printed in the United States of America

Library of Congress Cataloging in Publication Data

Main entry under title:
Congressional elections.

(Sage electoral studies yearbook; v. 6)
Bibliography: p.
1. United States. Congress—Elections, 1978—Addresses, essays, lectures. I. Maisel, Louis. II. Cooper, Joseph.
JK1968 1978.C64 324.973'0926 80-28704
ISBN 0-8039-1568-3
ISBN 0-8039-1569-1 (pbk.)

FIRST PRINTING

CONTENTS

INTRODUCTION

This sixth volume of the Sage Electoral Studies Yearbook is unique in many ways. First, all of the articles deal with one dataset, the 1978 American National Election Study conducted by the Center for Political Studies of the Institute for Social Research at the University of Michigan. Second, each of the articles was written by a scholar who was directly involved in the design of that study. Warren Miller directed the study; Alan Abramowitz, Barbara Hinckley, Gary Jacobson, Tom Mann, Glenn Parker, and Ray Wolfinger were 6 of the 10 congressional elections research scholars who served on the Standing Committee, chaired by Richard Fenno, whose advice was incorporated into the planning of the 1978 study.

In addition, each of these scholars and the editors of this volume were participants in the University of Houston-Rice University Conference on Congressional Elections, held in January 1980. The purpose of that conference, organized by David Brady and Joseph Cooper, was to begin the dissemination of the findings from analysis of the 1978 data.

As editors, our original intent was to publish the best papers from the Houston-Rice Conference. We abandoned that plan for two reasons. First, we knew that two important papers which had been presented elsewhere should be included in any volume collecting articles based on this dataset; the Mann-Wolfinger article and the one by Barbara Hinckley—each first presented as papers at the 1979 Annual Meeting of the American Political Science Association and each already accepted for publication in scholarly journals—are already the subject of intense discussion and certainly merit wider dissemination. Second, Warren Miller presented us with the intriguing possibility of presenting much of the basic data itself to our readership.

We felt immediately that a volume which combined scholarly articles with a presentation of much of the basic data on which these articles were based would be tremendously useful to researchers and to classroom teachers as well. For the research community, this volume provides a ready reference to the key variables explored in the 1978 National Election Study. This volume, then, is of the same genre as the *American National Elections Study Sourcebook, 1952–1978* (Miller et al., 1980), which was published last year and has already proven so helpful to many scholars. This volume is also unique in the opportunities it presents for classroom use. The basic dataset and the five substantive chapters should provide the core reading for an important section of any course on the Congress or on the electoral process. Further, because of the opportunities for comparative analysis, the volume should be most appropriate for a case study approach in courses on research methodology. Rarely have aspiring researchers been given such a clear opportunity to see how leading political scientists make use of the same dataset to attack similar problems.

The organization of this volume is straightforward. In the first chapter, Warren Miller and Jack Kotash explain the study design for the 1978 study and lay out the basic data in a conceptual framework which should ease the task of researchers as they work their way through this wealth of information. In addition, they provide a detailed explication of where the scholars whose articles follow have relied on the same variables in analyzing the data.

While each is unique and important in its own right, the five articles which follow raise a number of recurring themes. Tom Mann and Ray Wolfinger begin the examination of why incumbents are so successful in House elections by exploring what the voters know about the candidates among whom they are choosing. Mann and Wolfinger conclude that previous scholars have underestimated voter awareness by relying too heavily on questions relating to name recall. Voters know a good deal about incumbents and are able to form positive or negative opinions about incumbents even if they cannot recall the incumbents' names. The authors emphasize that the incumbents' uses of the communications resources available to members of the House are important in this regard. They also stress that the seriousness or lack of seriousness of the challengers is a key factor in incumbents' successes which should not be underplayed.

In parallel articles Alan Abramowitz and Barbara Hinckley take up this theme and explore House and Senate differences. Abramowitz examines two models of electoral accountability: a party model in which a judgment of the performance of the President is used as a basis to reward or punish his party in off-Presidential year congressional elections and an individual model in which the judgment is based on the performance of the incumbent. He concludes that the individual accountability model has more explanatory power, that incumbents have more success because they are better known and more positively evaluated than are their challengers. He further concludes that this is more the case in House elections than in Senate elections. Hinckley develops the same theme, in exploring the question of why House incumbents have been much more successful than their Senate counterparts in recent elections. She also finds that the strength of Senate challengers as opposed to the near invisibility of many House challengers (not to mention the number of House incumbents who run unopposed) is the factor which offsets the advantage in recognition and positive evaluation held by incumbents.

In his chapter, Gary Jacobson goes further into the exploration of voter evaluation of incumbents. Jacobson shows that the key factor is not merely incumbency or renown, but the fact that the incumbents are viewed positively by the electorate. Jacobson's contribution is also important because in its final section he cautions scholars about some of the difficulties in drawing general conclusions from a single study. Jacobson shows that the sample used in the 1978 study exaggerates the strengths of incumbents and the weaknesses of challengers in House races.

In the final chapter, Glenn Parker combines data from the 1978 National Election Study with that compiled by the House of Representatives Commission on Administrative Review (the Obey Commission) in 1977 in order to explore why House members are evaluated so positively. Parker maintains that this positive evaluation, with its resultant electoral advantage, can be explained by combining the conclusions of Richard Fenno (1978), Morris Fiorina (1977), and David Mayhew (1974). Parker demonstrates that members do develop individual ways to cultivate their own districts (Fenno's homestyle), that the opportunity to do constituent service leads to a tremendous advantage as Fiorina claims, and that members are adept at translating this advantage into votes by self-advertising (Mayhew's electoral connection). Parker's conclusion is that incumbent popularity and concomitant electoral success can be explained in terms of members' raising their constituents' consciousness of those activities which generate positive images.

Taken together, these articles provide important insights into the congressional elections process and how scholars study it. In presenting this volume of the Sage Electoral Studies Yearbook, we want to acknowledge our debt to the scholars who have contributed to it and helped us develop this means of presenting new data on congressional elections. We would be remiss if we did not single out Warren Miller for special thanks. We share with the entire community of congressional elections research scholars the knowledge that not only this book but all of our efforts in the years ahead will be enhanced because of his enterprise, foresight, and skill.

Louis Sandy Maisel
Joseph Cooper

REFERENCES

FENNO, R. F., Jr. (1978) Home Style: House Members in Their Districts. Boston: Little, Brown.

FIORINA, M. P. (1977) Congress: Keystone of the Washington Establishment. New Haven, CT: Yale University Press.

MAYHEW, D. (1974) Congress: The Electoral Connection. New Haven, CT: Yale University Press.

MILLER, W. E. et al. (1980) American National Elections Study Sourcebook, 1952–1978. Cambridge, MA: Harvard University Press.

1

DESIGN AND CORE DATA FOR THE 1978 ELECTION STUDY

WARREN E. MILLER
JOHN P. KATOSH

I
STUDY DESCRIPTION

The American National Election Study, 1978, was conducted by the Center for Political Studies of the Institute for Social Research, The University of Michigan, under the direction of Warren E. Miller. It is the 15th in a series of studies of national elections produced by the Political Behavior Program of the Survey Research Center and the Center for Political Studies. Although 15th in the series, the 1978 study is the first to be conducted under a grant from the National Science Foundation (Grant # SOC77-08885) providing long-term support for national election studies.

A total of 2304 respondents were interviewed in a sample of 108 congressional districts after the 1978 congressional elections.

The research design called for the selection of about 100 congressional districts where approximately 2500 interviews would be conducted following the 1978 congressional elections. The design stipulated that, on the average, 25 personal interviews were desired from each congressional district. Congressional districts constituted the primary sampling areas. The sample for the 1978 election study met two objectives:

(1) a probability sample of U.S. citizens 18 years of age or older who resided in housing units within the 48 contiguous states (the District of Columbia was excluded) exclusive of housing units on military bases

(2) a probability sample of congressional districts in coterminous United States, inclusive of states with at-large districts.

Region, as defined by the Census Bureau four-fold classification, was another valid level of analysis for the 1978 election sample: State, however, was not.

The universe of 432 eligible congressional districts constituted a rather heterogeneous collection. For sampling purposes, these districts were divided into 108 strata, each containing four congressional districts of roughly comparable characteristics that included, insofar as possible, homogeneity with respect to geographic region, state, urbanization, and recent voting behavior. From each of the 108 strata, one district was then selected with probability of selection in proportion to the 1975 estimated population for a total of 108 districts in the 1978 election study sample.

Sampling districts with probabilities proportionate to 1975 estimated populations was an attempt to counteract shifts in population since 1970. However, creating strata that were homogeneous with respect to state contributed to inequalities in strata sizes and, consequently, in sample sizes when a self-weighting sample of housing was to be maintained. In spite of all reasonable efforts to locate areas of major new construction or demolition within sample areas, achievement was imperfect; these conditions accounted for some of the variations in district sizes.

While the 1978 election study sample was designed to yield estimates for congressional districts, the sample was *not* intended to produce estimates of *each* district's constituency. The within-district sampling of constituents was conducted so as to keep sampling and field costs within reasonable bounds. Ideally, the within-district sampling would have distributed sample selections across the district. However, this specification would have been impossible to satisfy within the constraints of a number of interviews at reasonable costs. When the district was part of a major city, the sample of 8 or 10 clusters was distributed across the district. But as population density declined, the district sample was confined to a part of the geographic area. When the district included many counties, generally only one was selected for the sample. In all districts and at each stage of sampling, strict probability sampling procedures were used. Selections of household clusters were spread within the defined district sample areas as much as possible with the understanding, however, that such selections would never mirror within-district heterogeneity or serve as a basis for district estimates.

At the overall sampling rate of 1 in 5040, approximately 948 clusters averaging about four housing units were designated for the sample. A total of 3346 households were contacted for participation in the study. In 2304 of these (68.9%), an interview was completed with the household member designated as the respondent through an objective selection procedure allowing for no substitutions. Refusals accounted for 22.6% of the noninterviews; still other reasons including sickness, language difficulties, being away on vacation, and so on accounted for the remaining 8.5% of the noninterviews.

The primary objective of this study was to analyze the attitudes and behavior of the American electorate in the context of the 1978 congressional elections. Major emphasis was placed on the respondents' evaluations of their district's candidates—both the incumbent and opponent—along several dimensions. They were asked to assess the candidates in terms of their issue orientation, performance in office and behavior during the campaign, and the ability of each candidate to represent the interests of the constituency. Respondents were also asked whether they had ever had any personal contact with their representative. Similar questions were asked about the Senate candidates in the states where such elections were held in 1978.

Respondents were also asked to evaluate the media coverage of the various electoral contests. Other items dealt with the respondents' interest in the campaign and their actual voting behavior in the 1978 election. In addition, the respondents were asked to report their feelings about potential presidential candidates in 1980. A series of questions focused on President Carter and his handling of specific issues, such as the economy.

As in the past, the questionnaire included an inquiry into the major problems facing the country. A series of scales measured the respondent's position, as well as the perceived position of the political parties and of certain political leaders—including congressional and Senate candidates—with regard to such issues as urban unrest, protection of the rights of the accused, aid to minority groups, a government insurance plan, and women's role in society.

The personal data section contained information on the respondent's education, occupation, age, sex, marital status, socioeconomic status, ethnic background, and religious affiliation. Parallel information on education and occupation was ascertained for the spouse.

The preparation of the 1978 interview schedule was a collaborative venture involving the Center for Political Studies (CPS) staff, the National Election Studies Board of Overseers, and a Standing Committee of congressional elections research scholars. The substantive decisions and recommendations of these groups were formed by opinions and preferences voiced at board-sponsored conferences attended by other members of the political science discipline and the social science community at large. The content of the interview schedule emphasizes questions and issues relevant to the study of the dynamics of congressional elections. To further facilitate this line of inquiry, the sampling frame had been redefined for this study, with congressional districts designated as primary areas for sampling purposes as described above.

During planning for the 1978 study, members of the Board of Overseers were: Heinz Eulau, Chair, Stanford University; Kristi Andersen, Ohio State University; Richard F. Fenno, Jr., University of Rochester; John E. Jackson, University of Pennsylvania; Warren E. Miller, ex officio, University of Michigan; Benjamin I. Page, University of Chicago; David O. Sears, University of California, Los Angeles; J. Merrill Shanks, University of California, Berkeley; and John Sprague, Washington University.

The composition of the Standing Committee during the planning for the 1978 study was as follows: Committee Chairman, Richard F.

Fenno, Jr., University of Rochester; Subcommittee on Contextual Data: Gerald C. Wright, Jr., Chair, Florida Atlantic University; Alan I. Abramowitz, The College of William and Mary; Gary C. Jacobson, Trinity College; and Glenn R. Parker, Miami University. Subcommittee on Interview Design: David R. Mayhew, Yale University, Chair; Morris P. Fiorina, California Institute for Technology; Barbara Hinckley, University of Wisconsin—Madison; Thomas E. Mann, Assistant Director, American Political Science Association; Raymond E. Wolfinger, University of California, Berkeley. (For a detailed account of the planning of this study, see Board of Overseers, 1979: 4–14.)

CONTEXTUAL DATA STUDY

Included in the 1978 election study are "contextual" data which were collected from various sources and then added to the respondent's file. Some of these data pertain to the voting returns at the county, congressional district, and state levels for the 1972, 1976, and 1978 national elections. Others contain information on the congressional candidates and incumbents from the 108 congressional districts included in the survey. The eight contextual datasets that have been added to the 1978 election study survey data are: (1) historical election returns (1972, 1974, and 1976); (2) the 1978 election returns; (3) incumbency characteristics; (4) candidate characteristics; (5) registration and voting records check; (6) election materials checklist; (7) media structure; and (8) Federal Election Commission data.

The Historical Election Returns Data contain state, congressional district, and county returns for the 1972 and 1976 presidential elections plus state, county, and congressional district returns for the 1972, 1974, and 1976 senatorial and gubernatorial election. With the exception of the 1976 election returns at the congressional district level for the offices of President, Senator, and Governor, which were supplied by Congressional Quarterly, Inc., the returns reported have been provided by the Inter-university Consortium for Political and Social Research.

The 1978 Election Returns Data have information on the Democratic and Republican primary election winners and runners-up as well as the returns from the general election. These data include county level primary election returns for the U.S. Senate and gubernatorial races; congressional district primary election returns for the congressional race; state and county election returns for the senatorial and gubernatorial general elections; and county and congressional district returns for the congressional elections. These data were obtained from official reports produced by state and county election officials.

The Incumbency Characteristics Data include information pertaining to the incumbent U.S. Representative of the 95th Congress in each of the 108 congressional districts sampled in the survey. Biographical data on the incumbents were obtained from the following sources: U.S. Congress, Congressional Directory, 1978, 1979; congressional Quarterly, Inc., Washington Information Directory, 1978–79, 1978; Bronson, Charles B., Congressional Staff Directory, 1978; Michael Barone, Grant Ujifusa, and Douglas Matthews, The Almanac of American Politics, 1976 and 1978; Congressional Quarterly, Inc., Electing Congress, 1978. A major feature of this dataset is the series of performance ratings that each member of Congress received from certain interest groups and also from the Congressional Quarterly. The 11 interest groups included in this series were selected mainly because of their prior appearance in the Almanac of American Politics, 1978. The ratings for the incumbents in 1977 and 1978 were obtained directly from the reporting groups' national offices in Washington, D.C., and are not contained in the 1978 edition of the almanac. In two instances, the AFL-CIO Committee on Political Education and the National Farmers Union, "scores" were not reported by the group. Rather, they were calculated by the CPS staff by dividing the number of "correct" votes by the total number of votes considered by the group. The six Congressional Quarterly ratings were obtained from that organization's Weekly Report appearing in January and December of 1978.

The Candidate Characteristics Data apply to the Democratic and Republican candidates for the office of U.S. House of Representatives in the 1978 general election. These data were obtained from a 1978 candidate questionnaire that was administered by Congressional Quarterly, Inc., and sent to all candidates. If a questionnaire was not returned or returned incomplete, other sources were used to retrieve biographical information for the candidate. These additional sources included: Congressional Quarterly's candidate questionnaires from a previous election year; biographical information that was supplied by the candidate's campaign headquarters or that appeared in a Congressional Quarterly Weekly Report; the special election issue of Congressional Quarterly's Weekly Report issued on October 14, 1978; and for the candidates who were incumbents, the Incumbency Characteristics dataset.

The Registration and Voting Records Check Data report the effort to validate the responses about registration and voting behavior made by all of the respondents in the study. For the first time, in 1978 respondents were asked not only whether they were registered to vote but also the address at which they were registered. Personal visits were made by members of the Survey Research Center field staff during February and March 1979 to the local governmental offices charged with the responsibility for maintaining registration and voting records in places where the survey respondents resided. Telephone calls were made by CPS staff members to those places outside the study sample when a respondent claimed to be registered in such an area. In the cases of 35 respondents who did not provide the interviewers with their names and another 4 respondents who reported being registered at a different address but who did not provide that address to the interviewer, it was impossible to perform the records check. Additionally, this dataset includes two groups of precinct level primary and general election returns for the 1978 gubernatorial, senatorial, and congressional elections.

The 1978 Election Materials Checklist contains information collected by the Survey Research Center staff at the same time they conducted the Registration and Voting Records Check. The Survey Research Center staff was instructed to collect a series of items pertaining to the administration of elections in the local area. The materials included: sample ballots, the precinct level election returns and registration figures, lists of polling places, poll hours, election maps, and information about registering and voting. The materials themselves are stored at the Center for Political Studies in Ann Arbor. Anyone may ask for and obtain access to this data by visiting the center. However, individuals who desire such access should make their request in writing and allow enough lead time so the center staff can provide the necessary materials, facilities, and workplace.

The Media Structure Data contain information about the television coverage of each county in which a respondent resides as well as the Area of Dominant Influence (ADI) which covers that county. These data include the number of television households in the county and ADI, the relative ranking of the ADI, and the number of congressional districts covered completely or partially by the ADI.

The Campaign Finance Data contain information about the total amount of campaign receipts and disbursements for the 1976 and 1978 Senate and House election campaigns. The data are reported separately for each of the major party candidates and summed when there were two or more minor party candidates on the ballot (and filing a report).

The data for the 1976 elections were obtained from the Federal Elections Commission (FEC) Disclosure Series; No. 6: 1976 Senatorial Campaigns Receipts and Expenditures (April, 1977); and No. 9: 1976 House of Representatives Campaigns Receipts and Expenditures (September 1977). The data for the 1978 elections were obtained from the Federal Elections Commission Reports on Financial Activity 1977–1978; Interim Report No. 5: U.S. Senate and House Campaigns (June 1979). The FEC figures reported for the 1976 elections cover all campaign finance activity for the period of January 1, 1975, to December 31, 1976. The FEC figures reported for the 1978 elections are of an interim nature and cover the period beginning January 1, 1977. The final report will not be issued until "the end of the 1977–1978 election cycle." The figures for 1976 and 1978, therefore, represent a combination of primary and general election receipts and disbursements.

CENSUS DATA

In addition to the contextual data that were added to the 1978 election study, special subsets of the Congressional District Data Book (93rd Congress) and the County and City Data Book, 1972—data files for the 108 congressional districts and the 123 counties contained in the survey—have been prepared by the Inter-university Consortium for Political and Social Research.

All variables that are contained in the present consortium Congressional District Data Book file and in the County and City Data Book file (at the county level) are included in these subsets. Further information including technical details is contained in the consortium codebook for the 1978 Election Study from which this description of the study has been abstracted.

II.
SAGE: A SOURCEBOOK OF SELECTED DATA

One of the signs of maturation of a social science discipline is provided by the extent to which private insights are subjected to public examination under common rules extracted from the logic of inquiry. Independent examination of the *evidence* supporting or testing an argument is essential to this transformation of knowledge from the private personal domain of the individual scholar to the public domain shared by a community of scholars. This first chapter of this volume has been prepared in the spirit of enhancing the reader's opportunity to make an independent assessment of many of the arguments presented in the five substantive chapters and to permit exploration of some of the implications of extending or interrelating important conclusions suggested by the various authors.

The following presentation of data is, however, by no means exhaustive, and the further extension of many lines of inquiry is possible only by going to the entire file of original data maintained for public use by the Inter-university Consortium for Political and Social Research.[1] Indeed, a secondary motive for the following presentation of data is that of stimulating scholars to go beyond the work presented in this book and pursue independent investigations of questions that may be suggested but not fully explored here. Our own examination of the data as presented suggests that they raise as many new questions as they resolve; and wonderment about the new questions should lead the reader to the formulation of possible answers (the articulation of hypotheses) that can be tested within the full array of the 1978 dataset. The dual objective of this presentation of data is, therefore, to give the reader an independent base from which to query the work contained in the five chapters which follow the presentation of the data and to stimulate the reader to initiate further research through exploring the full dataset in independent research.

The investigations reported below take particular advantage of many of the data that are more or less unique to the 1978 congressional election study. Although these data were collected to address questions previously raised in the published literature, the data themselves are often "new." Therefore, the individual chapters, and the collections of supporting data, are not centered on the array of data that CPS has collected in earlier studies of congressional elections. Many of those data, including the full array of data pertaining to the social, economic, and political attributes of members of the mass electorate, are presented in the volume of time series data, *The American National Election Studies Data Sourcebook, 1952–1978* (Miller et al., 1980).

ORGANIZATION OF TABLES

Although the data presentation is only partial and limited in the various ways just described, it is a relatively systematic and full presentation within those limits. We have not eliminated individual tables because they seem uninteresting or contain relationships that do not meet some test of statistical significance. Given the ubiquitous influence of party, most of the tables present party affiliation or party identification, either as a descriptor or as a "control" so that one can examine relationships apart from the confounding relationships with partisanship. With candidate incumbency and electoral competition as central themes of the substantive chapters, three of the subsections present data using the "Type of Race" as a constant basis for comparisons. Finally, the ultimate party vote choice of the voters is widely used as the crucial "dependent" variable for assessing the political importance of other variables and variable relationships.

Each of the subsections is characterized by a distinct analytic pattern which is then repeated a number of times as single variables are substituted one for another. A recognition of this repetitive format will help reduce the impression of a massive presentation of data to a realization that there are only a very limited number of analytic themes that are followed. The reader should also come to recognize that the logic connecting various analyses, and interpretations across many tables, can be explicated and enhanced by attention to the marginal totals that are presented. The marginals are always presented for both dimensions of any data array in which a third variable, usually the "dependent" variable, is displayed *within* the categories formed by the bivariate array of two "independent" or control variables.

The first subsection, Tables 1-1 to 1-12, looks at three dependent variables, Turnout, Party Vote Division, and Vote for Incumbent

(text continued on p. 27)

TABLE 1-1

RESPONDENT'S PARTY IDENTIFICATION
BY TYPE OF RACE

Respondent's Party I.D.	Type of Race: Democr. Incumb. Running Contested	Democr. Incumb. Running Uncontested	Repub. Incumb. Running Contested	Repub. Incumb. Running Uncontested	Op.Seat Contested (Dem. Incum.)	Op.Seat Uncontested (Dem. Incum.)	Op.Seat Contested (Rep. Incum.)	Total	
Str. Dem.	18%	17%	11%	11%	17%	13%	16%	15%	[340]
Weak Dem.	27	28	19	25	32	26	24	25	[557]
Ind. Dem.	14	14	15	21	12	29	12	15	[328]
Ind. Ind.	13	14	17	15	9	18	9	14	[312]
Ind. Rep.	11	7	10	10	13	5	6	10	[217]
Weak Rep.	11	12	18	11	9	5	22	13	[292]
Str. Rep.	6	9	10	8	8	3	12	8	[178]
[N]	[886]	[319]	[631]	[121]	[161]	[38]	[68]		[2224]

TABLE 1-2

RESPONDENT'S PARTY IDENTIFICATION
BY TYPE(S) OF RACE

Respondent's Party I.D.	Type(s) of Race: Incumbent Running? Yes	Incumbent Running? No	Contested Race? Yes	Contested Race? No	Totals	
Str. Dem.	15%	16%	15%	15%	15%	[340]
Weak Dem.	25	19	25	27	25	[557]
Ind. Dem.	15	14	14	17	15	[328]
Ind. Ind.	15	11	14	15	14	[312]
Ind. Rep.	10	10	11	7	10	[217]
Weak Rep.	13	12	14	11	13	[292]
Str. Rep.	8	8	8	8	8	[178]
[N]	[1957]	[267]	[1746]	[478]		[2224]

TABLE 1-3

RESPONDENT'S PARTY IDENTIFICATION
BY INCUMBENT'S PARTY AND OPPOSITION

Respondent's Party I.D.	Incumbent's Party and Opposition: Incumbent Running? Yes: Demo-crat	Yes: Repub-lican	No: Open Seat	Incumbent Running? Yes: Con-tested	Yes: Uncon-tested	No: Con-tested	No: Uncon-tested	Totals	
Str. Dem.	18%	11%	16%	15%	15%	17%	13%	15%	[340]
Weak Dem.	27	20	29	24	27	30	26	25	[557]
Ind. Dem.	14	16	14	15	16	12	29	15	[328]
Ind. Ind.	13	16	11	15	14	9	18	14	[312]
Ind. Rep.	9	10	10	10	7	11	5	10	[217]
Weak Rep.	11	17	12	14	12	13	5	13	[292]
Str. Rep.	7	10	8	8	9	9	3	8	[178]
[N]	[1205]	[752]	[267]	[1517]	[440]	[229]	[38]		[2224]

TABLE 1-4

TURNOUT BY TYPE OF RACE
AND RESPONDENT'S PARTY IDENTIFICATION

Respondent's Party I.D.	Type of Race: Democr. Incumb. Running Contested	Democr. Incumb. Running Uncontested	Repub. Incumb. Running Contested	Repub. Incumb. Running Uncontested	Op. Seat Contested (Dem. Incum.)	Op. Seat Uncontested (Dem. Incum.)	Op. Seat Contested (Rep. Incum.)	Total	
Str. Dem.	68	53	60	33	74	...	73	64	[319]
Weak Dem.	46	30	47	09	43	30	56	42	[528]
Ind. Dem.	43	35	58	31	37	36	...	45	[316]
Ind. Ind.	35	39	37	24	27	...	...	35	[307]
Ind. Rep.	48	40	66	64	62	...	...	54	[215]
Weak Rep.	59	45	55	50	43	...	71	55	[273]
Str. Rep.	79	36	79	25	75	...	...	72	[165]
Total	52	38	55	30	51	34	61	50	
[N]	[869]	[277]	[626]	[88]	[159]	[38]	[66]		[2123]

Cell entries are the proportion of respondents who reported voting in the House race in their district.

TABLE 1-5

TURNOUT BY TYPE(S) OF RACE
AND RESPONDENT'S PARTY IDENTIFICATION

Respondent's Party I.D.	Type(s) of Race: Incumbent Running? Yes	Incumbent Running? No	Contested Race? Yes	Contested Race? No	Totals	
Str. Dem.	63	72	67	50	64	[319]
Weak Dem.	42	44	46	25	42	[528]
Ind. Dem.	46	34	34	66	45	[316]
Ind. Ind.	36	25	36	32	35	[307]
Ind. Rep.	54	58	56	49	54	[215]
Weak Rep.	55	57	57	46	55	[273]
Str. Rep.	70	81	80	33	72	[165]
Total	50	51	53	36	50	
[N]	[1860]	[263]	[1720]	[403]		[2123]

Cell entries are the proportion of respondents who reported voting in the House race in their district.

TABLE 1-6

TURNOUT BY INCUMBENT'S PARTY AND OPPOSITION
AND RESPONDENT'S PARTY IDENTIFICATION

Respondent's Party I.D.	Incumbent's Party and Opposition							Totals	
	Incumbent Running?								
	Yes		No	Yes		No			
	Democrat	Republican	Open Seat	Contested	Uncontested	Contested	Uncontested		
Str. Dem.	65	57	72	66	49	74	...	64	[319]
Weak Dem.	42	40	44	46	25	46	30	42	[528]
Ind. Dem.	40	55	34	49	34	33	36	45	[316]
Ind. Ind.	36	35	25	36	34	29	...	35	[307]
Ind. Rep.	47	66	58	55	48	58	...	54	[215]
Weak Rep.	56	55	57	57	46	57	...	55	[273]
Str. Rep.	65	76	81	79	35	85	...	72	[165]
Total	48	52	51	53	36	54	34	50	
[N]	[1146]	[714]	[263]	[1495]	[365]	[225]	[38]		[2123]

Cell entries are the proportion of respondents who reported voting in the House race in their district.

TABLE 1-7

PARTY VOTE BY TYPE OF RACE
AND RESPONDENT'S PARTY IDENTIFICATION

Respondent's Party I.D.	Type of Race							Total	
	Democr. Incumb. Running Contested	Democr. Incumb. Running Uncontested	Repub. Incumb. Running Contested	Repub. Incumb. Running Uncontested	Op.Seat Contested (Dem. Incum.)	Op.Seat Uncontested (Dem. Incum.)	Op.Seat Contested (Rep. Incum.)		
Str. Dem.	97	100	66	...	85	...	...	87	[200]
Weak Dem.	93	100	42	...	96	...	...	80	[210]
Ind. Dem.	92	100	29	...	...	...	...	62	[129]
Ind. Ind.	76	100	17	...	...	...	...	57	[98]
Ind. Rep.	67	...	05	...	...	...	...	38	[109]
Weak Rep.	56	100	05	...	...	...	...	34	[146]
Str. Rep.	30	100	00	...	...	...	...	20	[115]
Total	80	100	23	00	62	100	39	59	
[N]	[430]	[98]	[326]	[25]	[77]	[12]	[39]		[1007]

Cell entries are the proportion of voters who reported voting Democratic in the House race in their district.

TABLE 1-8

PARTY VOTE BY TYPE(S) OF RACE
AND RESPONDENT'S PARTY IDENTIFICATION

Respondent's Party I.D.	Type(s) of Race: Incumbent Running? Yes	Incumbent Running? No	Contested Race? Yes	Contested Race? No	Totals	
Str. Dem.	88	77	86	89	87	[200]
Weak Dem.	79	88	78	92	80	[210]
Ind. Dem.	62	64	60	75	62	[129]
Ind. Ind.	54	100	51	80	57	[98]
Ind. Rep.	41	08	33	60	37	[109]
Weak Rep.	35	25	27	78	34	[146]
Str. Rep.	21	13	13	90	20	[115]
Total	59	59	55	82	59	
[N]	[879]	[128]	[872]	[135]		[1007]

Cell entries are the proportion of voters who reported voting Democratic in the House race in their district.

TABLE 1-9

PARTY VOTE BY INCUMBENT'S PARTY AND OPPOSITION
AND RESPONDENT'S PARTY IDENTIFICATION

Respondent's Party I.D.	Incumbent's Party and Opposition: Incumbent Running? Yes: Demo-crat	Yes: Repub-lican	No: Open Seat	Yes: Con-tested	Yes: Uncon-tested	No: Con-tested	No: Uncon-tested	Totals	
Str. Dem.	98	61	77	88	87	75	100	87	[200]
Weak Dem.	94	40	88	77	91	87	100	80	[210]
Ind. Dem.	94	27	64	60	71	50	100	62	[129]
Ind. Ind.	83	15	100	47	79	100	100	57	[98]
Ind. Rep.	73	05	08	38	57	00	100	37	[109]
Weak Rep.	64	05	25	28	77	20	100	34	[146]
Str. Rep.	43	00	13	14	90	13	...	20	[145]
Total	83	21	59	55	80	54	100	59	
[N]	[528]	[351]	[128]	[756]	[123]	[116]	[12]		[1007]

Cell entries are the proportion of voters who reported voting Democratic in the House race in their district.

TABLE 1-10

INCUMBENCY VOTE BY TYPE OF RACE
AND RESPONDENT'S PARTY IDENTIFICATION

Respondent's Party I.D.	Type of Race								
	Democr. Incumb. Running Contested	Democr. Incumb. Running Uncontested	Repub. Incumb. Running Contested	Repub. Incumb. Running Uncontested	Op.Seat Contested (Dem. Incum.)	Op.Seat Uncontested (Dem. Incum.)	Op.Seat Contested (Rep. Incum.)	Total	
Str. Dem.	97	...	34	...	...	...	...	82	[169]
Weak Dem.	93	...	58	...	...	...	...	84	[176]
Ind. Dem.	92	...	69	...	...	...	...	83	[119]
Ind. Ind.	76	...	83	...	...	...	...	84	[91]
Ind. Rep.	67	...	95	...	...	...	...	83	[96]
Weak Rep.	56	...	95	...	...	...	...	80	[130]
Str. Rep.	30	...	100	...	...	...	...	72	[99]
Total	80	100	77	100	...	...	...	82	
[N]	[430]	[98]	[327]	[25]	[0]	[0]	[0]		[880]

Cell entries are the proportion of voters who reported voting for the Incumbent in the House race in their district.

TABLE 1-11

INCUMBENCY VOTE BY TYPE(S) OF RACE
AND RESPONDENT'S PARTY IDENTIFICATION

Respondent's Party I.D.	Type(s) of Race					
	Incumbent Running?		Contested Race?			
	Yes	No	Yes	No	Totals	
Str. Dem.	82	...	80	100	82	[169]
Weak Dem.	84	...	82	100	84	[176]
Ind. Dem.	83	...	80	100	83	[119]
Ind. Ind.	84	...	79	100	84	[91]
Ind. Rep.	83	...	81	100	83	[96]
Weak Rep.	80	...	77	100	80	[130]
Str. Rep.	72	...	69	100	72	[99]
Total	82	...	79	100	82	
[N]	[880]	[0]	[757]	[123]		[880]

Cell entries are the proportion of voters who reported voting for the Incumbent in the House race in their district.

TABLE 1-12

INCUMBENCY VOTE BY INCUMBENT'S PARTY AND OPPOSITION
AND RESPONDENT'S PARTY IDENTIFICATION

Respondent's Party I.D.	Incumbent's Party and Opposition								
	Incumbent Running? Yes		No	Yes		No		Totals	
	Demo-crat	Repub-lican	Open Seat	Con-tested	Uncon-tested	Con-tested	Uncon-tested		
Str. Dem.	98	39	...	80	100	...	...	82	[169]
Weak Dem.	95	60	...	82	100	...	...	84	[176]
Ind. Dem.	94	72	...	80	100	...	...	83	[119]
Ind. Ind.	83	85	...	79	100	...	...	84	[91]
Ind. Rep.	73	96	...	81	100	...	...	83	[96]
Weak Rep.	65	94	...	77	100	...	...	80	[130]
Str. Rep.	43	100	...	69	100	...	...	72	[99]
Total	83	79	...	79	100	...	...	82	
[N]	[528]	[352]	[0]	[757]	[123]	[0]	[0]		[880]

Cell entries are the proportion of voters who reported voting for the Incumbent in the House race in their district.

Candidates. Each variable, in turn, is summarized within categories of the Party Identification of the mass electorate who are constituents located in various types of congressional districts. The types of districts are described exhaustively in Figure 1. The eight types reflect the complete disaggregation describing any election as (1) contested or uncontested, (2) involving an incumbent as one candidate or an open seat with no incumbent candidate, *and* (3) as an election for a seat previously held by a Democrat or Republican. The five different levels of aggregation or disaggregation of combinations of these three sets of district attributes are displayed in Figure 1 and then first presented in Tables 1-1 to 1-3 (where Tables 1-2 and 1-3 are, in fact, two-part tables, with the parts separated by a double vertical line but combined in one table, to save space, with one level of aggregation presented in each part). Tables 1-4 to 1-6 follow the format of 1-1, 1-2, and 1-3, but present data on Turnout (proportion reporting having voted in their congressional election) *within* each of the 49 cate-

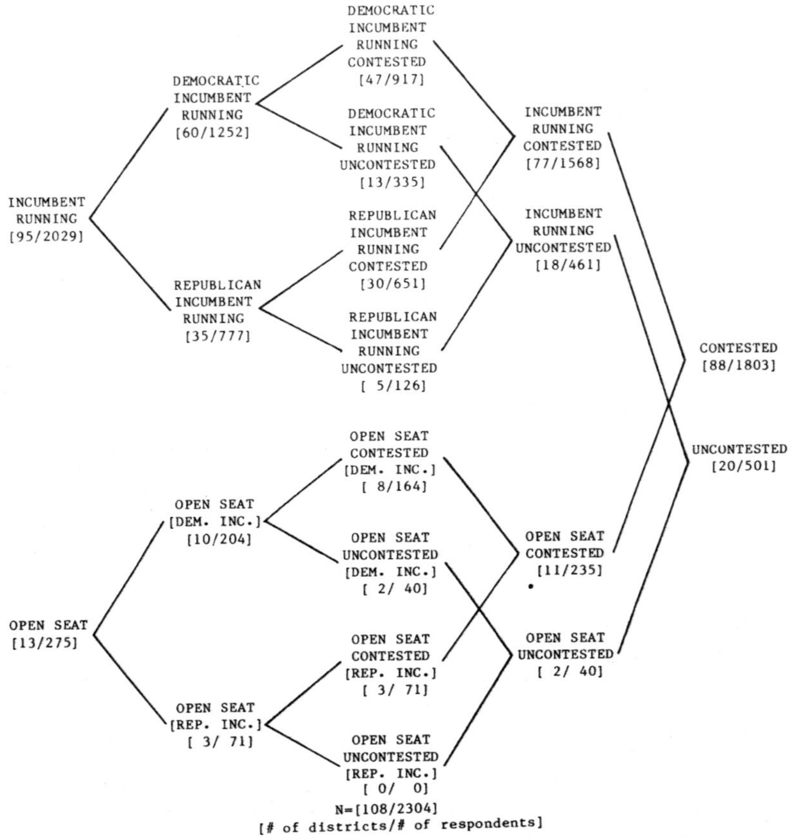

Figure 1: Types of Races

gories of citizens defined by the intersection of Party Identification and Type of Race. (Note there are only seven of the eight possible types of races represented in the study sample of 108 congressional districts. The sample did not include any uncontested races in districts where a Republican incumbent was not running for reelection in the general fall election. Three dots are used here and throughout to denote a cell in which the sample base for an estimate contained fewer than 10 persons.) Tables 1-7 and 1-9 repeat the format, substituting Democratic proportion of the two-party vote for the Turnout estimates presented in Tables 1-4 to 1-6. (Twelve respondents in the national sample who reported a minor party vote or who refused to indicate how they voted were excluded from all Party Vote calculations.) Finally, Tables 1-10 to 1-12 present the proportion of the total vote given to the Incumbent.

The second subsection is concerned with various indicators of the citizens' involvement in politics and selects three indicators for study: (1) interest in the election campaign, (2) caring about which party wins the elections, and more general interest in (3) following what goes on in government and public affairs. Each is presented as an independent variable and, after the mode of the first subsection, Turnout, Party Vote, and Incumbent Vote are examined, in turn, as dependent variables.

The analytic scheme of the second subsection differs from the first because none of the "independent" variables appears to differentiate, or be differentiated by, Type of Race (see Tables 2-1 to 2-3, 2-8 to 2-10 and 2-13 to 2-15). Consequently, the heart of this section emphasizes partisanship. Following each set of tables based on Type of Race and the relationship between citizen Party Identification and

TABLE 2-1

INTEREST IN THE POLITICAL CAMPAIGNS
BY TYPE OF RACE

Level of Campaign Interest	Type of Race: Democr. Incumb. Running Con-tested	Democr. Incumb. Running Uncon-tested	Repub. Incumb. Running Con-tested	Repub. Incumb. Running Uncon-tested	Op.Seat Con-tested (Dem. Incum.)	Op.Seat Uncon-tested (Dem. Incum.)	Op.Seat Con-tested (Rep. Incum.)	Total	
Very Much	22%	22%	20%	27%	23%	28%	24%	22%	[496]
Somewhat	45	42	46	40	37	49	55	45	[1025]
Not Much	33	36	34	33	40	23	21	34	[778]
[N]	[916]	[334]	[650]	[126]	[163]	[39]	[71]		[2299]

TABLE 2-2

INTEREST IN THE POLITICAL CAMPAIGNS
BY TYPE(S) OF RACE

Level of Campaign Interest	Type(s) of Race: Incumbent Running? Yes	No	Contested Race? Yes	No	Totals
Very Much	21%	24%	21%	23%	22% [496]
Somewhat	45	44	45	42	45 [1025]
Not Much	34	33	34	35	34 [778]
[N]	[2026]	[273]	[1800]	[499]	[2299]

TABLE 2-3

INTEREST IN THE POLITICAL CAMPAIGNS
BY INCUMBENT'S PARTY AND OPPOSITION

Level of Campaign Interest	Incumbent's Party and Opposition: Incumbent Running? Yes: Democrat	Yes: Republican	No: Open Seat	Contested? Yes: Contested	Yes: Uncontested	No: Contested	No: Uncontested	Totals
Very Much	22%	21%	24%	21%	23%	23%	28%	22% [496]
Somewhat	45	45	44	46	42	43	49	45 [1025]
Not Much	34	34	33	34	35	34	23	34 [778]
[N]	[1250]	[776]	[273]	[1566]	[460]	[234]	[39]	[2299]

TABLE 2-4

INTEREST IN THE POLITICAL CAMPAIGNS
BY RESPONDENT'S PARTY IDENTIFICATION

Level of Campaign Interest	Respondent's Party Identification: Str. Dem.	Weak Dem.	Ind. Dem.	Ind. Ind.	Ind. Rep.	Weak Rep.	Str. Rep.	Total
Very Much	37%	15%	21%	12%	24%	29%	39%	22% [494]
Somewhat	40	46	46	44	52	53	41	46 [1018]
Not Much	23	39	33	44	24	27	20	32 [708]
[N]	[338]	[557]	[328]	[311]	[217]	[292]	[177]	[2220]

TABLE 2-5

TURNOUT BY INTEREST IN THE POLITICAL CAMPAIGNS AND RESPONDENT'S PARTY IDENTIFICATION

Level of Campaign Interest	Respondent's Party Identification							
	Str. Dem.	Weak Dem.	Ind. Dem.	Ind. Ind.	Ind. Rep.	Weak Rep.	Str. Rep.	Total
Very Much	74	62	80	66	70	82	77	73 [468]
Somewhat	70	52	46	41	57	57	82	55 [972]
Not Much	39	22	22	19	32	33	41	26 [679]
Total	64	42	45	35	54	55	71	50
[N]	[317]	[528]	[316]	[306]	[215]	[273]	[164]	[2119]

Cell entries are the proportion of respondents who reported voting in the House race in their district.

TABLE 2-6

PARTY VOTE BY INTEREST IN THE POLITICAL CAMPAIGNS AND RESPONDENT'S PARTY IDENTIFICATION

Level of Campaign Interest	Respondent's Party Identification							
	Str. Dem.	Weak Dem.	Ind. Dem.	Ind. Ind.	Ind. Rep.	Weak Rep.	Str. Rep.	Total
Very Much	89	78	67	55	39	34	24	60 [328]
Somewhat	83	77	57	61	36	41	17	57 [512]
Not Much	89	91	65	48	33	08	17	59 [164]
Total	86	80	62	57	37	34	20	59
[N]	[199]	[210]	[129]	[97]	[109]	[146]	[114]	[1004]

Cell entries are the proportion of voters who reported voting Democratic in the House race in their district.

citizen involvement is a series of three tables: (1) Turnout, and (2) Party Vote, within each category defined by partisanship and involvement, and (3) Vote for the Incumbent as it may be jointly affected by the involvement variable and the congruence or mismatch of citizen and incumbent candidate partisanship.

The third subsection of the data presentation follows exactly the scheme of the second part and for the same empirical reasons. This section is concerned with retrospective voting, vote decisions based on the past record of governmental performance. It treats three such assessments: two appraisals of the president, a rating of President Carter's performance and an effective rating of feeling toward Carter (the thermometer scores), and a simple rating of the performance of Congress. In this section as elsewhere, the categorization of feeling thermometer appraisals describe those who score a person between 76 and 100 on the thermometer as "very positive," 51–75 as "posi-

TABLE 2-7

INCUMBENCY VOTE BY INTEREST IN THE POLITICAL CAMPAIGNS AND RESPONDENT'S PARTY IDENTIFICATION AND INCUMBENT'S PARTY

Level of Campaign Interest	Respondent's Party Identification and Incumbent's Party: Same	Resp. is Ind. Ind.	Different	Total	
Very Much	95	75	48	75	[243]
Somewhat	96	83	61	81	[380]
Not Much	95	75	43	78	[132]
Total	95	79	54	78	
[N]	[405]	[72]	[278]		[755]

Cell entries are the proportion of voters who reported voting for the Incumbent in districts where the Incumbent was opposed.

TABLE 2-8

CARE ABOUT THE CONGRESSIONAL ELECTION OUTCOME BY TYPE OF RACE

Care About Outcome	Type of Race: Democr. Incumb. Running Con-tested	Democr. Incumb. Running Uncon-tested	Repub. Incumb. Running Con-tested	Repub. Incumb. Running Uncon-tested	Op.Seat Con-tested (Dem. Incum.)	Op.Seat Uncon-tested (Dem. Incum.)	Op.Seat Con-tested (Rep. Incum.)	Total	
Very Much	14%	16%	15%	17%	17%	13%	16%	15%	[334]
Pretty Much	29	31	31	28	24	37	30	30	[653]
Not Very Much	36	35	39	37	45	37	44	38	[832]
Not At All	21	18	14	18	14	13	10	17	[384]
[N]	[876]	[312]	[630]	[122]	[156]	[38]	[69]		[2203]

tive," 50 as "neutral," and below 50 (0–49) as "negative." Following the demonstration that none of the appraisals is very clearly related to Type of Race, each assessment, in turn, is revealed to be a clear correlate of the citizen's Party Identification but, at best, a weak correlate of the dependent assessments. Even though Democratic and Republican incumbents may gain office because of the predominance

TABLE 2-9

CARE ABOUT THE CONGRESSIONAL ELECTION OUTCOME
BY TYPE(S) OF RACE

Care About Outcome	Type(s) of Race: Incumbent Running? Yes	No	Contested Race? Yes	No	Totals	
Very Much	15%	16%	15%	16%	15%	[334]
Pretty Much	30	28	29	31	30	[653]
Not Very Much	37	43	38	35	38	[832]
Not At All	18	13	17	18	17	[384]
[N]	[1940]	[263]	[1731]	[472]		[2203]

TABLE 2-10

CARE ABOUT THE CONGRESSIONAL ELECTION OUTCOME
BY INCUMBENT'S PARTY AND OPPOSITION

Care About Outcome	Incumbent's Party and Opposition: Incumbent Running? Yes: Demo-crat	Yes: Repub-lican	No: Open Seat	Yes: Con-tested	Yes: Uncon-tested	No: Con-tested	No: Uncon-tested	Totals	
Very Much	15%	16%	16%	15%	17%	16%	13%	15%	[334]
Pretty Much	30	31	28	30	30	26	37	30	[653]
Not Very Much	36	39	43	38	35	44	37	38	[332]
Not At All	20	15	13	18	18	13	13	17	[384]
[N]	[1188]	[752]	[263]	[1506]	[434]	[225]	[38]		[2203]

of fellow partisans among their constituents, the partisan implications of the three appraisals are not clearly reflected in the distribution of appraisals across the types of races. Some sense of the looseness of connections and the discontinuities within the system are, therefore,

TABLE 2-11

CARE ABOUT THE CONGRESSIONAL ELECTION OUTCOME
BY RESPONDENT'S PARTY IDENTIFICATION

Care About Outcome	Respondent's Party Identification								
	Str. Dem.	Weak Dem.	Ind. Dem.	Ind. Ind.	Ind. Rep.	Weak Rep.	Str. Rep.	Total	
Very Much	24%	11%	10%	9%	20%	15%	32%	16%	[332]
Pretty Much	36	29	29	26	27	31	38	31	[651]
Not Very Much	30	42	43	38	44	41	19	38	[813]
Not At All	10	18	18	27	9	12	10	16	[340]
[N]	[324]	[532]	[318]	[299]	[213]	[280]	[170]		[2136]

TABLE 2-12

TURNOUT BY CARE ABOUT THE CONGRESSIONAL ELECTION OUTCOME
AND RESPONDENT'S PARTY IDENTIFICATION

Care About Outcome	Respondent's Party Identification								
	Str. Dem.	Weak Dem.	Ind. Dem.	Ind. Ind.	Ind. Rep.	Weak Rep.	Str. Rep.	Total	
Very Much	70	59	79	70	67	68	87	71	[313]
Pretty Much	75	51	63	51	74	66	74	63	[620]
Not Very Much	55	40	39	30	46	51	64	43	[786]
Not At All	50	27	14	15	11	36	31	24	[323]
Total	64	42	45	35	54	55	71	50	
[N]	[307]	[505]	[306]	[294]	[211]	[261]	[158]		[2042]

Cell entries are the proportion of respondents who reported voting in the House race in their district.

portrayed and the possible importance of congressional candidate incumbency status against the influence of candidate partisanship is suggested.

The fourth subsection follows from this and shifts to an examina-

TABLE 2-13

PARTY VOTE BY CARE ABOUT THE CONGRESSIONAL ELECTION OUTCOME AND RESPONDENT'S PARTY IDENTIFICATION

Care About Outcome	Respondent's Party Identification								
	Str. Dem.	Weak Dem.	Ind. Dem.	Ind. Ind.	Ind. Rep.	Weak Rep.	Str. Rep.	Total	
Very Much	90	86	57	44	39	38	15	54	[212]
Pretty Much	86	72	63	69	34	36	23	59	[379]
Not Very Much	80	82	63	59	39	27	19	59	[324]
Not At All	100	87	71	44	50	46	40	72	[71]
Total	86	79	63	59	37	34	20	59	
[N]	[197]	[205]	[128]	[94]	[108]	[143]	[111]		[986]

Cell entries are the proportion of voters who reported voting Democratic in the House race in their district.

TABLE 2-14

INCUMBENCY VOTE BY CARE ABOUT THE CONGRESSIONAL ELECTION OUTCOME AND RESPONDENT'S PARTY IDENTIFICATION AND INCUMBENT'S PARTY

Care About Outcome	Respondent's Party Identification and Incumbent's Party				
	Same	Resp. is Ind. Ind.	Different	Total	
Very Much	93	93	34	73	[147]
Pretty Much	94	78	59	79	[287]
Not Very Much	99	81	61	83	[247]
Not At All	94	67	41	71	[59]
Total	95	81	54	79	
[N]	[398]	[68]	[274]		[740]

Cell entries are the proportion of voters who reported voting for the Incumbent in districts where the Incumbent was opposed.

tion of constituency response to congressional incumbents. Eight different aspects of citizens' response to incumbents are examined, in turn. The 16 tables of this subsection are, therefore, eight repetitive presentations of responses to the incumbent for the two sets of constituents—those who have been represented by Democrats and those who have been represented by Republicans. Each of the eight

TABLE 2-15

FOLLOW WHAT'S GOING ON IN GOVERNMENT AND PUBLIC AFFAIRS BY TYPE OF RACE

Follow What's Going On	Type of Race							
	Democr. Incumb. Running Con-tested	Democr. Incumb. Running Uncon-tested	Repub. Incumb. Running Con-tested	Repub. Incumb. Running Uncon-tested	Op.Seat Con-tested (Dem. Incum.)	Op.Seat Uncon-tested (Dem. Incum.)	Op.Seat Con-tested (Rep. Incum.)	Total
Most Times	25%	21%	21%	25%	23%	24%	24%	23% [528]
Some Times	33	31	37	35	32	38	32	34 [771]
Now And Then	25	26	26	18	23	22	34	25 [571]
Hardly At All	17	22	15	22	21	16	10	18 [396]
[N]	[903]	[328]	[642]	[126]	[159]	[37]	[71]	[2266]

TABLE 2-16

FOLLOW WHAT'S GOING ON IN GOVERNMENT AND PUBLIC AFFAIRS BY TYPE(S) OF RACE

Follow What's Going On	Type(s) of Race				
	Incumbent Running?		Contested Race?		
	Yes	No	Yes	No	Totals
Most Times	23%	24%	24%	23%	23% [528]
Some Times	34	33	35	32	34 [771]
Now And Then	25	26	26	24	25 [571]
Hardly At All	18	18	16	21	18 [396]
[N]	[1999]	[267]	[1775]	[491]	[2266]

pairs of tables first relates the citizens' Party Identification to a given response (such as a rating of the congressman's performance in Table 4-1) and, second, portrays the vote for the incumbent (in Table 4-2), first for Democratic incumbents and then for Republican incumbents.

The fifth section continues the study of citizen response to candidate characteristics, but it returns to the emphasis on respondents'

TABLE 2-17

FOLLOW WHAT'S GOING ON IN GOVERNMENT AND PUBLIC AFFAIRS BY INCUMBENT'S PARTY AND OPPOSITION

Follow What's Going On	Incumbent's Party and Opposition: Incumbent Running? Yes: Democrat	Yes: Republican	No: Open Seat	Yes: Contested	Yes: Uncontested	No: Contested	No: Uncontested	Totals	
Most Times	24%	22%	24%	24%	23%	24%	24%	23%	[528]
Some Times	33	37	33	35	32	32	38	34	[771]
Now And Then	25	25	26	26	24	27	22	25	[571]
Hardly At All	18	16	18	16	22	18	16	18	[396]
[N]	[1231]	[768]	[267]	[1545]	[454]	[230]	[37]		[2266]

TABLE 2-18

FOLLOW WHAT'S GOING ON IN GOVERNMENT AND PUBLIC AFFAIRS BY RESPONDENT'S PARTY IDENTIFICATION

Follow What's Going On	Respondent's Party Identification: Str. Dem.	Weak Dem.	Ind. Dem.	Ind. Ind.	Ind. Rep.	Weak Rep.	Str. Rep.	Total	
Most Times	28%	17%	25%	19%	27%	23%	43%	24%	[526]
Some Times	42	30	35	30	42	35	37	35	[765]
Now And Then	18	30	25	32	24	29	15	26	[568]
Hardly At All	12	23	16	19	7	14	5	15	[337]
[N]	[332]	[553]	[323]	[310]	[214]	[289]	[175]		[2196]

TABLE 2-19

TURNOUT BY FOLLOW WHAT'S GOING ON IN GOVERNMENT AND PUBLIC AFFAIRS AND RESPONDENT'S PARTY IDENTIFICATION

Follow What's Going On	Respondent's Party Identification							
	Str. Dem.	Weak Dem.	Ind. Dem.	Ind. Ind.	Ind. Rep.	Weak Rep.	Str. Rep.	Total
Most Times	82	59	73	54	71	63	76	69 [502]
Some Times	61	48	51	36	59	63	77	55 [735]
Now And Then	59	40	28	30	33	47	60	40 [545]
Hardly At All	44	23	14	23	31	41	...	26 [314]
Total	65	42	45	35	54	56	72	50
[N]	[311]	[525]	[311]	[305]	[212]	[270]	[162]	[2096]

Cell entries are the proportion of respondents who reported voting in the House race in their district.

TABLE 2-20

PARTY VOTE BY FOLLOW WHAT'S GOING ON IN GOVERNMENT AND PUBLIC AFFAIRS AND RESPONDENT'S PARTY IDENTIFICATION

Follow What's Going On	Respondent's Party Identification							
	Str. Dem.	Weak Dem.	Ind. Dem.	Ind. Ind.	Ind. Rep.	Weak Rep.	Str. Rep.	Total
Most Times	86	81	62	55	45	43	20	59 [330]
Some Times	84	80	61	63	31	32	23	57 [381]
Now And Then	90	79	60	56	35	33	14	60 [208]
Hardly At All	94	79	67	50	...	13	...	61 [77]
Total	86	80	61	57	37	33	20	58
[N]	[197]	[209]	[127]	[98]	[107]	[145]	[113]	[996]

Cell entries are the proportion of voters who reported voting Democratic in the House race in their district.

TABLE 2-21

INCUMBENCY VOTE BY FOLLOW WHAT'S GOING ON IN GOVERNMENT AND PUBLIC AFFAIRS AND RESPONDENT'S PARTY IDENTIFICATION AND INCUMBENT'S PARTY

Follow What's Going On	Respondent's Party Identification and Incumbent's Party				
	Same	Resp. is Ind. Ind.	Different	Total	
Most Times	95	77	48	73	[241]
Some Times	96	79	60	32	[282]
Now And Then	96	79	62	82	[164]
Hardly At All	92	86	39	76	[52]
Total	95	79	54	79	
[N]	[403]	[72]	[274]		[749]

Cell entries are the proportion of voters who reported voting for the Incumbent in districts where the Incumbent was opposed.

Party Identification *and* Type of Race presented in the very first subsection of this data presentation. The variables chosen for presentation here include: constituent's recognition of a candidate, recall of a candidate's name, constituent liked something about the candidate, disliked something about the candidate, was contacted by the candidate, and a feeling thermometer rating of the constituent's affect toward the candidate. The first two parts of this subsection present citizen reactions to Democratic candidates in Tables 5-1 to 5-14 and, then, Republican candidates in Tables 5-15 to 5-28. The tables are again presented in pairs, two each for each of six independent variables that may influence the citizen's party vote. The first table of a pair reveals the incidence of the independent variable (such as candidate recognition in 5-1) within each of the 49 categories in the Party Identification-Type of Race matrix; the second then shows the Party Vote within categories of Party Identification and the independent variable (candidate recognition in 5-2). The same format is repeated through the additional five independent variables (Tables 5-3 to 5-14). Because of the widespread use of the feeling thermometer measures, the presentation of thermometer assessments is preceded by the simple bivariate relationships between the thermometer rating and Type of Race and Citizen's Party Identification, respectively, in Tables 5-11 and 5-12 and in 5-25 and 5-26.

The third and fourth parts of this section reorganize the data to present citizen reactions first to *incumbent candidates* (Tables 5-29 to

TABLE 3-1

RATING THE JOB PRESIDENT CARTER HAS DONE
BY TYPE OF RACE

Rate Carter's Job	Type of Race: Democr. Incumb. Running Con-tested	Democr. Incumb. Running Uncon-tested	Repub. Incumb. Running Con-tested	Repub. Incumb. Running Uncon-tested	Op. Seat Con-tested (Dem. Incum.)	Op. Seat Uncon-tested (Dem. Incum.)	Op. Seat Con-tested (Rep. Incum.)	Total
Very Good	7%	10%	4%	7%	8%	8%	6%	7% [148]
Good	28	29	29	30	26	38	13	28 [627]
Fair	50	47	50	47	43	35	58	49 [1088]
Poor	12	8	13	11	13	15	10	12 [261]
Very Poor	3	6	4	6	6	5	9	4 [96]
[N]	[883]	[314]	[634]	[123]	[155]	[40]	[71]	[2220]

TABLE 3-2

RATING THE JOB PRESIDENT CARTER HAS DONE
BY TYPE(S) OF RACE

Rate Carter's Job	Type(s) of Race: Incumbent Running? Yes	No	Contested Race? Yes	No	Totals
Very Good	7%	7%	6%	9%	7% [148]
Good	29	26	28	30	28 [627]
Fair	49	49	50	46	49 [1088]
Poor	12	12	12	9	12 [261]
Very Poor	4	6	4	6	4 [96]
[N]	[1954]	[256]	[1743]	[477]	[2220]

5-42) and then to *nonincumbent challengers* (Tables 5-43 to 5-56). Since some incumbents, but no nonincumbent challengers, ran in uncontested races, there are no entries in Tables 5-43 to 5-56 for nonincumbent challengers for this latter type of race. Given the fact that both incumbents and nonincumbent challengers included both

TABLE 3-3

RATING THE JOB PRESIDENT CARTER HAS DONE
BY INCUMBENT'S PARTY AND OPPOSITION

Rate Carter's Job	Incumbent's Party and Opposition							
	Incumbent Running?							
	Yes		No	Yes		No		
	Demo-crat	Repub-lican	Open Seat	Con-tested	Uncon-tested	Con-tested	Uncon-tested	Totals
Very Good	8%	5%	7%	6%	9%	7%	8%	7% [148]
Good	28	30	26	29	29	24	38	28 [627]
Fair	49	49	49	50	47	51	35	49 [1088]
Poor	11	12	12	13	9	12	15	12 [261]
Very Poor	4	4	6	4	6	7	5	4 [96]
[N]	[1197]	[757]	[266]	[1517]	[437]	[226]	[40]	[2220]

TABLE 3-4

RATING THE JOB PRESIDENT CARTER HAS DONE
BY RESPONDENT'S PARTY IDENTIFICATION

Rate Carter's Job	Respondent's Party Identification							
	Str. Dem.	Weak Dem.	Ind. Dem.	Ind. Ind.	Ind. Rep.	Weak Rep.	Str. Rep.	Total
Very Good	16%	7%	7%	4%	2%	3%	4%	7% [147]
Good	40	33	35	28	19	14	12	28 [605]
Fair	34	53	48	54	52	60	39	49 [1060]
Poor	7	6	8	10	20	17	32	12 [253]
Very Poor	3	1	2	3	7	7	13	4 [90]
[N]	[333]	[539]	[321]	[294]	[210]	[282]	[176]	[2155]

Democrats and Republicans, the Party Identification variables in all of the tables are simplified, summarized combinations of citizen and candidate partisanship, and they reveal only the match or mismatch of citizen-candidate partisanship. This seems appropriate where the interest is in incumbency and not partisanship as presented in the first half of this subsection.

TABLE 3-5

TURNOUT BY RATING THE JOB PRESIDENT CARTER HAS DONE AND RESPONDENT'S PARTY IDENTIFICATION

Rate Carter's Job	Respondent's Party Identification: Str. Dem.	Weak Dem.	Ind. Dem.	Ind. Ind.	Ind. Rep.	Weak Rep.	Str. Rep.	Total	
Very Good	61	39	64	67	...	...	...	57	[137]
Good	67	48	37	40	50	38	55	48	[576]
Fair	65	42	49	29	52	56	72	49	[1018]
Poor	54	23	40	32	65	62	72	53	[246]
Very Poor	56	...	...	...	57	71	90	57	[82]
Total	64	42	45	35	55	56	72	50	
[N]	[313]	[512]	[309]	[289]	[208]	[265]	[163]		[2059]

Cell entries are the proportion of respondents who reported voting in the House race in their district.

TABLE 3-6

PARTY VOTE BY RATING THE JOB PRESIDENT CARTER HAS DONE AND RESPONDENT'S PARTY IDENTIFICATION

Rate Carter's Job	Respondent's Party Identification: Str. Dem.	Weak Dem.	Ind. Dem.	Ind. Ind.	Ind. Rep.	Weak Rep.	Str. Rep.	Total	
Very Good	90	86	85	57	...	...	...	80	[75]
Good	85	76	70	69	26	36	18	69	[268]
Fair	85	83	49	53	40	29	21	55	[473]
Poor	83	43	78	38	36	37	14	38	[122]
Very Poor	100	...	...	...	14	42	29	45	[51]
Total	86	80	62	57	36	34	20	58	
[N]	[196]	[207]	[128]	[93]	[107]	[143]	[115]		[989]

Cell entries are the proportion of voters who reported voting Democratic in the House race in their district.

The final two subsections of the presentation of basic data focus on issue voting. Section six is divided into two parts. The first part contains data on five questions of public policy: government guarantees of jobs and standard of living, protection of the civil rights of those accused of crimes, government help to minority groups, government health insurance, and women's role in society. The second

TABLE 3-7

INCUMBENCY VOTE BY RATING THE JOB PRESIDENT CARTER HAS DONE AND RESPONDENT'S PARTY IDENTIFICATION AND INCUMBENT'S PARTY

Rate Carter's Job	Respondent's Party Identification and Incumbent's Party				
	Same	Resp. is Ind. Ind.	Different	Total	
Very Good	100	60	47	80	[50]
Good	96	75	53	79	[204]
Fair	94	85	57	78	[360]
Poor	96	88	49	78	[97]
Very Poor	95	67	36	73	[33]
Total	95	80	54	78	
[N]	[399]	[69]	[276]		[744]

Cell entries are the proportion of voters who reported voting for the Incumbent in districts where the Incumbent was opposed.

TABLE 3-8

RATING FOR JIMMY CARTER ON THE FEELING THERMOMETER BY RATING THE JOB PRESIDENT CARTER HAS DONE

Feeling Therm. Rating	Rate Carter's Job						
	Very Good	Good	Fair	Poor	Very Poor	Total	
Very Pos.	88%	58%	13%	23%	5%	29%	[638]
Positive	9	39	62	20	10	45	[977]
Neutral	2	2	14	16	10	10	[208]
Negative	1	1	11	61	76	16	[357]
[N]	[146]	[616]	[1067]	[257]	[94]		[2180]

part provides a more limited treatment of another five issues: racial segregation/desegregation, taxes, abortion, preferential treatment for women and minorities, and the Equal Rights Amendment.

In the first part of this sixth subsection, each issue is presented in a series of six tables. The first shows the distributions of policy prefer-

TABLE 3-9

RATING FOR JIMMY CARTER ON THE FEELING THERMOMETER BY TYPE OF RACE

Feeling Therm. Rating	Type of Race							
	Democr. Incumb. Running Con- tested	Democr. Incumb. Running Uncon- tested	Repub. Incumb. Running Con- tested	Repub. Incumb. Running Uncon- tested	Op.Seat Con- tested (Dem. Incum.)	Op.Seat Uncon- tested (Dem. Incum.)	Op.Seat Con- tested (Rep. Incum.)	Total
Very Pos.	29%	33%	27%	30%	29%	36%	19%	29% [651]
Positive	46	43	44	47	42	44	49	45 [1006]
Neutral	9	10	11	9	10	5	14	10 [223]
Negative	15	14	19	15	19	15	19	16 [363]
[N]	[901]	[311]	[641]	[124]	[157]	[39]	[70]	[2243]

TABLE 3-10

RATING FOR JIMMY CARTER ON THE FEELING THERMOMETER BY TYPE(S) OF RACE

Feeling Therm. Rating	Type(s) of Race				
	Incumbent Running?		Contested Race?		
	Yes	No	Yes	No	Totals
Very Pos.	29%	27%	28%	33%	29% [651]
Positive	45	44	45	44	45 [1006]
Neutral	10	11	10	9	10 [223]
Negative	16	18	17	14	16 [363]
[N]	[1977]	[266]	[1769]	[474]	[2243]

ences by party identification and the second shows the Party Vote within each category of the Policy Preference-Party Identification matrix. The next four tables relate the citizen's policy preference to the perceived issue position of a candidate, first presenting data pertaining to the Democratic candidate, then the Republican, then the

TABLE 3-11

RATING FOR JIMMY CARTER ON THE FEELING THERMOMETER
BY INCUMBENT'S PARTY AND OPPOSITION

Feeling Therm. Rating	Incumbent's Party and Opposition							
	Incumbent Running?							
	Yes		No	Yes		No		
	Democrat	Republican	Open Seat	Contested	Uncontested	Contested	Uncontested	Totals
Very Pos.	30%	28%	27%	28%	32%	26%	36%	29% [651]
Positive	46	44	44	45	44	44	44	45 [1006]
Neutral	10	10	11	10	10	12	5	10 [223]
Negative	15	18	18	17	14	19	15	16 [363]
[N]	[1212]	[765]	[266]	[1542]	[435]	[227]	[39]	[2243]

TABLE 3-12

RATING FOR JIMMY CARTER ON THE FEELING THERMOMETER
BY RESPONDENT'S PARTY IDENTIFICATION

Feeling Therm. Rating	Respondent's Party Identification							
	Str. Dem.	Weak Dem.	Ind. Dem.	Ind. Ind.	Ind. Rep.	Weak Rep.	Str. Rep.	Total
Very Pos.	53%	37%	28%	26%	17%	12%	13%	29% [636]
Positive	34	49	54	49	40	48	31	45 [979]
Neutral	9	7	8	12	14	12	9	10 [210]
Negative	5	7	11	14	29	29	47	16 [355]
[N]	[333]	[545]	[323]	[303]	[215]	[286]	[175]	[2180]

Incumbent, and finally the Challenger. In each of the four tables, the relationships between the citizen's position on an issue and the citizen's perception of the candidate's position are presented within (or "controlling on") the citizen's party identification and separately for voters and nonvoters.

TABLE 3-13

TURNOUT BY RATING FOR JIMMY CARTER ON THE FEELING THERMOMETER AND RESPONDENT'S PARTY IDENTIFICATION

Feeling Therm. Rating	Respondent's Party Identification: Str. Dem.	Weak Dem.	Ind. Dem.	Ind. Ind.	Ind. Rep.	Weak Rep.	Str. Rep.	Total	
Very Pos.	62	48	44	45	56	46	58	51	[604]
Positive	71	43	47	33	50	55	69	49	[938]
Neutral	53	18	36	31	55	41	50	39	[199]
Negative	64	37	44	30	61	65	79	58	[341]
Total	64	42	45	35	55	55	71	50	
[N]	[313]	[516]	[311]	[298]	[213]	[269]	[162]		[2082]

Cell entries are the proportion of respondents who reported voting in the House race in their district.

TABLE 3-14

PARTY VOTE BY RATING FOR JIMMY CARTER ON THE FEELING THERMOMETER AND RESPONDENT'S PARTY IDENTIFICATION

Feeling Therm. Rating	Respondent's Party Identification: Str. Dem.	Weak Dem.	Ind. Dem.	Ind. Ind.	Ind. Rep.	Weak Rep.	Str. Rep.	Total	
Very Pos.	86	80	75	59	25	33	36	71	[300]
Positive	88	80	55	57	43	37	19	60	[433]
Neutral	81	86	67	30	50	25	0	51	[76]
Negative	88	77	64	70	30	30	20	37	[188]
Total	86	80	63	56	37	33	20	58	
[N]	[197]	[209]	[128]	[96]	[109]	[145]	[113]		[997]

Cell entries are the proportion of voters who reported voting Democratic in the House race in their district.

The second part of the subsection on issues is less elaborate and presents only the first two tables for each issue. The first shows the distribution of policy preferences by Party Identification, and the second shows the Party Vote within each category of the Policy

TABLE 3-15

INCUMBENCY VOTE BY RATING FOR JIMMY CARTER ON THE FEELING THERMOMETER AND RESPONDENT'S PARTY IDENTIFICATION AND INCUMBENT'S PARTY

Feeling Therm. Rating	Respondent's Party Identification and Incumbent's Party: Same	Resp. is Ind. Ind.	Different	Total	
Very Pos.	96	73	50	77	[219]
Positive	95	76	58	78	[328]
Neutral	94	88	71	88	[58]
Negative	96	100	45	76	[144]
Total	95	79	54	78	
[N]	[402]	[71]	[276]		[749]

Cell entries are the proportion of voters who reported voting for the Incumbent in districts where the Incumbent was opposed.

TABLE 3-16

RATING THE JOB THE CONGRESS HAS DONE BY TYPE OF RACE

Rate Congress' Job	Type of Race: Democr. Incumb. Running Con- tested	Democr. Incumb. Running Uncon- tested	Repub. Incumb. Running Con- tested	Repub. Incumb. Running Uncon- tested	Op.Seat Con- tested (Dem. Incum.)	Op.Seat Uncon- tested (Dem. Incum.)	Op.Seat Con- tested (Rep. Incum.)	Total	
Very Good	1%	5%	1%	0%	0%	0%	0%	1%	[24]
Good	18	21	20	14	15	29	12	19	[341]
Fair	50	52	55	49	58	54	57	52	[966]
Poor	24	17	18	28	21	17	23	21	[386]
Very Poor	7	6	7	9	6	0	8	7	[125]
[N]	[724]	[248]	[539]	[109]	[127]	[35]	[60]		[1842]

Preference-Party Identification matrix. The last four tables for each issue that are presented in the first part of this subsection are not presented in the second part because the candidate placement questions were not asked for these particular issues.

TABLE 3-17

RATING THE JOB THE CONGRESS HAS DONE BY TYPE(S) OF RACE

Rate Congress' Job	Type(s) of Race: Incumbent Running? Yes	Incumbent Running? No	Contested Race? Yes	Contested Race? No	Totals	
Very Good	2%	0%	1%	3%	1%	[24]
Good	19	16	18	19	19	[341]
Fair	52	57	53	51	52	[966]
Poor	21	21	21	20	21	[386]
Very Poor	7	5	7	6	7	[125]
[N]	[1620]	[222]	[1450]	[392]		[1842]

TABLE 3-18

RATING THE JOB THE CONGRESS HAS DONE BY INCUMBENT'S PARTY AND OPPOSITION

Rate Congress' Job	Incumbent's Party and Opposition							Totals	
	Incumbent Running?								
	Yes		No	Yes		No			
	Demo-crat	Repub-lican	Open Seat	Con-tested	Uncon-tested	Con-tested	Uncon-tested		
Very Good	2%	1%	0%	1%	4%	0%	0%	1%	[24]
Good	19	19	16	19	19	14	29	19	[341]
Fair	51	54	57	52	51	58	54	52	[966]
Poor	22	19	21	21	20	22	17	21	[386]
Very Poor	7	7	5	7	7	6	0	7	[125]
[N]	[972]	[648]	[222]	[1263]	[357]	[187]	[35]		[1842]

The seventh and final subsection is centered on citizen's self-placement on a scale of ideological position. As with the first part of the previous section, it presents the distribution of ideological positions within party identification (Table 7-1), the Party Vote within

TABLE 3-19

RATING THE JOB THE CONGRESS HAS DONE
BY RESPONDENT'S PARTY IDENTIFICATION

Rate Congress' Job	Respondent's Party Identification								
	Str. Dem.	Weak Dem.	Ind. Dem.	Ind. Ind.	Ind. Rep.	Weak Rep.	Str. Rep.	Total	
Very Good	3%	2%	1%	1%	1%	1%	1%	1%	[24]
Good	25	21	17	21	12	16	10	19	[337]
Fair	52	55	54	48	48	55	51	52	[948]
Poor	16	18	20	21	32	21	29	21	[380]
Very Poor	5	4	8	10	7	8	9	7	[124]
[N]	[291]	[426]	[280]	[229]	[189]	[244]	[154]		[1813]

TABLE 3-20

TURNOUT BY RATING THE JOB THE CONGRESS HAS DONE
AND RESPONDENT'S PARTY IDENTIFICATION

Rate Congress' Job	Respondent's Party Identification								
	Str. Dem.	Weak Dem.	Ind. Dem.	Ind. Ind.	Ind. Rep.	Weak Rep.	Str. Rep.	Total	
Very Good	...	...	...	...	...	...	...	23	[22]
Good	65	36	33	28	52	62	75	46	[326]
Fair	69	48	50	45	58	58	74	56	[897]
Poor	65	51	56	39	59	53	74	56	[364]
Very Poor	79	53	60	55	69	78	100	69	[116]
Total	66	45	49	41	58	57	76	54	
[N]	[271]	[404]	[268]	[225]	[187]	[227]	[143]		[1725]

Cell entries are the proportion of respondents who reported voting in the House race in their district.

categories of the Ideology-Party Identification matrix (Table 7-3), and the relationships of citizen self-placement to perceptions of candidate positions, for Democratic and Republican candidates as well as Incumbent and Nonincumbent challengers, *controlling* on citizens' Party Identification and Turnout (Tables 7-5 to 7-8). The other

(text continued on p. 120)

TABLE 3-21

PARTY VOTE BY RATING THE JOB THE CONGRESS HAS DONE AND RESPONDENT'S PARTY IDENTIFICATION

Rate Congress' Job	Respondent's Party Identification: Str. Dem.	Weak Dem.	Ind. Dem.	Ind. Ind.	Ind. Rep.	Weak Rep.	Str. Rep.	Total	
Very Good	...	...	...	...	...	...	...	75	[4]
Good	87	79	56	85	55	27	18	66	[146]
Fair	81	78	60	51	38	33	22	57	[480]
Poor	96	85	61	50	34	42	14	56	[190]
Very Poor	90	75	75	55	13	43	21	51	[73]
Total	86	80	61	56	37	35	20	58	
[N]	[176]	[174]	[120]	[86]	[101]	[129]	[107]		[893]

Cell entries are the proportion of voters who reported voting Democratic in the House race in their district.

TABLE 3-22

INCUMBENCY VOTE BY RATING THE JOB THE CONGRESS HAS DONE AND RESPONDENT'S PARTY IDENTIFICATION AND INCUMBENT'S PARTY

Rate Congress' Job	Respondent's Party Identification and Incumbent's Party: Same	Resp. is Ind. Ind.	Different	Total	
Very Good	100	0	...	67	[3]
Good	95	100	62	83	[108]
Fair	97	73	59	80	[343]
Poor	96	79	43	72	[156]
Very Poor	88	90	35	73	[60]
Total	96	79	54	78	
[N]	[352]	[65]	[253]		[670]

Cell entries are the proportion of voters who reported voting for the Incumbent in districts where the Incumbent was opposed.

TABLE 3-23

RATING THE JOB THE CONGRESS HAS DONE
BY RATING THE JOB THE INCUMBENT CONGRESSMAN HAS DONE

Rate Congress' Job	Rate Incumbent's Job: Very Good	Good	Fair	Poor	Very Poor	Total	
Very Good	4%	1%	1%	0%	0%	1%	[17]
Good	27	20	15	17	6	19	[274]
Fair	48	54	58	24	29	52	[738]
Poor	14	21	21	37	24	20	[287]
Very Poor	8	5	6	22	41	7	[95]
[N]	[305]	[616]	[414]	[59]	[17]		[1411]

TABLE 4-1

RATING THE JOB THE INCUMBENT CONGRESSMAN HAS DONE
BY RESPONDENT'S PARTY IDENTIFICATION,
CONTROLLING FOR INCUMBENT'S PARTY

Rate Incumbent's Job	Respondent's Party Identification: Str. Dem.	Weak Dem.	Ind. Dem.	Ind. Ind.	Ind. Rep.	Weak Rep.	Str. Rep.	Total	
DEMOCRATIC CONGRESSMEN									
Very Good	41%	23%	16%	25%	13%	11%	18%	23%	[231]
Good	38	43	44	36	49	43	36	41	[413]
Fair	18	31	34	32	31	43	33	30	[304]
Poor	2	3	4	4	6	3	10	4	[37]
Very Poor	2	.....	2	3	1	1	3	1	[14]
[N]	[194]	[275]	[136]	[114]	[97]	[105]	[78]		[999]
REPUBLICAN CONGRESSMEN									
Very Good	12%	15%	10%	12%	27%	18%	33%	17%	[107]
Good	46	39	45	54	51	52	51	48	[294]
Fair	38	42	36	29	16	27	16	30	[186]
Poor	4	4	8	2	6	3	0	4	[24]
Very Poor	0	1	1	2	0	0	0	1	[4]
[N]	[69]	[124]	[89]	[85]	[70]	[105]	[73]		[615]

TABLE 4-2

INCUMBENCY VOTE BY RATING THE JOB THE INCUMBENT CONGRESSMAN HAS DONE AND RESPONDENT'S PARTY IDENTIFICATION, CONTROLLING FOR INCUMBENT'S PARTY

Rate Incumbent's Job	Respondent's Party Identification: Str. Dem.	Weak Dem.	Ind. Dem.	Ind. Ind.	Ind. Rep.	Weak Rep.	Str. Rep.	Total	
DEMOCRATIC CONGRESSMEN									
Very Good	100	100	100	100	...	...	89	99	[122]
Good	95	92	100	94	91	93	40	90	[202]
Fair	95	96	80	67	70	32	23	67	[110]
Poor	...	...	...	...	...	...	...	35	[17]
Very Poor	...	...	...	...	...	...	...	60	[5]
Total	97	95	95	84	79	68	43	85	
[N]	[114]	[101]	[55]	[43]	[43]	[56]	[44]		[456]
REPUBLICAN CONGRESSMEN									
Very Good	...	88	...	...	100	100	100	97	[61]
Good	52	82	92	86	100	97	100	88	[173]
Fair	27	45	67	88	50	92	100	61	[77]
Poor	...	...	...	...	...	...	...	9	[11]
Very Poor	...	...	...	...	...	...	...	100	[2]
Total	42	63	76	85	95	95	100	80	
[N]	[41]	[48]	[49]	[34]	[43]	[60]	[49]		[324]

Cell entries are the proportion of voters who reported voting for the Incumbent in the House race in their district.

TABLE 4-3

RATING FOR INCUMBENT CONGRESSMAN ON THE FEELING THERMOMETER BY RESPONDENT'S PARTY IDENTIFICATION, CONTROLLING FOR INCUMBENT'S PARTY

Feeling Therm. Rating	Respondent's Party Identification								
	Str. Dem.	Weak Dem.	Ind. Dem.	Ind. Ind.	Ind. Rep.	Weak Rep.	Str. Rep.	Total	
DEMOCRATIC CONGRESSMEN									
Very Pos.	61%	40%	35%	31%	25%	24%	17%	37%	[405]
Positive	24	32	38	32	38	40	39	33	[364]
Neutral	10	21	14	28	21	24	18	19	[208]
Negative	5	6	13	10	17	12	27	11	[115]
[N]	[205]	[293]	[153]	[133]	[109]	[120]	[79]		[1092]
REPUBLICAN CONGRESSMEN									
Very Pos.	33%	26%	30%	32%	45%	35%	50%	35%	[231]
Positive	35	46	38	34	32	41	40	39	[256]
Neutral	17	18	18	25	15	16	6	17	[112]
Negative	15	10	15	9	8	7	4	10	[65]
[N]	[72]	[126]	[104]	[97]	[73]	[116]	[76]		[664]

TABLE 4-4

INCUMBENCY VOTE BY RATING FOR INCUMBENT CONGRESSMAN ON THE FEELING THERMOMETER AND RESPONDENT'S PARTY IDENTIFICATION, CONTROLLING FOR INCUMBENT'S PARTY

Feeling Therm. Rating	Respondent's Party Identification								
	Str. Dem.	Weak Dem.	Ind. Dem.	Ind. Ind.	Ind. Rep.	Weak Rep.	Str. Rep.	Total	
DEMOCRATIC CONGRESSMEN									
Very Pos.	100	100	96	100	85	100	...	98	[206]
Positive	100	97	96	81	95	70	47	85	[162]
Neutral	100	79	100	89	78	50	...	77	[64]
Negative	...	80	60	...	14	...	8	27	[44]
Total	97	95	93	81	77	69	41	84	
[N]	[114]	[108]	[57]	[47]	[48]	[58]	[44]		[476]
REPUBLICAN CONGRESSMEN									
Very Pos.	67	100	95	93	100	100	100	96	[137]
Positive	39	70	76	87	100	97	100	81	[144]
Neutral	...	29	33	100	...	100	...	62	[26]
Negative	...	...	...	50	...	...	...	23	[26]
Total	42	63	74	89	100	95	100	81	
[N]	[41]	[49]	[53]	[35]	[43]	[63]	[49]		[333]

Cell entries are the proportion of voters who reported voting for the Incumbent in the House race in their district.

TABLE 4-5

RECOGNIZE NAME OF INCUMBENT CONGRESSMAN
BY RESPONDENT'S PARTY IDENTIFICATION,
CONTROLLING FOR INCUMBENT'S PARTY

Recognize Incumbent's Name?	Respondent's Party Identification								
	Str. Dem.	Weak Dem.	Ind. Dem.	Ind. Ind.	Ind. Rep.	Weak Rep.	Str. Rep.	Total	
DEMOCRATIC CONGRESSMEN									
Yes	91%	89%	86%	86%	88%	89%	93%	89%	[1237]
No	9	11	14	14	12	11	8	11	[157]
[N]	[244]	[389]	[199]	[182]	[138]	[149]	[93]		[1394]
REPUBLICAN CONGRESSMEN									
Yes	88%	87%	88%	86%	96%	92%	98%	90%	[733]
No	12	13	13	14	4	8	2	10	[83]
[N]	[94]	[164]	[128]	[127]	[78]	[143]	[82]		[816]

TABLE 4-6

INCUMBENCY VOTE BY RECOGNIZE NAME OF INCUMBENT CONGRESSMAN
AND RESPONDENT'S PARTY IDENTIFICATION,
CONTROLLING FOR INCUMBENT'S PARTY

Recognize Incumbent's Name?	Respondent's Party Identification								
	Str. Dem.	Weak Dem.	Ind. Dem.	Ind. Ind.	Ind. Rep.	Weak Rep.	Str. Rep.	Total	
DEMOCRATIC CONGRESSMEN									
Yes	98	95	93	82	74	68	45	84	[506]
No	100	83	100	100	0	0	0	65	[20]
Total	98	94	94	83	73	65	43	83	
[N]	[123]	[124]	[62]	[52]	[51]	[65]	[49]		[526]
REPUBLICAN CONGRESSMEN									
Yes	41	62	71	84	96	95	100	79	[344]
No	0	0	100	100	...	100	...	50	[8]
Total	39	60	72	84	96	96	100	79	
[N]	[44]	[52]	[57]	[39]	[45]	[65]	[50]		[352]

Cell entries are the proportion of voters who reported voting for the Incumbent in the House race in their district.

TABLE 4-7

CONTACTED BY INCUMBENT CONGRESSMAN
BY RESPONDENT'S PARTY IDENTIFICATION,
CONTROLLING FOR INCUMBENT'S PARTY

Contacted by Incumbent?	Respondent's Party Identification								
	Str. Dem.	Weak Dem.	Ind. Dem.	Ind. Ind.	Ind. Rep.	Weak Rep.	Str. Rep.	Total	
DEMOCRATIC CONGRESSMEN									
Yes	80%	73%	75%	71%	81%	77%	78%	76%	[1062]
No	20	27	25	29	19	24	22	24	[341]
[N]	[245]	[392]	[199]	[184]	[139]	[149]	[95]		[1403]
REPUBLICAN CONGRESSMEN									
Yes	81%	80%	80%	75%	91%	79%	90%	81%	[665]
No	19	20	20	25	9	21	10	19	[154]
[N]	[94]	[165]	[128]	[128]	[78]	[143]	[83]		[819]

TABLE 4-8

INCUMBENCY VOTE BY CONTACTED BY INCUMBENT CONGRESSMAN
AND RESPONDENT'S PARTY IDENTIFICATION,
CONTROLLING FOR INCUMBENT'S PARTY

Contacted by Incumbent?	Respondent's Party Identification								
	Str. Dem.	Weak Dem.	Ind. Dem.	Ind. Ind.	Ind. Rep.	Weak Rep.	Str. Rep.	Total	
DEMOCRATIC CONGRESSMEN									
Yes	97	95	95	83	78	67	40	85	[458]
No	100	90	75	83	20	50	55	76	[70]
Total	98	94	94	83	73	65	43	83	
[N]	[125]	[124]	[62]	[52]	[51]	[65]	[49]		[528]
REPUBLICAN CONGRESSMEN									
Yes	41	63	73	89	96	95	100	80	[329]
No	0	33	60	50	...	100	100	57	[23]
Total	39	60	72	85	96	95	100	79	
[N]	[44]	[52]	[57]	[39]	[45]	[65]	[50]		[352]

Cell entries are the proportion of voters who reported voting for the Incumbent in the House race in their district.

TABLE 4-9

EVER CONTACT INCUMBENT CONGRESSMAN
BY RESPONDENT'S PARTY IDENTIFICATION,
CONTROLLING FOR INCUMBENT'S PARTY

Ever Contact Incumbent?	Respondent's Party Identification							Total	
	Str. Dem.	Weak Dem.	Ind. Dem.	Ind. Ind.	Ind. Rep.	Weak Rep.	Str. Rep.		
DEMOCRATIC CONGRESSMEN									
Yes	18%	13%	17%	11%	14%	14%	15%	14%	[197]
No	83	87	83	89	86	86	85	86	[1176]
[N]	[240]	[379]	[198]	[180]	[137]	[147]	[92]		[1373]
REPUBLICAN CONGRESSMEN									
Yes	13%	11%	16%	11%	27%	20%	37%	18%	[143]
No	87	89	84	89	73	80	63	82	[665]
[N]	[94]	[163]	[126]	[126]	[78]	[142]	[79]		[808]

TABLE 4-10

INCUMBENCY VOTE BY EVER CONTACT INCUMBENT CONGRESSMAN
AND RESPONDENT'S PARTY IDENTIFICATION,
CONTROLLING FOR INCUMBENT'S PARTY

Ever Contact Incumbent?	Respondent's Party Identification							Total	
	Str. Dem.	Weak Dem.	Ind. Dem.	Ind. Ind.	Ind. Rep.	Weak Rep.	Str. Rep.		
DEMOCRATIC CONGRESSMEN									
Yes	96	94	100	92	50	60	50	83	[94]
No	98	96	92	82	77	64	42	84	[422]
Total	98	96	93	84	73	64	44	84	
[N]	[123]	[120]	[61]	[50]	[51]	[63]	[48]		[516]
REPUBLICAN CONGRESSMEN									
Yes	63	100	67	100	94	96	100	91	[90]
No	33	54	72	81	97	96	100	74	[258]
Total	39	60	71	84	96	96	100	78	
[N]	[44]	[52]	[56]	[39]	[45]	[65]	[47]		[348]

Cell entries are the proportion of voters who reported voting for the Incumbent in the House race in their district.

TABLE 4-11

HAS INCUMBENT CONGRESSMAN DONE ANYTHING SPECIAL FOR THE DISTRICT BY RESPONDENT'S PARTY IDENTIFICATION, CONTROLLING FOR INCUMBENT'S PARTY

Incumbent Done Anything Special?	Respondent's Party Identification								
	Str. Dem.	Weak Dem.	Ind. Dem.	Ind. Ind.	Ind. Rep.	Weak Rep.	Str. Rep.	Total	
	DEMOCRATIC CONGRESSMEN								
Yes	33%	20%	21%	17%	23%	15%	26%	22%	[311]
No	67	80	79	84	77	85	74	78	[1089]
[N]	[245]	[392]	[199]	[182]	[139]	[148]	[95]		[1400]
	REPUBLICAN CONGRESSMEN								
Yes	18%	12%	16%	13%	27%	17%	29%	18%	[143]
No	82	89	84	87	73	83	71	83	[674]
[N]	[93]	[165]	[129]	[128]	[77]	[143]	[82]		[817]

TABLE 4-12

INCUMBENCY VOTE BY HAS INCUMBENT CONGRESSMAN DONE ANYTHING SPECIAL FOR THE DISTRICT AND RESPONDENT'S PARTY IDENTIFICATION, CONTROLLING FOR INCUMBENT'S PARTY

Incumbent Done Anything Special?	Respondent's Party Identification								
	Str. Dem.	Weak Dem.	Ind. Dem.	Ind. Ind.	Ind. Rep.	Weak Rep.	Str. Rep.	Total	
	DEMOCRATIC CONGRESSMEN								
Yes	100	94	100	93	71	83	42	88	[168]
No	96	95	90	79	73	60	44	81	[360]
Total	98	94	94	83	73	65	43	83	
[N]	[125]	[124]	[62]	[52]	[51]	[65]	[49]		[528]
	REPUBLICAN CONGRESSMEN								
Yes	55	67	77	100	100	94	100	88	[97]
No	34	58	71	79	92	96	100	76	[254]
Total	40	60	72	85	96	96	100	79	
[N]	[43]	[52]	[57]	[39]	[45]	[65]	[50]		[351]

Cell entries are the proportion of voters who reported voting for the Incumbent in the House race in their district.

TABLE 4-13

WOULD INCUMBENT CONGRESSMAN BE HELPFUL WITH PROBLEM
BY RESPONDENT'S PARTY IDENTIFICATION,
CONTROLLING FOR INCUMBENT'S PARTY

Would Incumbent Be Helpful?	Respondent's Party Identification								
	Str. Dem.	Weak Dem.	Ind. Dem.	Ind. Ind.	Ind. Rep.	Weak Rep.	Str. Rep.	Total	
DEMOCRATIC CONGRESSMEN									
Very Helpful	62%	40%	29%	34%	40%	23%	37%	40%	[400]
Somewhat Helpful	32	49	51	47	42	63	47	46	[466]
Not Very Helpful	6	11	21	19	18	14	16	14	[138]
[N]	[187]	[280]	[144]	[121]	[95]	[107]	[70]		[1004]
REPUBLICAN CONGRESSMEN									
Very Helpful	33%	27%	34%	26%	48%	33%	56%	35%	[206]
Somewhat Helpful	46	62	49	55	44	62	38	53	[312]
Not Very Helpful	21	11	17	19	8	4	6	13	[74]
[N]	[67]	[125]	[90]	[94]	[63]	[90]	[63]		[592]

TABLE 4-14

INCUMBENCY VOTE BY WOULD INCUMBENT CONGRESSMAN BE HELPFUL WITH PROBLEM AND RESPONDENT'S PARTY IDENTIFICATION, CONTROLLING FOR INCUMBENT'S PARTY

Would Incumbent Be Helpful?	Respondent's Party Identification: Str. Dem.	Weak Dem.	Ind. Dem.	Ind. Ind.	Ind. Rep.	Weak Rep.	Str. Rep.	Total	
DEMOCRATIC CONGRESSMEN									
Very Helpful	99	96	100	87	88	71	77	93	[202]
Somewhat Helpful	97	94	96	87	82	77	30	83	[197]
Not Very Helpful	...	80	50	50	17	...	...	48	[40]
Total	97	93	93	85	74	70	42	84	
[N]	[106]	[103]	[56]	[40]	[39]	[54]	[41]		[439]
REPUBLICAN CONGRESSMEN									
Very Helpful	78	92	89	100	100	96	100	95	[121]
Somewhat Helpful	40	48	78	88	95	94	100	76	[164]
Not Very Helpful	...	...	...	...	...	...	...	26	[19]
Total	45	60	76	85	95	95	100	80	
[N]	[38]	[45]	[45]	[33]	[43]	[55]	[45]		[304]

Cell entries are the proportion of voters who reported voting for the Incumbent in the House race in their district.

TABLE 4-15

AGREE/DISAGREE WITH INCUMBENT CONGRESSMAN'S VOTING RECORD
BY RESPONDENT'S PARTY IDENTIFICATION,
CONTROLLING FOR INCUMBENT'S PARTY

Opinion of Incumbent's Voting Record	Respondent's Party Identification								
	Str. Dem.	Weak Dem.	Ind. Dem.	Ind. Ind.	Ind. Rep.	Weak Rep.	Str. Rep.	Total	
	DEMOCRATIC CONGRESSMEN								
Agree	43%	26%	27%	23%	18%	10%	15%	26%	[152]
Agree Somewhat	38	46	43	45	48	48	44	44	[257]
Neutral	12	20	21	24	13	30	15	19	[110]
Disagree Somewhat	5	7	7	5	13	12	15	8	[46]
Disagree	3	1	3	3	8	0	13	3	[20]
[N]	[133]	[138]	[73]	[62]	[62]	[69]	[48]		[585]
	REPUBLICAN CONGRESSMEN								
Agree	18%	8%	9%	18%	29%	14%	40%	18%	[67]
Agree Somewhat	46	52	40	37	44	58	40	46	[168]
Neutral	23	31	32	33	18	22	15	25	[92]
Disagree Somewhat	8	8	12	6	9	5	6	8	[28]
Disagree	5	2	7	6	0	2	0	3	[11]
[N]	[39]	[62]	[57]	[51]	[45]	[64]	[48]		[366]

TABLE 4-16

INCUMBENCY VOTE BY AGREE/DISAGREE WITH INCUMBENT CONGRESSMAN'S VOTING RECORD AND RESPONDENT'S PARTY IDENTIFICATION, CONTROLLING FOR INCUMBENT'S PARTY

Opinion of Incumbent's Voting Record	Respondent's Party Identification								
	Str. Dem.	Weak Dem.	Ind. Dem.	Ind. Ind.	Ind. Rep.	Weak Rep.	Str. Rep.	Total	
DEMOCRATIC CONGRESSMEN									
Agree	100	100	100	100	80	100	100	99	[81]
Agree Somewhat	96	93	96	86	84	86	57	88	[147]
Neutral	100	88	0	72	100	50	20	71	[41]
Disagree Somewhat	...	...	...	...	...	...	...	35	[17]
Disagree	...	...	...	...	...	...	...	40	[10]
Total	99	94	94	82	76	69	44	84	
[N]	[80]	[51]	[36]	[28]	[33]	[36]	[32]		[296]
REPUBLICAN CONGRESSMEN									
Agree	...	100	100	100	100	100	100	95	[42]
Agree Somewhat	73	67	94	100	100	100	100	92	[106]
Neutral	...	20	60	...	...	...	...	62	[29]
Disagree Somewhat	...	...	...	...	...	...	...	73	[15]
Disagree	...	...	...	...	...	...	...	14	[7]
Total	47	58	78	91	97	97	100	84	
[N]	[19]	[26]	[32]	[22]	[30]	[35]	[35]		[199]

Cell entries are the proportion of voters who reported voting for the Incumbent in the House race in their district.

TABLE 5-1

RECOGNIZE NAME OF DEMOCRATIC CONGRESSIONAL CANDIDATE
BY TYPE OF RACE AND RESPONDENT'S PARTY IDENTIFICATION

Respondent's Party I.D.	Type of Race							Total	
	Democr. Incumb. Running Con-tested	Democr. Incumb. Running Uncon-tested	Repub. Incumb. Running Con-tested	Repub. Incumb. Running Uncon-tested	Op.Seat Con-tested (Dem. Incum.)	Op.Seat Uncon-tested (Dem. Incum.)	Op.Seat Con-tested (Rep. Incum.)		
Str. Dem.	92	89	59	...	89	...	82	84	[325]
Weak Dem.	87	91	64	...	89	100	94	33	[524]
Ind. Dem.	89	76	66	...	84	78	...	79	[302]
Ind. Ind.	86	80	68	...	87	...	...	78	[291]
Ind. Rep.	87	95	55	...	91	...	...	78	[205]
Weak Rep.	87	92	72	...	79	...	80	81	[279]
Str. Rep.	94	93	72	...	92	...	...	85	[166]
Total	88	87	66	...	88	84	85	81	
[N]	[881]	[315]	[629]	[0]	[161]	[38]	[68]		[2092]

Cell entries are the proportion of respondents who could recognize the name of the Democratic congressional candidate from their district.

TABLE 5-2

PARTY VOTE BY
RECOGNIZE NAME OF DEMOCRATIC CONGRESSIONAL CANDIDATE
AND RESPONDENT'S PARTY IDENTIFICATION

Recognize Democratic Candidate's Name?	Respondent's Party Identification							Total	
	Str. Dem.	Weak Dem.	Ind. Dem.	Ind. Ind.	Ind. Rep.	Weak Rep.	Str. Rep.		
Yes	91	83	71	66	48	40	24	65	[849]
No	67	60	33	10	0	0	0	28	[131]
Total	88	81	65	60	39	35	20	60	
[N]	[195]	[208]	[124]	[94]	[103]	[142]	[114]		[980]

Cell entries are the proportion of voters who reported voting Democratic in the House race in their district.

TABLE 5-3

RECALL NAME OF DEMOCRATIC CONGRESSIONAL CANDIDATE
BY TYPE OF RACE AND RESPONDENT'S PARTY IDENTIFICATION

Respondent's Party I.D.	Type of Race								
	Democr. Incumb. Running Contested	Democr. Incumb. Running Uncontested	Repub. Incumb. Running Contested	Repub. Incumb. Running Uncontested	Op.Seat Contested (Dem. Incum.)	Op.Seat Uncontested (Dem. Incum.)	Op.Seat Contested (Rep. Incum.)	Total	
Str. Dem.	44	40	11	...	33	...	18	35	[327]
Weak Dem.	32	28	9	...	27	20	44	26	[527]
Ind. Dem.	31	20	13	...	16	0	...	21	[303]
Ind. Ind.	21	16	9	...	27	...	...	16	[294]
Ind. Rep.	38	35	16	...	29	...	...	30	[205]
Weak Rep.	39	32	12	...	36	...	27	26	[279]
Str. Rep.	48	28	23	...	46	...	...	36	[168]
Total	35	28	13	...	29	21	34	26	
[N]	[886]	[319]	[631]	[0]	[161]	[38]	[68]		[2103]

Cell entries are the proportion of respondents who could recall the name of the Democratic congressional candidate from their district.

TABLE 5-4

PARTY VOTE BY
RECALL NAME OF DEMOCRATIC CONGRESSIONAL CANDIDATE
AND RESPONDENT'S PARTY IDENTIFICATION

Recall Democratic Candidate's Name?	Respondent's Party Identification								
	Str. Dem.	Weak Dem.	Ind. Dem.	Ind. Ind.	Ind. Rep.	Weak Rep.	Str. Rep.	Total	
Yes	95	90	88	63	54	53	24	71	[370]
No	83	75	54	58	31	24	18	54	[612]
Total	88	81	65	60	39	35	20	60	
[N]	[197]	[208]	[124]	[94]	[103]	[142]	[114]		[982]

Cell entries are the proportion of voters who reported voting Democratic in the House race in their district.

TABLE 5-5

LIKED SOMETHING ABOUT DEMOCRATIC CONGRESSIONAL CANDIDATE
BY TYPE OF RACE AND RESPONDENT'S PARTY IDENTIFICATION

Respondent's Party I.D.	Type of Race: Democr. Incumb. Running Contested	Democr. Incumb. Running Uncontested	Repub. Incumb. Running Contested	Repub. Incumb. Running Uncontested	Op.Seat Contested (Dem. Incum.)	Op.Seat Uncontested (Dem. Incum.)	Op.Seat Contested (Rep. Incum.)	Total	
Str. Dem.	77	76	44	...	71	...	40	72	[229]
Weak Dem.	58	65	24	...	62	57	54	54	[342]
Ind. Dem.	59	37	21	...	31	25	...	43	[210]
Ind. Ind.	33	45	23	...	40	...	...	33	[179]
Ind. Rep.	56	...	13	...	42	...	...	41	[133]
Weak Rep.	53	42	17	...	40	...	8	36	[174]
Str. Rep.	55	77	19	...	33	...	...	45	[106]
Total	58	55	23	...	52	50	40	48	
[N]	[681]	[210]	[316]	[0]	[97]	[24]	[45]		[1373]

Cell entries are the proportion of respondents who reported liking something about the Democratic congressional candidate from their district.

TABLE 5-6

PARTY VOTE BY
LIKED SOMETHING ABOUT DEMOCRATIC CONGRESSIONAL CANDIDATE
AND RESPONDENT'S PARTY IDENTIFICATION

Liked Something About Democratic Candidate?	Respondent's Party Identification: Str. Dem.	Weak Dem.	Ind. Dem.	Ind. Ind.	Ind. Rep.	Weak Rep.	Str. Rep.	Total	
Yes	97	95	95	90	70	79	39	87	[400]
No	75	67	44	55	33	23	14	45	[337]
Total	91	84	73	68	50	42	26	67	
[N]	[156]	[160]	[97]	[72]	[76]	[98]	[78]		[737]

Cell entries are the proportion of voters who reported voting Democratic in the House race in their district.

TABLE 5-7

DID NOT LIKE SOMETHING ABOUT DEMOCRATIC CONGRESSIONAL CANDIDATE
BY TYPE OF RACE AND RESPONDENT'S PARTY IDENTIFICATION

Respondent's Party I.D.	Type of Race							
	Democr. Incumb. Running Con-tested	Democr. Incumb. Running Uncon-tested	Repub. Incumb. Running Con-tested	Repub. Incumb. Running Uncon-tested	Op.Seat Con-tested (Dem. Incum.)	Op.Seat Uncon-tested (Dem. Incum.)	Op.Seat Con-tested (Rep. Incum.)	Total
Str. Dem.	9	2	13	...	33	...	14	11 [237]
Weak Dem.	16	2	14	...	14	0	17	13 [352]
Ind. Dem.	22	7	7	...	22	0	...	15 [214]
Ind. Ind.	11	0	16	...	55	...	...	15 [190]
Ind. Rep.	28	6	29	...	42	...	...	26 [133]
Weak Rep.	15	4	22	...	25	...	9	16 [176]
Str. Rep.	50	22	32	...	29	...	...	38 [107]
Total	18	5	18	...	27	24	22	17
[N]	[693]	[215]	[323]	[0]	[107]	[25]	[46]	[1409]

Cell entries are the proportion of respondents who reported not liking something about the Democratic congressional candidate from their district.

TABLE 5-8

PARTY VOTE BY
DID NOT LIKE SOMETHING ABOUT DEMOCRATIC CONGRESSIONAL CANDIDATE
AND RESPONDENT'S PARTY IDENTIFICATION

Did Not Like Something About Democratic Candidate?	Respondent's Party Identification							
	Str. Dem.	Weak Dem.	Ind. Dem.	Ind. Ind.	Ind. Rep.	Weak Rep.	Str. Rep.	Total
Yes	72	67	55	36	21	24	17	40 [159]
No	93	87	77	78	65	46	33	75 [596]
Total	90	84	72	69	51	41	26	67
[N]	[160]	[167]	[101]	[72]	[75]	[102]	[78]	[755]

Cell entries are the proportion of voters who reported voting Democratic in the House race in their district.

TABLE 5-9

CONTACTED BY DEMOCRATIC CONGRESSIONAL CANDIDATE
BY TYPE OF RACE AND RESPONDENT'S PARTY IDENTIFICATION

Respondent's Party I.D.	Type of Race: Democr. Incumb. Running Con-tested	Democr. Incumb. Running Uncon-tested	Repub. Incumb. Running Con-tested	Repub. Incumb. Running Uncon-tested	Op.Seat Con-tested (Dem. Incum.)	Op.Seat Uncon-tested (Dem. Incum.)	Op.Seat Con-tested (Rep. Incum.)	Total	
Str. Dem.	81	72	44	...	81	...	64	71	[326]
Weak Dem.	75	67	49	...	64	50	75	66	[527]
Ind. Dem.	82	58	51	...	67	55	...	66	[301]
Ind. Ind.	71	67	44	...	80	...	...	61	[294]
Ind. Rep.	78	90	48	...	71	...	...	70	[205]
Weak Rep.	77	74	44	...	71	...	60	62	[279]
Str. Rep.	83	66	65	...	54	...	...	67	[168]
Total	77	69	48	...	69	55	72	66	
[N]	[886]	[319]	[631]	[0]	[159]	[38]	[67]		[2100]

Cell entries are the proportion of respondents who reported coming into contact with the Democratic congressional candidate from their district.

TABLE 5-10

PARTY VOTE BY
CONTACTED BY DEMOCRATIC CONGRESSIONAL CANDIDATE
AND RESPONDENT'S PARTY IDENTIFICATION

Contacted By Democratic Candidate?	Respondent's Party Identification: Str. Dem.	Weak Dem.	Ind. Dem.	Ind. Ind.	Ind. Rep.	Weak Rep.	Str. Rep.	Total	
Yes	93	85	69	66	50	46	22	67	[738]
No	71	68	46	38	7	9	17	39	[243]
Total	88	81	65	60	39	35	20	60	
[N]	[196]	[208]	[124]	[94]	[103]	[142]	[114]		[981]

Cell entries are the proportion of voters who reported voting Democratic in the House race in their district.

TABLE 5-11

RATING FOR DEMOCRATIC CANDIDATE ON THE FEELING THERMOMETER
BY TYPE OF RACE

Feeling Therm. Rating	Type of Race: Democr. Incumb. Running Contested	Democr. Incumb. Running Uncontested	Repub. Incumb. Running Contested	Repub. Incumb. Running Uncontested	Op.Seat Contested (Dem. Incum.)	Op.Seat Uncontested (Dem. Incum.)	Op.Seat Contested (Rep. Incum.)	Total	
Very Pos.	36%	44%	8%	...	25%	43%	16%	30%	[433]
Positive	35	31	28	...	33	20	36	32	[465]
Neutral	19	19	47	...	24	30	32	26	[371]
Negative	11	6	17	...	19	7	16	12	[171]
[N]	[724]	[232]	[300]	[0]	[110]	[30]	[44]		[1440]

TABLE 5-12

RATING FOR DEMOCRATIC CANDIDATE ON THE FEELING THERMOMETER
BY RESPONDENT'S PARTY IDENTIFICATION

Feeling Therm. Rating	Respondent's Party Identification: Str. Dem.	Weak Dem.	Ind. Dem.	Ind. Ind.	Ind. Rep.	Weak Rep.	Str. Rep.	Total	
Very Pos.	55%	37%	26%	21%	18%	18%	12%	30%	[426]
Positive	25	33	36	35	31	35	33	32	[454]
Neutral	13	24	23	35	30	33	30	26	[363]
Negative	8	5	15	10	20	14	24	12	[167]
[N]	[241]	[353]	[205]	[182]	[137]	[177]	[115]		[1410]

TABLE 5-13

AVERAGE FEELING THERMOMETER RATING FOR DEMOCRATIC CANDIDATE BY TYPE OF RACE AND RESPONDENT'S PARTY IDENTIFICATION

Respondent's Party I.D.	Type of Race: Democr. Incumb. Running Con-tested	Democr. Incumb. Running Uncon-tested	Repub. Incumb. Running Con-tested	Repub. Incumb. Running Uncon-tested	Op.Seat Con-tested (Dem. Incum.)	Op.Seat Uncon-tested (Dem. Incum.)	Op.Seat Con-tested (Rep. Incum.)	Total	
Str. Dem.	79	79	55	...	69	...	62	75	[241]
Weak Dem.	70	76	57	...	70	79	64	69	[253]
Ind. Dem.	67	65	55	...	54	57	...	62	[205]
Ind. Ind.	62	73	56	...	50	...	...	61	[182]
Ind. Rep.	60	65	49	...	49	...	...	57	[137]
Weak Rep.	65	65	50	...	56	...	48	59	[177]
Str. Rep.	55	64	46	...	40	...	...	53	[115]
Total	68	72	53	...	60	70	56	64	
[N]	[707]	[227]	[295]	[0]	[109]	[29]	[43]		[1410]

Cell entries are the average feeling thermometer ratings reported by respondents for the Democratic congressional candidate in their district.

TABLE 5-14

PARTY VOTE BY RATING FOR DEMOCRATIC CANDIDATE ON THE FEELING THERMOMETER AND RESPONDENT'S PARTY IDENTIFICATION

Feeling Therm. Rating	Respondent's Party Identification: Str. Dem.	Weak Dem.	Ind. Dem.	Ind. Ind.	Ind. Rep.	Weak Rep.	Str. Rep.	Total	
Very Pos.	99	97	93	100	86	100	...	96	[248]
Positive	94	85	85	64	75	63	35	75	[243]
Neutral	85	65	40	67	30	22	17	44	[160]
Negative	50	57	23	0	7	0	4	17	[88]
Total	92	86	73	69	50	47	24	69	
[N]	[156]	[166]	[94]	[68]	[76]	[97]	[82]		[739]

Cell entries are the proportion of voters who reported voting Democratic in the House race in their district.

TABLE 5-15

RECOGNIZE NAME OF REPUBLICAN CONGRESSIONAL CANDIDATE BY TYPE OF RACE AND RESPONDENT'S PARTY IDENTIFICATION

Respondent's Party I.D.	Type of Race: Democr. Incumb. Running Contested	Democr. Incumb. Running Uncontested	Repub. Incumb. Running Contested	Repub. Incumb. Running Uncontested	Op.Seat Contested (Dem. Incum.)	Op.Seat Uncontested (Dem. Incum.)	Op.Seat Contested (Rep. Incum.)	Total	
Str. Dem.	54	...	96	69	93	...	90	70	[278]
Weak Dem.	48	...	87	83	79	...	94	66	[454]
Ind. Dem.	57	...	92	72	90	...	...	74	[270]
Ind. Ind.	52	...	86	83	87	...	...	70	[257]
Ind. Rep.	63	...	97	100	81	...	...	79	[195]
Weak Rep.	56	...	93	92	79	...	87	78	[252]
Str. Rep.	67	...	99	89	85	...	...	85	[147]
Total	54	...	92	83	84	...	89	73	
[N]	[878]	[0]	[628]	[120]	[161]	[0]	[66]		[1853]

Cell entries are the proportion of respondents who could recognize the name of the Republican congressional candidate from their district.

TABLE 5-16

PARTY VOTE BY RECOGNIZE NAME OF REPUBLICAN CONGRESSIONAL CANDIDATE AND RESPONDENT'S PARTY IDENTIFICATION

Recognize Republican Candidate's Name?	Respondent's Party Identification: Str. Dem.	Weak Dem.	Ind. Dem.	Ind. Ind.	Ind. Rep.	Weak Rep.	Str. Rep.	Total	
Yes	80	69	51	39	22	19	9	44	[700]
No	100	97	86	88	80	64	40	36	[193]
Total	85	77	57	49	31	27	13	53	
[N]	[173]	[186]	[114]	[82]	[100]	[132]	[106]		[893]

Cell entries are the proportion of voters who reported voting Democratic in the House race in their district.

TABLE 5-17

RECALL NAME OF REPUBLICAN CONGRESSIONAL CANDIDATE
BY TYPE OF RACE AND RESPONDENT'S PARTY IDENTIFICATION

Respondent's Party I.D.	Type of Race								
	Democr. Incumb. Running Con-tested	Democr. Incumb. Running Uncon-tested	Repub. Incumb. Running Con-tested	Repub. Incumb. Running Uncon-tested	Op.Seat Con-tested (Dem. Incum.)	Op.Seat Uncon-tested (Dem. Incum.)	Op.Seat Con-tested (Rep. Incum.)	Total	
Str. Dem.	9	...	31	7	22	...	9	16	[282]
Weak Dem.	8	...	28	27	23	...	38	17	[458]
Ind. Dem.	6	...	37	20	16	...	...	20	[272]
Ind. Ind.	5	...	27	17	20	...	...	16	[260]
Ind. Rep.	18	...	57	33	33	...	...	33	[195]
Weak Rep.	15	...	34	39	29	...	27	26	[252]
Str. Rep.	25	...	52	30	31	...	...	41	[148]
Total	10	...	36	24	24	...	32	22	
[N]	[886]	[0]	[631]	[121]	[161]	[0]	[68]		[1867]

Cell entries are the proportion of respondents who could recall the name of the Republican congressional candidate from their district.

TABLE 5-18

PARTY VOTE BY
RECALL NAME OF REPUBLICAN CONGRESSIONAL CANDIDATE
AND RESPONDENT'S PARTY IDENTIFICATION

Recall Republican Candidate's Name?	Respondent's Party Identification								
	Str. Dem.	Weak Dem.	Ind. Dem.	Ind. Ind.	Ind. Rep.	Weak Rep.	Str. Rep.	Total	
Yes	74	55	35	24	9	14	2	27	[284]
No	87	85	63	60	49	35	25	66	[613]
Total	85	77	57	49	31	27	13	53	
[N]	[177]	[186]	[114]	[82]	[100]	[132]	[106]		[897]

Cell entries are the proportion of voters who reported voting Democratic in the House race in their district.

TABLE 5-19

LIKED SOMETHING ABOUT REPUBLICAN CONGRESSIONAL CANDIDATE
BY TYPE OF RACE AND RESPONDENT'S PARTY IDENTIFICATION

Respondent's Party I.D.	Type of Race: Democr. Incumb. Running Con-tested	Democr. Incumb. Running Uncon-tested	Repub. Incumb. Running Con-tested	Repub. Incumb. Running Uncon-tested	Op.Seat Con-tested (Dem. Incum.)	Op.Seat Uncon-tested (Dem. Incum.)	Op.Seat Con-tested (Rep. Incum.)	Total	
Str. Dem.	10	...	54	38	20	...	22	30	[141]
Weak Dem.	13	...	54	50	27	...	25	35	[230]
Ind. Dem.	6	...	58	50	44	...	...	39	[158]
Ind. Ind.	9	...	48	36	33	...	...	34	[146]
Ind. Rep.	30	...	68	82	67	...	...	57	[122]
Weak Rep.	29	...	65	56	33	...	50	53	[162]
Str. Rep.	46	...	86	57	78	...	...	74	[105]
Total	17	...	61	52	41	...	43	44	
[N]	[339]	[0]	[517]	[85]	[81]	[0]	[42]		[1064]

Cell entries are the proportion of respondents who reported liking something about the Republican congressional candidate from their district.

TABLE 5-20

PARTY VOTE BY
LIKED SOMETHING ABOUT REPUBLICAN CONGRESSIONAL CANDIDATE
AND RESPONDENT'S PARTY IDENTIFICATION

Liked Something About Republican Candidate?	Respondent's Party Identification: Str. Dem.	Weak Dem.	Ind. Dem.	Ind. Ind.	Ind. Rep.	Weak Rep.	Str. Rep.	Total	
Yes	53	27	15	12	4	5	0	13	[334]
No	83	88	81	64	71	32	28	70	[253]
Total	74	61	46	34	19	14	6	38	
[N]	[98]	[101]	[76]	[59]	[73]	[98]	[82]		[587]

Cell entries are the proportion of voters who reported voting Democratic in the House race in their district.

TABLE 5-21

DID NOT LIKE SOMETHING ABOUT REPUBLICAN CONGRESSIONAL CANDIDATE BY TYPE OF RACE AND RESPONDENT'S PARTY IDENTIFICATION

Respondent's Party I.D.	Democr. Incumb. Running Contested	Democr. Incumb. Running Uncontested	Repub. Incumb. Running Contested	Repub. Incumb. Running Uncontested	Op. Seat Contested (Dem. Incum.)	Op. Seat Uncontested (Dem. Incum.)	Op. Seat Contested (Rep. Incum.)	Total	
	Type of Race								
Str. Dem.	19	...	31	0	27	...	11	23	[149]
Weak Dem.	16	...	19	14	16	...	...	17	[242]
Ind. Dem.	25	...	10	11	33	...	...	17	[164]
Ind. Ind.	4	...	12	7	11	...	...	11	[152]
Ind. Rep.	32	...	16	9	19	...	...	21	[122]
Weak Rep.	11	...	8	11	20	...	0	9	[168]
Str. Rep.	30	...	19	0	22	...	...	19	[104]
Total	18	...	16	9	20	...	15	16	
[N]	[356]	[0]	[525]	[89]	[84]	[0]	[47]		[1101]

Cell entries are the proportion of respondents who reported not liking something about the Republican congressional candidate from their district.

TABLE 5-22

PARTY VOTE BY DID NOT LIKE SOMETHING ABOUT REPUBLICAN CONGRESSIONAL CANDIDATE AND RESPONDENT'S PARTY IDENTIFICATION

Did Not Like Something About Republican Candidate?	Str. Dem.	Weak Dem.	Ind. Dem.	Ind. Ind.	Ind. Rep.	Weak Rep.	Str. Rep.	Total	
	Respondent's Party Identification								
Yes	100	80	70	44	26	46	6	59	[124]
No	63	38	56	34	15	9	5	32	[474]
Total	73	63	44	36	18	13	5	38	
[N]	[100]	[104]	[79]	[59]	[73]	[102]	[81]		[598]

Cell entries are the proportion of voters who reported voting Democratic in the House race in their district.

TABLE 5-23

CONTACTED BY REPUBLICAN CONGRESSIONAL CANDIDATE
BY TYPE OF RACE AND RESPONDENT'S PARTY IDENTIFICATION

Respondent's Party I.D.	Type of Race: Democr. Incumb. Running Contested	Democr. Incumb. Running Uncontested	Repub. Incumb. Running Contested	Repub. Incumb. Running Uncontested	Op.Seat Contested (Dem. Incum.)	Op.Seat Uncontested (Dem. Incum.)	Op.Seat Contested (Rep. Incum.)	Total	
Str. Dem.	22	...	87	54	50	...	82	45	[281]
Weak Dem.	28	...	80	73	52	...	69	49	[457]
Ind. Dem.	28	...	85	60	61	...	...	55	[270]
Ind. Ind.	29	...	76	72	40	...	...	53	[260]
Ind. Rep.	38	...	92	92	62	...	100	62	[195]
Weak Rep.	43	...	79	69	57	...	80	64	[251]
Str. Rep.	52	...	92	70	75	...	...	75	[147]
Total	31	...	83	69	55	...	79	55	
[N]	[883]	[0]	[631]	[121]	[158]	[0]	[68]		[1861]

Cell entries are the proportion of respondents who reported coming into contact with the Republican congressional candidate from their district.

TABLE 5-24

PARTY VOTE BY
CONTACTED BY REPUBLICAN CONGRESSIONAL CANDIDATE
AND RESPONDENT'S PARTY IDENTIFICATION

Contacted By Republican Candidate?	Respondent's Party Identification: Str. Dem.	Weak Dem.	Ind. Dem.	Ind. Ind.	Ind. Rep.	Weak Rep.	Str. Rep.	Total	
Yes	70	63	41	28	18	14	4	35	[563]
No	98	94	38	84	67	60	52	85	[331]
Total	85	77	57	49	31	27	13	53	
[N]	[176]	[185]	[114]	[82]	[100]	[132]	[105]		[894]

Cell entries are the proportion of voters who reported voting Democratic in the House race in their district.

TABLE 5-25

RATING FOR REPUBLICAN CANDIDATE ON THE FEELING THERMOMETER BY TYPE OF RACE

Feeling Therm. Rating	Type of Race							
	Democr. Incumb. Running Con- tested	Democr. Incumb. Running Uncon- tested	Repub. Incumb. Running Con- tested	Repub. Incumb. Running Uncon- tested	Op.Seat Con- tested (Dem. Incum.)	Op.Seat Uncon- tested (Dem. Incum.)	Op.Seat Con- tested (Rep. Incum.)	Total
Very Pos.	8%	...	35%	26%	19%	...	23%	25% [265]
Positive	28	...	39	45	40	...	34	36 [390]
Neutral	47	...	16	21	28	...	28	27 [294]
Negative	17	...	10	8	12	...	15	12 [129]
[N]	[315]	[0]	[535]	[89]	[92]	[0]	[47]	[1078]

TABLE 5-26

RATING FOR REPUBLICAN CANDIDATE ON THE FEELING THERMOMETER BY RESPONDENT'S PARTY IDENTIFICATION

Feeling Therm. Rating	Respondent's Party Identification							
	Str. Dem.	Weak Dem.	Ind. Dem.	Ind. Ind.	Ind. Rep.	Weak Rep.	Str. Rep.	Total
Very Pos.	18%	18%	18%	23%	32%	28%	49%	25% [264]
Positive	31	43	33	32	29	45	38	36 [386]
Neutral	30	29	30	36	27	23	11	27 [288]
Negative	21	11	20	9	12	5	3	12 [125]
[N]	[142]	[216]	[162]	[144]	[130]	[164]	[105]	[1063]

TABLE 5-27

AVERAGE FEELING THERMOMETER RATING FOR REPUBLICAN CANDIDATE BY TYPE OF RACE AND RESPONDENT'S PARTY IDENTIFICATION

Respondent's Party I.D.	Type of Race: Democr. Incumb. Running Contested	Democr. Incumb. Running Uncontested	Repub. Incumb. Running Contested	Repub. Incumb. Running Uncontested	Op.Seat Contested (Dem. Incum.)	Op.Seat Uncontested (Dem. Incum.)	Op.Seat Contested (Rep. Incum.)	Total	
Str. Dem.	49	...	66	61	51	...	47	57	[142]
Weak Dem.	53	...	65	65	63	...	59	60	[216]
Ind. Dem.	44	...	65	67	52	...	...	58	[162]
Ind. Ind.	55	...	65	67	61	...	...	62	[144]
Ind. Rep.	52	...	70	76	67	...	...	64	[130]
Weak Rep.	59	...	71	62	67	...	68	57	[164]
Str. Rep.	70	...	78	71	68	...	...	76	[105]
Total	53	...	68	67	60	...	59	63	
[N]	[311]	[0]	[526]	[88]	[92]	[0]	[46]		[1063]

Cell entries are the average feeling thermometer ratings reported by respondents for the Republican congressional candidate in their district.

TABLE 5-28

PARTY VOTE BY RATING FOR REPUBLICAN CANDIDATE ON THE FEELING THERMOMETER AND RESPONDENT'S PARTY IDENTIFICATION

Feeling Therm. Rating	Respondent's Party Identification: Str. Dem.	Weak Dem.	Ind. Dem.	Ind. Ind.	Ind. Rep.	Weak Rep.	Str. Rep.	Total	
Very Pos.	43	28	5	11	0	3	0	8	[178]
Positive	72	49	27	25	17	8	7	30	[231]
Neutral	87	89	78	55	46	67	25	71	[103]
Negative	88	91	89	67	57	50	0	81	[68]
Total	75	60	42	29	17	17	5	37	
[N]	[97]	[96]	[79]	[52]	[75]	[100]	[81]		[580]

Cell entries are the proportion of voters who reported voting Democratic in the House race in their district.

TABLE 5-29

RECOGNIZE NAME OF INCUMBENT CONGRESSIONAL CANDIDATE BY TYPE OF RACE AND RESPONDENT'S PARTY IDENTIFICATION

Respondent's Party I.D. and Incumbent's Party	Type of Race: Democr. Incumb. Running Con-tested	Democr. Incumb. Running Uncon-tested	Repub. Incumb. Running Con-tested	Repub. Incumb. Running Uncon-tested	Total	
Same	89	87	96	94	90	[984]
Resp. Is Ind. Ind.	86	80	86	...	85	[281]
Different	89	93	91	77	89	[679]
Total	88	87	92	83	89	
[N]	[881]	[315]	[628]	[120]		[1944]

Cell entries are the proportion of respondents who could recognize the name of the Incumbent congressional candidate from their district.

TABLE 5-30

INCUMBENCY VOTE BY RECOGNIZE NAME OF INCUMBENT CONGRESSIONAL CANDIDATE AND RESPONDENT'S PARTY IDENTIFICATION AND INCUMBENT'S PARTY

Recognize Incumbent Candidate's Name?	Respondent's Party Identification and Incumbent's Party: Same	Resp. is Ind. Ind.	Different	Total	
Yes	96	83	61	82	[850]
No	...	...	...	61	[28]
Total	96	84	59	81	
[N]	[469]	[91]	[318]		[878]

Cell entries are the proportion of voters who reported voting for the Incumbent in the House race in their district.

TABLE 5-31

RECALL NAME OF INCUMBENT CONGRESSIONAL CANDIDATE
BY TYPE OF RACE AND RESPONDENT'S PARTY IDENTIFICATION

Respondent's Party I.D. and Incumbent's Party	Type of Race: Democr. Incumb. Running Con-tested	Democr. Incumb. Running Uncon-tested	Repub. Incumb. Running Con-tested	Repub. Incumb. Running Uncon-tested	Total	
Same	35	29	45	34	36	[990]
Resp. Is Ind. Ind.	21	16	27	...	22	[284]
Different	40	31	32	21	34	[683]
Total	35	28	36	24	33	
[N]	[886]	[319]	[631]	[121]		[1957]

Cell entries are the proportion of respondents who could recall the name of the Incumbent congressional candidate from their district.

TABLE 5-32

INCUMBENCY VOTE BY RECALL NAME OF INCUMBENT CONGRESSIONAL CANDIDATE
AND RESPONDENT'S PARTY IDENTIFICATION AND INCUMBENT'S PARTY

Recall Incumbent Candidate's Name?	Respondent's Party Identification and Incumbent's Party: Same	Resp. is Ind. Ind.	Different	Total	
Yes	98	76	63	84	[435]
No	94	89	56	79	[445]
Total	96	84	59	82	
[N]	[471]	[91]	[318]		[880]

Cell entries are the proportion of voters who reported voting for the Incumbent in the House race in their district.

TABLE 5-33

LIKED SOMETHING ABOUT INCUMBENT CONGRESSIONAL CANDIDATE BY TYPE OF RACE AND RESPONDENT'S PARTY IDENTIFICATION

Respondent's Party I.D. and Incumbent's Party	Type of Race: Democr. Incumb. Running Con- tested	Democr. Incumb. Running Uncon- tested	Repub. Incumb. Running Con- tested	Repub. Incumb. Running Uncon- tested	Total	
Same	64	62	72	67	67	[773]
Resp. Is Ind. Ind.	33	45	46	...	41	[202]
Different	54	48	55	48	53	[518]
Total	58	55	61	52	58	
[N]	[681]	[210]	[517]	[85]		[1493]

Cell entries are the proportion of respondents who reported liking something about the Incumbent congressional candidate from their district.

TABLE 5-34

INCUMBENCY VOTE BY LIKED SOMETHING ABOUT INCUMBENT CONGRESSIONAL CANDIDATE AND RESPONDENT'S PARTY IDENTIFICATION AND INCUMBENT'S PARTY

Liked Something About Incumbent Candidate?	Respondent's Party Identification and Incumbent's Party: Same	Resp. is Ind. Ind.	Different	Total	
Yes	99	94	76	91	[558]
No	87	69	39	63	[243]
Total	96	83	62	82	
[N]	[432]	[84]	[285]		[801]

Cell entries are the proportion of voters who reported voting for the Incumbent in the House race in their district.

TABLE 5-35

DID NOT LIKE SOMETHING ABOUT INCUMBENT CONGRESSIONAL CANDIDATE BY TYPE OF RACE AND RESPONDENT'S PARTY IDENTIFICATION

Respondent's Party I.D. and Incumbent's Party	Type of Race: Democr. Incumb. Running Contested	Democr. Incumb. Running Uncontested	Repub. Incumb. Running Contested	Repub. Incumb. Running Uncontested	Total	
Same	15	3	13	7	12	[786]
Resp. Is Ind. Ind.	11	0	12	...	10	[210]
Different	28	10	19	10	20	[526]
Total	18	5	16	9	15	
[N]	[693]	[215]	[525]	[89]		[1522]

Cell entries are the proportion of respondents who reported not liking something about the Incumbent congressional candidate from their district.

TABLE 5-36

INCUMBENCY VOTE BY DID NOT LIKE SOMETHING ABOUT INCUMBENT CONGRESSIONAL CANDIDATE AND RESPONDENT'S PARTY IDENTIFICATION AND INCUMBENT'S PARTY

Did Not Like Something About Incumbent Candidate?	Respondent's Party Identification and Incumbent's Party: Same	Resp. is Ind. Ind.	Different	Total	
Yes	82	...	45	50	[145]
No	98	90	75	90	[654]
Total	96	84	62	83	
[N]	[433]	[83]	[283]		[799]

Cell entries are the proportion of voters who reported voting for the Incumbent in the House race in their district.

TABLE 5-37

CONTACTED BY INCUMBENT CONGRESSIONAL CANDIDATE
BY TYPE OF RACE AND RESPONDENT'S PARTY IDENTIFICATION

Respondent's Party I.D. and Incumbent's Party	Type of Race: Democr. Incumb. Running Con-tested	Democr. Incumb. Running Uncon-tested	Repub. Incumb. Running Con-tested	Repub. Incumb. Running Uncon-tested	Total	
Same	78	66	86	77	78	[990]
Resp. Is Ind. Ind.	71	68	76	72	72	[284]
Different	79	75	84	65	79	[683]
Total	77	69	83	69	77	
[N]	[886]	[319]	[631]	[121]		[1957]

Cell entries are the proportion of respondents who reported coming into contact with the Incumbent congressional candidate from their district.

TABLE 5-38

INCUMBENCY VOTE BY CONTACTED BY INCUMBENT CONGRESSIONAL CANDIDATE
AND RESPONDENT'S PARTY IDENTIFICATION AND INCUMBENT'S PARTY

Contacted By Incumbent Candidate?	Respondent's Party Identification and Incumbent's Party: Same	Resp. is Ind. Ind.	Different	Total	
Yes	96	85	62	83	[787]
No	94	...	43	71	[93]
Total	96	84	59	82	
[N]	[471]	[91]	[318]		[880]

Cell entries are the proportion of voters who reported voting for the Incumbent in the House race in their district.

TABLE 5-39

RATING FOR INCUMBENT CANDIDATE ON THE FEELING THERMOMETER BY TYPE OF RACE

Feeling Therm. Rating	Type of Race				
	Democr. Incumb. Running Con-tested	Democr. Incumb. Running Uncon-tested	Repub. Incumb. Running Con-tested	Repub. Incumb. Running Uncon-tested	Total
Very Pos.	36%	44%	35%	26%	36% [574]
Positive	35	31	39	45	36 [572]
Neutral	19	19	16	21	18 [287]
Negative	10	6	10	8	9 [147]
[N]	[724]	[232]	[535]	[89]	[1580]

TABLE 5-40

RATING FOR INCUMBENT CANDIDATE ON THE FEELING THERMOMETER BY RESPONDENT'S PARTY IDENTIFICATION AND INCUMBENT'S PARTY

Feeling Therm. Rating	Respondent's Party Identification and Incumbent's Party			
	Same	Resp. is Ind. Ind.	Different	Total
Very Pos.	46%	30%	26%	37% [568]
Positive	34	34	41	36 [560]
Neutral	15	27	19	18 [277]
Negative	6	9	14	9 [143]
[N]	[796]	[208]	[544]	[1548]

TABLE 5-41

AVERAGE FEELING THERMOMETER RATING FOR INCUMBENT CANDIDATE BY TYPE OF RACE AND RESPONDENT'S PARTY IDENTIFICATION AND INCUMBENT'S PARTY

Respondent's Party I.D. and Incumbent's Party	Type of Race				
	Democr. Incumb. Running Con-tested	Democr. Incumb. Running Uncon-tested	Repub. Incumb. Running Con-tested	Repub. Incumb. Running Uncon-tested	Total
Same	72	75	73	70	73 [796]
Resp. Is Ind. Ind.	62	73	65	...	65 [208]
Different	60	65	65	65	63 [544]
Total	68	71	68	67	68
[N]	[707]	[227]	[526]	[88]	[1548]

Cell entries are the average feeling thermometer ratings reported by respondents for the Incumbent congressional candidate in their district.

TABLE 5-42

INCUMBENCY VOTE BY RATING FOR INCUMBENT CANDIDATE ON THE FEELING THERMOMETER AND RESPONDENT'S PARTY IDENTIFICATION AND INCUMBENT'S PARTY

Feeling Therm. Rating	Respondent's Party Identification and Incumbent's Party			
	Same	Resp. is Ind. Ind.	Different	Total
Very Pos.	100	97	89	97 [343]
Positive	98	84	67	83 [306]
Neutral	92	92	48	72 [90]
Negative	60	...	12	26 [70]
Total	97	84	62	83
[N]	[434]	[82]	[293]	[809]

Cell entries are the proportion of voters who reported voting for the Incumbent in the House race in their district.

TABLE 5-43

RECOGNIZE NAME OF INCUMBENT CHALLENGER
BY TYPE OF RACE AND RESPONDENT'S PARTY IDENTIFICATION

Respondent's Party I.D. and Incumbent's Party	Type of Race: Democr. Incumb. Running Contested	Democr. Incumb. Running Uncontested	Repub. Incumb. Running Contested	Repub. Incumb. Running Uncontested	Total	
Same	52	...	68	...	57	[762]
Resp. Is Ind. Ind.	52	...	68	...	59	[218]
Different	61	...	63	...	62	[527]
Total	54	...	66	...	59	
[N]	[878]	[0]	[629]	[0]		[1507]

Cell entries are the proportion of respondents who could recognize the name of the Incumbent challenger from their district.

TABLE 5-44

INCUMBENCY VOTE BY RECOGNIZE NAME OF INCUMBENT CHALLENGER
AND RESPONDENT'S PARTY IDENTIFICATION AND INCUMBENT'S PARTY

Recognize Incumbent Challenger's Name?	Respondent's Party Identification and Incumbent's Party: Same	Resp. is Ind. Ind.	Different	Total	
Yes	93	71	49	74	[477]
No	98	96	63	87	[277]
Total	95	79	54	79	
[N]	[404]	[72]	[278]		[754]

Cell entries are the proportion of voters who reported voting for the Incumbent in the House race in their district.

TABLE 5-45

RECALL NAME OF INCUMBENT CHALLENGER
BY TYPE OF RACE AND RESPONDENT'S PARTY IDENTIFICATION

Respondent's Party I.D. and Incumbent's Party	Type of Race: Democr. Incumb. Running Con-tested	Democr. Incumb. Running Uncon-tested	Repub. Incumb. Running Con-tested	Repub. Incumb. Running Uncon-tested	Total	
Same	8	...	16	...	11	[768]
Resp. Is Ind. Ind.	5	...	9	...	7	[221]
Different	18	...	11	...	14	[528]
Total	10	...	13	...	11	
[N]	[886]	[0]	[631]	[0]		[1517]

Cell entries are the proportion of respondents who could recall the name of the Incumbent challenger from their district.

TABLE 5-46

INCUMBENCY VOTE BY RECALL NAME OF INCUMBENT CHALLENGER
AND RESPONDENT'S PARTY IDENTIFICATION AND INCUMBENT'S PARTY

Recall Incumbent Challenger's Name?	Respondent's Party Identification and Incumbent's Party: Same	Resp. is Ind. Ind.	Different	Total	
Yes	93	55	26	60	[124]
No	96	84	61	82	[633]
Total	95	79	54	79	
[N]	[407]	[72]	[278]		[757]

Cell entries are the proportion of voters who reported voting for the Incumbent in the House race in their district.

TABLE 5-47

LIKED SOMETHING ABOUT INCUMBENT CHALLENGER
BY TYPE OF RACE AND RESPONDENT'S PARTY IDENTIFICATION

Respondent's Party I.D. and Incumbent's Party	Type of Race: Democr. Incumb. Running Contested	Democr. Incumb. Running Uncontested	Repub. Incumb. Running Contested	Repub. Incumb. Running Uncontested	Total	
Same	10	...	17	...	13	[309]
Resp. Is Ind. Ind.	9	...	23	...	17	[97]
Different	33	...	27	...	30	[249]
Total	17	...	23	...	20	
[N]	[339]	[0]	[316]	[0]		[655]

Cell entries are the proportion of respondents who reported liking something about the Incumbent challenger from their district.

TABLE 5-48

INCUMBENCY VOTE BY LIKED SOMETHING ABOUT INCUMBENT CHALLENGER
AND RESPONDENT'S PARTY IDENTIFICATION AND INCUMBENT'S PARTY

Liked Something About Incumbent Challenger?	Respondent's Party Identification and Incumbent's Party: Same	Resp. is Ind. Ind.	Different	Total	
Yes	79	...	16	35	[87]
No	95	82	63	83	[280]
Total	93	69	46	71	
[N]	[182]	[36]	[149]		[367]

Cell entries are the proportion of voters who reported voting for the Incumbent in the House race in their district.

TABLE 5-49

DID NOT LIKE SOMETHING ABOUT INCUMBENT CHALLENGER
BY TYPE OF RACE AND RESPONDENT'S PARTY IDENTIFICATION

Respondent's Party I.D. and Incumbent's Party	Type of Race: Democr. Incumb. Running Contested	Democr. Incumb. Running Uncontested	Repub. Incumb. Running Contested	Repub. Incumb. Running Uncontested	Total	
Same	19	...	26	...	22	[324]
Resp. Is Ind. Ind.	4	...	16	...	11	[102]
Different	22	...	11	...	16	[253]
Total	18	...	18	...	18	
[N]	[356]	[0]	[323]	[0]		[679]

Cell entries are the proportion of respondents who reported not liking something about the Incumbent challenger from their district.

TABLE 5-50

INCUMBENCY VOTE BY DID NOT LIKE SOMETHING ABOUT INCUMBENT CHALLENGER
AND RESPONDENT'S PARTY IDENTIFICATION AND INCUMBENT'S PARTY

Did Not Like Something About Incumbent Challenger?	Respondent's Party Identification and Incumbent's Party: Same	Resp. is Ind. Ind.	Different	Total	
Yes	93	...	49	76	[96]
No	92	67	44	69	[286]
Total	92	69	45	71	
[N]	[189]	[36]	[157]		[382]

Cell entries are the proportion of voters who reported voting for the Incumbent in the House race in their district.

TABLE 5-51

CONTACTED BY INCUMBENT CHALLENGER
BY TYPE OF RACE AND RESPONDENT'S PARTY IDENTIFICATION

Respondent's Party I.D. and Incumbent's Party	Type of Race: Democr. Incumb. Running Contested	Democr. Incumb. Running Uncontested	Repub. Incumb. Running Contested	Repub. Incumb. Running Uncontested	Total	
Same	26	...	48	...	33	[766]
Resp. Is Ind. Ind.	29	...	44	...	36	[221]
Different	43	...	48	...	46	[527]
Total	31	...	48	...	38	
[N]	[883]	[0]	[631]	[0]		[1514]

Cell entries are the proportion of respondents who reported coming into contact with the Incumbent challenger from their district.

TABLE 5-52

INCUMBENCY VOTE BY CONTACTED BY INCUMBENT CHALLENGER
AND RESPONDENT'S PARTY IDENTIFICATION AND INCUMBENT'S PARTY

Contacted By Incumbent Challenger?	Respondent's Party Identification and Incumbent's Party: Same	Resp. is Ind. Ind.	Different	Total	
Yes	92	71	46	70	[336]
No	97	87	63	86	[420]
Total	95	79	54	78	
[N]	[406]	[72]	[278]		[756]

Cell entries are the proportion of voters who reported voting for the Incumbent in the House race in their district.

TABLE 5-53

RATING FOR INCUMBENT CHALLENGER ON THE FEELING THERMOMETER
BY TYPE OF RACE

Feeling Therm. Rating	Type of Race: Democr. Incumb. Running Contested	Democr. Incumb. Running Uncontested	Repub. Incumb. Running Contested	Repub. Incumb. Running Uncontested	Total	
Very Pos.	8%	...	8%	...	8%	[49]
Positive	28	...	28	...	28	[172]
Neutral	47	...	47	...	47	[289]
Negative	17	...	17	...	17	[105]
[N]	[315]	[0]	[300]	[0]		[615]

TABLE 5-54

RATING FOR INCUMBENT CHALLENGER ON THE FEELING THERMOMETER
BY RESPONDENT'S PARTY IDENTIFICATION AND INCUMBENT'S PARTY

Feeling Therm. Rating	Respondent's Party Identification and Incumbent's Party: Same	Resp. is Ind. Ind.	Different	Total	
Very Pos.	4%	5%	14%	8%	[48]
Positive	22	31	34	28	[170]
Neutral	51	56	39	47	[285]
Negative	23	8	13	17	[103]
[N]	[280]	[84]	[242]		[606]

TABLE 5-55

AVERAGE FEELING THERMOMETER RATING FOR INCUMBENT CHALLENGER BY TYPE OF RACE AND RESPONDENT'S PARTY IDENTIFICATION AND INCUMBENT'S PARTY

Respondent's Party I.D. and Incumbent's Party	Type of Race				
	Democr. Incumb. Running Contested	Democr. Incumb. Running Uncontested	Repub. Incumb. Running Contested	Repub. Incumb. Running Uncontested	Total
Same	49	...	48	...	49 [280]
Resp. Is Ind. Ind.	55	...	56	...	55 [84]
Different	59	...	56	...	57 [242]
Total	53	...	53	...	53
[N]	[311]	[0]	[295]	[0]	[606]

Cell entries are the average feeling thermometer ratings reported by respondents for the Incumbent challenger in their district.

TABLE 5-56

INCUMBENCY VOTE BY RATING FOR INCUMBENT CHALLENGER ON THE FEELING THERMOMETER AND RESPONDENT'S PARTY IDENTIFICATION AND INCUMBENT'S PARTY

Feeling Therm. Rating	Respondent's Party Identification and Incumbent's Party			
	Same	Resp. is Ind. Ind.	Different	Total
Very Pos.	33	...	13	13 [30]
Positive	88	...	34	56 [100]
Neutral	95	...	68	84 [138]
Negative	96	...	67	88 [66]
Total	93	68	46	70
[N]	[161]	[28]	[145]	[334]

Cell entries are the proportion of voters who reported voting for the Incumbent in the House race in their district.

TABLE 6-1

RESPONDENT'S POSITION ON THE GOVERNMENT GUARANTEE JOB AND STANDARD OF LIVING SCALE BY RESPONDENT'S PARTY IDENTIFICATION

Respondent's Position	Respondent's Party Identification								
	Str. Dem.	Weak Dem.	Ind. Dem.	Ind. Ind.	Ind. Rep.	Weak Rep.	Str. Rep.	Total	
Gov. See To	19%	10%	8%	8%	1%	2%	4%	8%	[148]
(2)	4	4	7	5	3	2	1	4	[71]
(3)	10	13	11	8	6	5	3	9	[160]
(4)	25	28	25	26	16	24	16	24	[430]
(5)	16	14	20	20	24	21	23	19	[334]
(6)	8	13	13	13	28	19	18	15	[265]
Ahead On Own	17	18	17	20	23	28	35	21	[380]
[N]	[264]	[424]	[279]	[250]	[182]	[238]	[151]		[1788]

TABLE 6-2

PARTY VOTE BY RESPONDENT'S POSITION ON THE GOVERNMENT GUARANTEE JOB AND STANDARD OF LIVING SCALE AND RESPONDENT'S PARTY IDENTIFICATION

Respondent's Position	Respondent's Party Identification								
	Str. Dem.	Weak Dem.	Ind. Dem.	Ind. Ind.	Ind. Rep.	Weak Rep.	Str. Rep.	Total	
Gov. See To	95	86	86	57	...	...	...	81	[52]
(2)	...	75	82	...	...	...	...	80	[30]
(3)	95	67	44	86	20	...	...	62	[66]
(4)	84	85	61	73	21	35	29	65	[200]
(5)	72	81	48	39	32	46	27	53	[175]
(6)	87	67	50	60	33	32	16	44	[140]
Ahead On Own	88	83	62	31	46	34	21	50	[176]
Total	86	80	69	56	34	35	22	57	
[N]	[159]	[163]	[112]	[82]	[96]	[122]	[105]		[839]

Cell entries are the proportion of voters who reported voting Democratic in the House race in their district.

TABLE 6-3

RESPONDENT'S PLACEMENT OF DEMOCRATIC CONGRESSIONAL CANDIDATE ON THE GOVERNMENT GUARANTEE JOB AND STANDARD OF LIVING SCALE BY RESPONDENT'S OWN POSITION ON THE SCALE, CONTROLLING FOR PARTY IDENTIFICATION AND TURNOUT

Respondent's Placement of Democratic Candidate	Respondent's Position: Govt. See To A Job	(2)	(3)	(4)	(5)	(6)	Let Each Get Ahead On Own	Total	
Party I.D.: DEMOCRAT									
Gov. See To	72%	58%	56%	41%	32%	24%	32%	42%	[199]
(4)	10	31	28	36	32	28	25	28	[133]
Ahead On Own	17	12	15	23	37	49	43	30	[140]
[N]	[58]	[26]	[39]	[138]	[79]	[51]	[81]		[472]
Party I.D.: IND. INDEPENDENT									
Gov. See To	...	...	50%	54%	55%	23%	42%	45%	[41]
(4)	...	...	10	46	20	31	17	30	[27]
Ahead On Own	...	...	40	0	25	46	42	25	[23]
[N]	[8]	[2]	[10]	[26]	[20]	[13]	[12]		[91]
Party I.D.: REPUBLICAN									
Gov. See To	60%	100%	50%	44%	36%	40%	37%	40%	[93]
(4)	20	0	30	39	38	40	30	35	[81]
Ahead On Own	20	0	20	17	27	20	33	25	[57]
[N]	[5]	[2]	[10]	[41]	[45]	[55]	[73]		[231]
Turnout: VOTED									
Gov. See To	74%	67%	57%	45%	39%	33%	38%	44%	[209]
(4)	8	28	23	36	30	32	30	29	[139]
Ahead On Own	17	6	20	19	31	35	33	26	[124]
[N]	[35]	[18]	[35]	[114]	[94]	[75]	[101]		[472]
Turnout: DID NOT VOTE									
Gov. See To	57%	50%	50%	41%	30%	24%	32%	38%	[118]
(4)	23	25	29	38	36	37	24	32	[99]
Ahead On Own	20	25	21	21	34	39	44	30	[93]
[N]	[35]	[12]	[24]	[86]	[50]	[41]	[62]		[310]

TABLE 6-4

RESPONDENT'S PLACEMENT OF REPUBLICAN CONGRESSIONAL CANDIDATE ON THE GOVERNMENT GUARANTEE JOB AND STANDARD OF LIVING SCALE BY RESPONDENT'S OWN POSITION ON THE SCALE, CONTROLLING FOR PARTY IDENTIFICATION AND TURNOUT

Respondent's Placement of Republican Candidate	Respondent's Position: Govt. See To A Job	(2)	(3)	(4)	(5)	(6)	Let Each Get Ahead On Own	Total	
				Party I.D.: DEMOCRAT					
Gov. See To	50%	25%	39%	35%	28%	23%	32%	34%	[105]
(4)	10	19	29	26	24	29	30	25	[78]
Ahead On Own	40	56	32	39	48	48	38	41	[129]
[N]	[30]	[16]	[41]	[94]	[50]	[31]	[50]		[312]
				Party I.D.: IND. INDEPENDENT					
Gov. See To	...	...		37%	26%	0%	29%	28%	[19]
(4)	...	...		47	21	22	14	29	[20]
Ahead On Own	...	...		16	53	78	57	44	[30]
[N]	[4]	[0]	[4]	[19]	[19]	[9]	[14]		[69]
				Party I.D.: REPUBLICAN					
Gov. See To	...	...	50%	30%	16%	8%	17%	20%	[48]
(4)	...	...	6	50	32	26	19	29	[69]
Ahead On Own	...	...	44	21	52	66	64	51	[123]
[N]	[4]	[3]	[16]	[44]	[50]	[53]	[70]		[240]
				Turnout: VOTED					
Gov. See To	56%	36%	42%	32%	18%	8%	23%	25%	[98]
(4)	17	7	19	38	23	22	21	24	[95]
Ahead On Own	28	57	39	30	60	71	57	51	[198]
[N]	[18]	[14]	[36]	[90]	[80]	[65]	[88]		[391]
				Turnout: DID NOT VOTE					
Gov. See To	43%	...	38%	35%	35%	19%	25%	32%	[71]
(4)	19	...	33	32	38	39	25	32	[71]
Ahead On Own	38	...	29	32	27	42	50	36	[80]
[N]	[21]	[5]	[24]	[65]	[37]	[26]	[44]		[222]

TABLE 6-5

RESPONDENT'S PLACEMENT OF INCUMBENT CONGRESSIONAL CANDIDATE ON THE GOVERNMENT GUARANTEE JOB AND STANDARD OF LIVING SCALE BY RESPONDENT'S OWN POSITION ON THE SCALE, CONTROLLING FOR PARTY IDENTIFICATION AND TURNOUT

Respondent's Placement of Incumbent Candidate	Respondent's Position: Govt. See To A Job	(2)	(3)	(4)	(5)	(6)	Let Each Get Ahead On Own	Total	
	Party I.D.: SAME AS INCUMBENT								
Gov. See To	79%	65%	68%	38%	25%	20%	26%	38%	[191]
(4)	9	25	16	39	30	25	16	26	[131]
Ahead On Own	13	10	16	23	45	55	59	37	[188]
[N]	[47]	[20]	[37]	[133]	[96]	[71]	[106]		[510]
	Party I.D.: R IS AN IND. INDEPENDENT								
Gov. See To	...	...	...	41%	33%	19%	32%	34%	[36]
(4)	...	...	...	48	21	13	16	27	[29]
Ahead On Own	...	...	...	10	46	69	53	39	[42]
[N]	[8]	[2]	[9]	[29]	[24]	[16]	[19]		[107]
	Party I.D.: DIFFERENT THAN INCUMBENT								
Gov. See To	72%	40%	48%	36%	27%	27%	32%	35%	[119]
(4)	5	10	23	30	31	38	33	30	[101]
Ahead On Own	22	50	29	34	42	35	35	35	[120]
[N]	[18]	[10]	[31]	[80]	[62]	[60]	[79]		[340]
	Turnout: VOTED								
Gov. See To	81%	68%	62%	37%	26%	20%	29%	36%	[208]
(4)	6	11	13	38	29	29	24	27	[156]
Ahead On Own	14	21	24	25	45	51	48	38	[218]
[N]	[36]	[19]	[45]	[139]	[124]	[100]	[119]		[582]
	Turnout: DID NOT VOTE								
Gov. See To	64%	39%	45%	38%	30%	25%	28%	36%	[128]
(4)	17	31	32	36	30	30	22	29	[101]
Ahead On Own	19	31	23	26	39	46	50	35	[123]
[N]	[36]	[13]	[31]	[94]	[56]	[44]	[78]		[352]

TABLE 6-6

RESPONDENT'S PLACEMENT OF INCUMBENT CHALLENGER ON THE GOVERNMENT GUARANTEE JOB AND STANDARD OF LIVING SCALE BY RESPONDENT'S OWN POSITION ON THE SCALE, CONTROLLING FOR PARTY IDENTIFICATION AND TURNOUT

Respondent's Placement of Challenger	Respondent's Position: Govt. See To A Job	(2)	(3)	(4)	(5)	(6)	Let Each Get Ahead On Own	Total	
Party I.D.: SAME AS INCUMBENT									
Gov. See To	39%	...	31%	42%	44%	59%	45%	43%	[61]
(4)	15	...	31	29	2	29	28	26	[37]
Ahead On Own	46	...	39	29	35	12	28	31	[43]
[N]	[13]	[5]	[13]	[41]	[23]	[17]	[29]		[141]
Party I.D.: R IS AN IND. INDEPENDENT									
Gov. See To	...	...	...	58%	52%	...	...	49%	[19]
(4)	...	...	...	42	15	...	...	28	[11]
Ahead On Own	...	...	...	0	23	...	...	23	[9]
[N]	[2]	[0]	[3]	[12]	[13]	[4]	[5]		[39]
Party I.D.: DIFFERENT THAN INCUMBENT									
Gov. See To	...	...	30%	33%	33%	0%	23%	26%	[32]
(4)	...	...	20	40	33	41	35	37	[45]
Ahead On Own	...	...	50	27	33	59	42	37	[45]
[N]	[7]	[6]	[10]	[30]	[21]	[22]	[26]		[122]
Turnout: VOTED									
Gov. See To	50%	...	27%	41%	45%	23%	37%	37%	[70]
(4)	10	...	27	33	18	30	23	26	[49]
Ahead On Own	40	...	47	26	38	47	40	37	[70]
[N]	[10]	[9]	[15]	[42]	[40]	[30]	[43]		[189]
Turnout: DID NOT VOTE									
Gov. See To	39%	...	36%	42%	41%	18%	32%	38%	[43]
(4)	39	...	18	37	41	64	42	39	[44]
Ahead On Own	23	...	46	22	18	18	26	24	[27]
[N]	[13]	[2]	[11]	[41]	[17]	[11]	[19]		[114]

TABLE 6-7

RESPONDENT'S POSITION ON THE RIGHTS OF THE ACCUSED SCALE BY RESPONDENT'S PARTY IDENTIFICATION

Respondent's Position	Respondent's Party Identification: Str. Dem.	Weak Dem.	Ind. Dem.	Ind. Ind.	Ind. Rep.	Weak Rep.	Str. Rep.	Total	
Prot. Rights	17%	14%	17%	15%	8%	8%	6%	13%	[248]
(2)	7	6	10	6	7	5	3	7	[129]
(3)	7	9	9	7	9	7	6	8	[148]
(4)	19	20	16	19	22	19	12	19	[352]
(5)	12	14	20	15	20	25	23	18	[336]
(6)	9	12	11	16	18	15	19	14	[257]
Stop Crime	28	24	16	22	16	22	32	23	[428]
[N]	[283]	[453]	[298]	[268]	[190]	[251]	[155]		[1898]

TABLE 6-8

PARTY VOTE BY RESPONDENT'S POSITION ON THE RIGHTS OF THE ACCUSED SCALE AND RESPONDENT'S PARTY IDENTIFICATION

Respondent's Position	Respondent's Party Identification: Str. Dem.	Weak Dem.	Ind. Dem.	Ind. Ind.	Ind. Rep.	Weak Rep.	Str. Rep.	Total	
Prot. Rights	90	80	68	43	80	27	0	68	[105]
(2)	80	80	56	...	...	40	...	60	[57]
(3)	83	78	73	67	..	25	20	55	[56]
(4)	87	83	67	59	44	40	25	65	[155]
(5)	84	81	48	44	33	32	15	50	[153]
(6)	81	76	55	79	24	30	13	48	[133]
Stop Crime	87	78	63	50	35	30	32	57	[195]
Total	86	80	61	55	34	32	21	57	
[N]	[171]	[173]	[118]	[87]	[100]	[131]	[104]		[884]

Cell entries are the proportion of voters who reported voting Democratic in the House race in their district.

TABLE 6-9

RESPONDENT'S PLACEMENT OF DEMOCRATIC CONGRESSIONAL CANDIDATE ON THE RIGHTS OF THE ACCUSED SCALE BY RESPONDENT'S OWN POSITION ON THE SCALE, CONTROLLING FOR PARTY IDENTIFICATION AND TURNOUT

Respondent's Placement of Democratic Candidate	Respondent's Position: Protect Rights Of Accused	(2)	(3)	(4)	(5)	(6)	Stop Crime Regardless Of Rights	Total	
Party I.D.: DEMOCRAT									
Prot. Rights	62%	59%	63%	33%	37%	9%	17%	36%	[168]
(4)	22	31	28	46	34	35	25	31	[144]
Stop Crime	17	10	9	22	29	57	57	33	[150]
[N]	[78]	[29]	[43]	[83]	[68]	[46]	[115]		[462]
Party I.D.: IND. INDEPENDENT									
Prot. Rights	62%	...	...	20%	50%	25%	11%	25%	[27]
(4)	15	...	...	67	30	25	16	30	[23]
Stop Crime	23	...	...	13	20	50	74	35	[27]
[N]	[13]	[3]	[5]	[15]	[10]	[12]	[19]		[77]
Party I.D.: REPUBLICAN									
Prot. Rights	58%	92%	72%	35%	41%	39%	30%	44%	[91]
(4)	42	8	22	51	33	36	25	33	[68]
Stop Crime	0	0	6	14	26	26	45	24	[50]
[N]	[12]	[12]	[18]	[37]	[46]	[31]	[53]		[209]
Turnout: VOTED									
Prot. Rights	72%	63%	62%	32%	36%	22%	23%	38%	[165]
(4)	12	33	35	49	38	34	26	32	[141]
Stop Crime	16	4	3	19	26	44	51	30	[129]
[N]	[58]	[24]	[29]	[73]	[77]	[64]	[110]		[435]
Turnout: DID NOT VOTE									
Prot. Rights	45%	74%	67%	33%	42%	23%	18%	38%	[115]
(4)	41	11	22	50	27	31	19	30	[91]
Stop Crime	14	16	11	17	31	46	63	31	[94]
[N]	[42]	[19]	[36]	[60]	[45]	[26]	[72]		[300]

TABLE 6-10

RESPONDENT'S PLACEMENT OF REPUBLICAN CONGRESSIONAL CANDIDATE ON THE RIGHTS OF THE ACCUSED SCALE BY RESPONDENT'S OWN POSITION ON THE SCALE, CONTROLLING FOR PARTY IDENTIFICATION AND TURNOUT

Respondent's Placement of Republican Candidate	Respondent's Position: Protect Rights Of Accused	(2)	(3)	(4)	(5)	(6)	Stop Crime Regardless Of Rights	Total	
				Party I.D.: DEMOCRAT					
Prot. Rights	54%	47%	39%	24%	27%	12%	18%	31%	[85]
(4)	19	33	23	44	29	35	30	30	[32]
Stop Crime	26	20	39	31	44	54	53	39	[108]
[N]	[57]	[15]	[26]	[45]	[45]	[26]	[61]		[275]
				Party I.D.: IND. INDEPENDENT					
Prot. Rights	...	...	...	19%	...	...	13%	31%	[20]
(4)	...	...	...	63	...	...	33	32	[21]
Stop Crime	...	...	...	19	...	...	53	37	[24]
[N]	[9]	[2]	[7]	[16]	[9]	[7]	[15]		[65]
				Party I.D.: REPUBLICAN					
Prot. Rights	...	77%	46%	26%	12%	11%	11%	23%	[49]
(4)	...	15	31	53	31	33	24	32	[68]
Stop Crime	...	7	23	21	57	56	65	45	[95]
[N]	[9]	[13]	[13]	[38]	[49]	[36]	[54]		[212]
				Turnout: VOTED					
Prot. Rights	51%	65%	42%	21%	17%	8%	11%	23%	[79]
(4)	21	17	21	48	29	31	27	29	[98]
Stop Crime	28	17	38	31	54	62	63	48	[160]
[N]	[39]	[23]	[24]	[48]	[65]	[52]	[86]		[337]
				Turnout: DID NOT VOTE					
Prot. Rights	65%	...	50%	28%	23%	24%	23%	34%	[72]
(4)	21	...	23	52	31	35	27	34	[71]
Stop Crime	15	...	27	20	46	42	50	32	[66]
[N]	[34]	[7]	[22]	[50]	[35]	[17]	[44]		[209]

TABLE 6-11

RESPONDENT'S PLACEMENT OF INCUMBENT CONGRESSIONAL CANDIDATE ON THE RIGHTS OF THE ACCUSED SCALE BY RESPONDENT'S OWN POSITION ON THE SCALE, CONTROLLING FOR PARTY IDENTIFICATION AND TURNOUT

Respondent's Placement of Incumbent Candidate	Respondent's Position: Protect Rights Of Accused	(2)	(3)	(4)	(5)	(6)	Stop Crime Regardless Of Rights	Total	
	Party I.D.: SAME AS INCUMBENT								
Prot. Rights	72%	77%	68%	29%	24%	9%	17%	34%	[160]
(4)	16	18	21	51	36	29	22	30	[139]
Stop Crime	13	6	12	20	40	63	60	36	[170]
[N]	[56]	[34]	[34]	[90]	[78]	[56]	[121]		[469]
	Party I.D.: R IS AN IND. INDEPENDENT								
Prot. Rights	77%	...	...	20%	9%	27%	8%	30%	[27]
(4)	8	...	...	65	36	18	21	30	[27]
Stop Crime	15	...	...	15	55	55	71	40	[36]
[N]	[13]	[3]	[8]	[20]	[11]	[11]	[24]		[90]
	Party I.D.: DIFFERENT THAN INCUMBENT								
Prot. Rights	69%	53%	56%	29%	33%	24%	18%	36%	[107]
(4)	15	27	25	50	30	37	25	31	[91]
Stop Crime	15	20	19	21	37	39	57	33	[98]
[N]	[39]	[15]	[32]	[52]	[54]	[41]	[63]		[296]
	Turnout: VOTED								
Prot. Rights	77%	66%	62%	25%	22%	15%	16%	33%	[166]
(4)	11	22	2	53	37	30	25	31	[156]
Stop Crime	11	13	15	22	41	55	59	37	[189]
[N]	[62]	[32]	[39]	[85]	[91]	[78]	[124]		[511]
	Turnout: DID NOT VOTE								
Prot. Rights	61%	74%	59%	33%	33%	17%	18%	37%	[118]
(4)	22	16	24	51	29	35	18	30	[95]
Stop Crime	17	11	18	16	38	48	64	34	[109]
[N]	[41]	[19]	[34]	[73]	[48]	[29]	[78]		[322]

TABLE 6-12

RESPONDENT'S PLACEMENT OF INCUMBENT CHALLENGER ON THE RIGHTS OF THE ACCUSED SCALE BY RESPONDENT'S OWN POSITION ON THE SCALE, CONTROLLING FOR PARTY IDENTIFICATION AND TURNOUT

Respondent's Placement of Challenger	Respondent's Position: Protect Rights Of Accused	(2)	(3)	(4)	(5)	(6)	Stop Crime Regardless Of Rights	Total	
	Party I.D.: SAME AS INCUMBENT								
Prot. Rights	40%	82%	...	29%	36%	40%	31%	38%	[49]
(4)	30	18	...	50	32	20	31	33	[42]
Stop Crime	30	0	...	21	32	40	38	30	[38]
[N]	[20]	[11]	[7]	[24]	[25]	[10]	[32]		[129]
	Party I.D.: R IS AN IND. INDEPENDENT								
Prot. Rights	...	...	...	...	...	...	...	36%	[14]
(4)	...	...	...	...	...	...	...	31	[12]
Stop Crime	...	...	...	...	...	...	...	33	[13]
[N]	[6]	[2]	[4]	[8]	[4]	[6]	[9]		[39]
	Party I.D.: DIFFERENT THAN INCUMBENT								
Prot. Rights	44%	...	38%	39%	42%	18%	11%	31%	[40]
(4)	31	...	50	30	19	44	30	34	[44]
Stop Crime	25	...	13	30	39	38	59	36	[47]
[N]	[16]	[7]	[16]	[23]	[26]	[16]	[27]		[131]
	Turnout: VOTED								
Prot. Rights	35%	62%	29%	39%	39%	21%	20%	32%	[57]
(4)	20	31	43	35	27	29	30	30	[54]
Stop Crime	45	8	29	27	33	50	50	38	[69]
[N]	[20]	[13]	[14]	[26]	[33]	[24]	[50]		[180]
	Turnout: DID NOT VOTE								
Prot. Rights	50%	...	62%	27%	38%	...	26%	38%	[45]
(4)	36	...	31	53	24	...	26	38	[45]
Stop Crime	14	...	7	20	38	...	47	25	[30]
[N]	[22]	[7]	[13]	[30]	[21]	[8]	[19]		[120]

TABLE 6-13

RESPONDENT'S POSITION ON THE GOVERNMENT HELP MINORITY GROUPS SCALE BY RESPONDENT'S PARTY IDENTIFICATION

Respondent's Position	Respondent's Party Identification								
	Str. Dem.	Weak Dem.	Ind. Dem.	Ind. Ind.	Ind. Rep.	Weak Rep.	Str. Rep.	Total	
Govern. Help	25%	12%	12%	9%	3%	5%	8%	12%	[228]
(2)	9	6	9	6	4	2	2	6	[116]
(3)	10	11	14	10	9	9	6	10	[204]
(4)	18	24	25	28	28	30	23	25	[494]
(5)	10	15	12	15	26	21	21	16	[324]
(6)	10	9	11	14	12	17	16	12	[238]
Minor. Help	19	23	17	18	18	16	25	19	[386]
[N]	[306]	[488]	[301]	[271]	[206]	[258]	[160]		[1990]

TABLE 6-14

PARTY VOTE BY RESPONDENT'S POSITION ON THE GOVERNMENT HELP MINORITY GROUPS SCALE AND RESPONDENT'S PARTY IDENTIFICATION

Respondent's Position	Respondent's Party Identification								
	Str. Dem.	Weak Dem.	Ind. Dem.	Ind. Ind.	Ind. Rep.	Weak Rep.	Str. Rep.	Total	
Govern. Help	85	91	77	67	...	...	...	74	[82]
(2)	88	69	77	...	...	...	...	72	[61]
(3)	95	73	71	44	60	36	29	66	[100]
(4)	83	76	63	64	41	34	23	57	[239]
(5)	90	82	62	50	26	38	19	52	[169]
(6)	59	88	43	46	17	30	24	45	[110]
Minor. Help	96	83	36	53	32	39	18	56	[168]
Total	86	80	61	56	36	35	21	58	
[N]	[181]	[195]	[116]	[90]	[107]	[131]	[109]		[929]

Cell entries are the proportion of voters who reported voting Democratic in the House race in their district.

TABLE 6-15

RESPONDENT'S PLACEMENT OF DEMOCRATIC CONGRESSIONAL CANDIDATE ON THE GOVERNMENT HELP MINORITY GROUPS SCALE BY RESPONDENT'S OWN POSITION ON THE SCALE, CONTROLLING FOR PARTY IDENTIFICATION AND TURNOUT

Respondent's Placement of Democratic Candidate	Respondent's Position: Government Should Help Min. Grps.	(2)	(3)	(4)	(5)	(6)	Min. Grps. Should Help Themselves	Total	
Party I.D.: DEMOCRAT									
Govern. Help	64%	68%	60%	41%	42%	36%	34%	48%	[244]
(4)	21	27	22	46	30	19	23	29	[146]
Minor. Help	15	5	17	13	28	45	43	23	[118]
[N]	[95]	[37]	[58]	[116]	[69]	[42]	[91]		[508]
Party I.D.: IND. INDEPENDENT									
Govern. Help	33%	...	...	32%	39%	27%	29%	39%	[36]
(4)	40	...	...	41	39	40	29	34	[31]
Minor. Help	27	...	...	27	23	33	43	27	[25]
[N]	[15]	[5]	[8]	[22]	[13]	[15]	[14]		[92]
Party I.D.: REPUBLICAN									
Govern. Help	72%	...	68%	34%	52%	45%	45%	48%	[113]
(4)	14	...	32	54	15	39	22	32	[75]
Minor. Help	14	...	0	12	33	16	33	20	[47]
[N]	[14]	[6]	[19]	[67]	[52]	[31]	[46]		[235]
Turnout: VOTED									
Govern. Help	71%	63%	54%	39%	44%	42%	40%	49%	[236]
(4)	19	31	22	46	27	25	21	29	[142]
Minor. Help	10	6	15	16	29	33	40	22	[107]
[N]	[63]	[32]	[55]	[122]	[89]	[48]	[76]		[485]
Turnout: DID NOT VOTE									
Govern. Help	47%	87%	66%	37%	49%	32%	36%	44%	[149]
(4)	28	13	24	51	21	34	27	32	[109]
Minor. Help	26	0	10	12	30	34	37	24	[82]
[N]	[58]	[15]	[29]	[81]	[43]	[41]	[73]		[340]

TABLE 6-16

RESPONDENT'S PLACEMENT OF REPUBLICAN CONGRESSIONAL CANDIDATE ON THE GOVERNMENT HELP MINORITY GROUPS SCALE BY RESPONDENT'S OWN POSITION ON THE SCALE, CONTROLLING FOR PARTY IDENTIFICATION AND TURNOUT

Respondent's Placement of Republican Candidate	Respondent's Position: Government Should Help Min. Grps.	(2)	(3)	(4)	(5)	(6)	Min. Grps. Should Help Themselves	Total	
				Party I.D.: DEMOCRAT					
Govern. Help	53%	27%	35%	35%	32%	33%	31%	36%	[110]
(4)	26	35	35	38	30	14	29	20	[92]
Minor. Help	21	39	30	27	38	53	40	34	[105]
[N]	[47]	[26]	[43]	[60]	[37]	[36]	[58]		[307]
				Party I.D.: IND. INDEPENDENT					
Govern. Help	...	...	...	13%	40%	...	40%	30%	[20]
(4)	...	...	...	73	20	...	20	38	[25]
Minor. Help	...	...	...	13	40	...	40	32	[21]
[N]	[6]	[5]	[6]	[15]	[15]	[9]	[10]		[66]
				Party I.D.: REPUBLICAN					
Govern. Help	...	...	77%	36%	25%	18%	19%	32%	[74]
(4)	...	...	15	46	30	30	21	30	[70]
Minor. Help	...	...	8	18	45	53	61	38	[87]
[N]	[9]	[7]	[13]	[66]	[53]	[40]	[43]		[231]
				Turnout: VOTED					
Govern. Help	48%	32%	36%	35%	27%	22%	24%	30%	[111]
(4)	19	29	36	41	31	13	27	29	[107]
Minor. Help	33	39	28	24	42	66	50	41	[150]
[N]	[27]	[28]	[36]	[83]	[71]	[55]	[68]		[368]
				Turnout: DID NOT VOTE					
Govern. Help	57%	50%	56%	32%	38%	29%	34%	40%	[93]
(4)	31	30	26	51	22	43	23	34	[79]
Minor. Help	11	20	19	18	41	29	43	26	[61]
[N]	[35]	[10]	[27]	[57]	[32]	[28]	[44]		[233]

TABLE 6-17

RESPONDENT'S PLACEMENT OF INCUMBENT CONGRESSIONAL CANDIDATE ON THE GOVERNMENT HELP MINORITY GROUPS SCALE BY RESPONDENT'S OWN POSITION ON THE SCALE, CONTROLLING FOR PARTY IDENTIFICATION AND TURNOUT

Respondent's Placement of Incumbent Candidate	Respondent's Position: Government Should Help Min. Grps.	(2)	(3)	(4)	(5)	(6)	Min. Grps. Should Help Themselves	Total	
	Party I.D.: SAME AS INCUMBENT								
Govern. Help	73%	73%	70%	40%	32%	32%	27%	44%	[230]
(4)	16	21	17	44	35	19	19	28	[146]
Minor. Help	10	6	13	16	34	49	54	28	[143]
[N]	[67]	[33]	[46]	[135]	[95]	[47]	[96]		[519]
	Party I.D.: R IS AN IND. INDEPENDENT								
Govern. Help	36%	...	...	22%	35%	13%	35%	34%	[36]
(4)	36	...	...	54	29	38	24	35	[37]
Minor. Help	29	...	...	25	35	50	41	32	[34]
[N]	[14]	[6]	[9]	[28]	[17]	[16]	[17]		[107]
	Party I.D.: DIFFERENT THAN INCUMBENT								
Govern. Help	69%	38%	52%	29%	33%	36%	38%	40%	[131]
(4)	16	19	31	54	22	27	29	32	[104]
Minor. Help	16	44	17	17	44	36	33	28	[91]
[N]	[32]	[16]	[48]	[72]	[45]	[44]	[69]		[326]
	Turnout: VOTED								
Govern. Help	73%	60%	57%	35%	28%	28%	32%	40%	[238]
(4)	14	16	27	46	35	22	22	30	[168]
Minor. Help	13	24	16	19	37	50	46	30	[170]
[N]	[56]	[37]	[63]	[138]	[106]	[60]	[106]		[566]
	Turnout: DID NOT VOTE								
Govern. Help	57%	71%	65%	34%	43%	35%	32%	43%	[160]
(4)	24	24	23	52	19	28	27	31	[116]
Minor. Help	19	6	13	14	38	37	41	25	[94]
[N]	[54]	[17]	[40]	[93]	[47]	[46]	[73]		[370]

TABLE 6-18

RESPONDENT'S PLACEMENT OF INCUMBENT CHALLENGER ON THE GOVERNMENT HELP MINORITY GROUPS SCALE BY RESPONDENT'S OWN POSITION ON THE SCALE, CONTROLLING FOR PARTY IDENTIFICATION AND TURNOUT

Respondent's Placement of Challenger	Respondent's Position: Government Should Help Min. Grps.	(2)	(3)	(4)	(5)	(6)	Min. Grps. Should Help Themselves	Total	
				Party I.D.: SAME AS INCUMBENT					
Govern. Help	33%	36%	...	46%	58%	42%	35%	43%	[65]
(4)	33	46	...	33	19	17	22	28	[42]
Minor. Help	33	18	...	22	23	42	44	29	[43]
[N]	[18]	[11]	[9]	[46]	[31]	[12]	[23]		[150]
				Party I.D.: R IS AN IND. INDEPENDENT					
Govern. Help	...	...	...	...	46%	...	...	35%	[14]
(4)	...	...	...	...	27	...	...	38	[15]
Minor. Help	...	...	...	...	27	...	...	28	[11]
[N]	[6]	[4]	[5]	[6]	[11]	[5]	[3]		[40]
				Party I.D.: DIFFERENT THAN INCUMBENT					
Govern. Help	18%	...	56%	47%	40%	19%	32%	36%	[48]
(4)	47	...	17	44	13	38	32	34	[46]
Minor. Help	35	...	28	9	47	43	36	30	[40]
[N]	[17]	[6]	[18]	[32]	[15]	[21]	[25]		[134]
				Turnout: VOTED					
Govern. Help	17%	29%	52%	49%	48%	32%	29%	39%	[78]
(4)	44	53	19	33	19	12	26	28	[55]
Minor. Help	39	18	29	18	33	56	45	33	[66]
[N]	[18]	[17]	[21]	[45]	[42]	[25]	[31]		[199]
				Turnout: DID NOT VOTE					
Govern. Help	26%	...	55%	38%	60%	15%	35%	38%	[48]
(4)	44	...	18	45	20	69	30	39	[49]
Minor. Help	30	...	27	18	20	15	35	23	[29]
[N]	[23]	[4]	[11]	[40]	[15]	[13]	[20]		[126]

TABLE 6-19

RESPONDENT'S POSITION ON THE HEALTH INSURANCE SCALE
BY RESPONDENT'S PARTY IDENTIFICATION

Respondent's Position	Respondent's Party Identification							
	Str. Dem.	Weak Dem.	Ind. Dem.	Ind. Ind.	Ind. Rep.	Weak Rep.	Str. Rep.	Total
Govt. Insur.	46%	34%	31%	28%	12%	13%	19%	28% [521]
(2)	8	9	11	10	7	8	8	9 [167]
(3)	5	9	11	6	11	8	2	8 [142]
(4)	11	13	13	15	16	15	8	13 [242]
(5)	7	9	8	9	12	12	7	9 [167]
(6)	8	10	8	9	17	13	15	11 [194]
Priv. Insur.	15	18	18	23	24	32	41	23 [415]
[N]	[280]	[452]	[281]	[243]	[186]	[248]	[158]	[1848]

TABLE 6-20

PARTY VOTE BY RESPONDENT'S POSITION ON THE HEALTH
INSURANCE SCALE AND RESPONDENT'S PARTY IDENTIFICATION

Respondent's Position	Respondent's Party Identification								
	Str. Dem.	Weak Dem.	Ind. Dem.	Ind. Ind.	Ind. Rep.	Weak Rep.	Str. Rep.	Total	
Govt. Insur.	88	85	65	65	58	30	24	72	[224]
(2)	82	88	50	38	...	36	43	55	[64]
(3)	...	90	81	...	42	29	...	71	[68]
(4)	87	80	38	55	20	30	38	56	[113]
(5)	87	65	80	17	43	23	13	52	[83]
(6)	87	64	57	17	24	28	10	41	[106]
Priv. Insur.	85	73	44	67	31	43	20	47	[201]
Total	87	78	59	54	35	34	21	57	
[N]	[166]	[175]	[113]	[80]	[96]	[123]	[106]		[859]

Cell entries are the proportion of voters who reported voting Democratic in the House race in their district.

TABLE 6-21

RESPONDENT'S PLACEMENT OF DEMOCRATIC CONGRESSIONAL CANDIDATE ON THE HEALTH INSURANCE SCALE BY RESPONDENT'S OWN POSITION ON THE SCALE, CONTROLLING FOR PARTY IDENTIFICATION AND TURNOUT

Respondent's Placement of Democratic Candidate	Respondent's Position: Government Insurance Plan	(2)	(3)	(4)	(5)	(6)	Private Insurance Plan	Total	
Party I.D.: DEMOCRAT									
Govt. Insur.	55%	46%	59%	32%	14%	37%	44%	46%	[177]
(4)	29	31	21	54	38	26	18	30	[116]
Priv. Insur.	16	23	21	14	48	37	39	24	[92]
[N]	[153]	[35]	[34]	[50]	[21]	[35]	[57]		[385]
Party I.D.: IND. INDEPENDENT									
Govt. Insur.	56%	40%	...	...	...	...	12%	34%	[23]
(4)	33	50	...	...	...	...	35	40	[27]
Priv. Insur.	11	10	...	...	...	...	53	25	[17]
[N]	[18]	[10]	[3]	[7]	[5]	[7]	[17]		[67]
Party I.D.: REPUBLICAN									
Govt. Insur.	44%	58%	55%	39%	44%	41%	41%	44%	[86]
(4)	22	26	36	46	33	31	27	31	[60]
Priv. Insur.	33	16	9	15	22	28	32	26	[50]
[N]	[27]	[19]	[11]	[26]	[18]	[29]	[66]		[196]
Turnout: VOTED									
Govt. Insur.	62%	58%	67%	41%	23%	46%	47%	51%	[192]
(4)	25	26	13	49	43	27	22	29	[107]
Priv. Insur.	13	16	20	10	33	27	31	21	[77]
[N]	[109]	[31]	[30]	[51]	[30]	[44]	[81]		[376]
Turnout: DID NOT VOTE									
Govt. Insur.	41%	36%	41%	26%	25%	27%	26%	33%	[85]
(4)	32	39	41	55	33	35	26	35	[91]
Priv. Insur.	27	24	18	19	42	39	48	32	[82]
[N]	[81]	[33]	[17]	[31]	[12]	[26]	[58]		[258]

TABLE 6-22

RESPONDENT'S PLACEMENT OF REPUBLICAN CONGRESSIONAL CANDIDATE ON THE HEALTH INSURANCE SCALE BY RESPONDENT'S OWN POSITION ON THE SCALE, CONTROLLING FOR PARTY IDENTIFICATION AND TURNOUT

Respondent's Placement of Republican Candidate	Respondent's Position: Government Insurance Plan	(2)	(3)	(4)	(5)	(6)	Private Insurance Plan	Total	
Party I.D.: DEMOCRAT									
Govt. Insur.	39%	39%	26%	25%	8%	14%	20%	29%	[69]
(4)	20	35	22	35	25	25	43	28	[66]
Priv. Insur.	40	26	52	40	67	61	38	44	[104]
[N]	[89]	[23]	[27]	[20]	[12]	[28]	[40]		[239]
Party I.D.: IND. INDEPENDENT									
Govt. Insur.	42%	...	...	...	...	...	25%	30%	[16]
(4)	33	...	...	...	...	...	50	43	[23]
Priv. Insur.	25	...	...	...	...	...	25	28	[15]
[N]	[12]	[8]	[2]	[9]	[6]	[5]	[12]		[54]
Party I.D.: REPUBLICAN									
Govt. Insur.	32%	47%	20%	12%	14%	10%	9%	17%	[31]
(4)	27	18	60	65	29	30	9	28	[52]
Priv. Insur.	41	35	20	23	57	60	83	55	[102]
[N]	[22]	[17]	[10]	[26]	[21]	[30]	[59]		[185]
Turnout: VOTED									
Govt. Insur.	36%	52%	23%	20%	14%	6%	11%	22%	[66]
(4)	23	20	27	53	23	32	16	27	[81]
Priv. Insur.	41	28	50	28	64	62	73	52	[156]
[N]	[70]	[25]	[26]	[40]	[22]	[47]	[73]		[303]
Turnout: DID NOT VOTE									
Govt. Insur.	39%	29%	36%	21%	14%	25%	22%	29%	[49]
(4)	26	46	46	43	29	19	41	34	[58]
Priv. Insur.	35	25	18	36	57	36	38	37	[63]

TABLE 6-23

RESPONDENT'S PLACEMENT OF INCUMBENT CONGRESSIONAL CANDIDATE ON THE HEALTH INSURANCE SCALE BY RESPONDENT'S OWN POSITION ON THE SCALE, CONTROLLING FOR PARTY IDENTIFICATION AND TURNOUT

Respondent's Placement of Incumbent Candidate	Respondent's Position: Government Insurance Plan	(2)	(3)	(4)	(5)	(6)	Private Insurance Plan	Total	
	Party I.D.: SAME AS INCUMBENT								
Govt. Insur.	59%	49%	39%	30%	14%	27%	26%	38%	[150]
(4)	28	26	36	54	31	25	12	29	[113]
Priv. Insur.	13	26	25	16	54	48	62	33	[128]
[N]	[115]	[35]	[28]	[57]	[35]	[44]	[77]		[391]
	Party I.D.: R IS AN IND. INDEPENDENT								
Govt. Insur.	55%	36%	...	...	...	...	17%	32%	[24]
(4)	32	64	...	...	...	...	33	42	[32]
Priv. Insur.	14	0	...	...	...	...	50	26	[20]
[N]	[22]	[11]	[4]	[7]	[6]	[8]	[18]		[76]
	Party I.D.: DIFFERENT THAN INCUMBENT								
Govt. Insur.	43%	52%	33%	30%	25%	15%	28%	33%	[91]
(4)	22	28	29	40	25	39	34	30	[83]
Priv. Insur.	36	21	38	30	50	46	39	37	[100]
[N]	[73]	[29]	[24]	[30]	[20]	[33]	[65]		[274]
	Turnout: VOTED								
Govt. Insur.	56%	58%	38%	33%	18%	22%	26%	37%	[163]
(4)	25	24	25	47	32	32	21	28	[124]
Priv. Insur.	19	18	38	21	50	47	53	35	[151]
[N]	[116]	[38]	[32]	[58]	[38]	[60]	[96]		[438]
	Turnout: DID NOT VOTE								
Govt. Insur.	46%	36%	36%	21%	17%	25%	24%	33%	[92]
(4)	29	42	46	62	22	33	24	35	[98]
Priv. Insur.	25	22	18	18	61	42	52	33	[93]
[N]	[87]	[36]	[22]	[34]	[18]	[24]	[62]		[283]

TABLE 6-24

RESPONDENT'S PLACEMENT OF INCUMBENT CHALLENGER ON THE HEALTH INSURANCE SCALE BY RESPONDENT'S OWN POSITION ON THE SCALE, CONTROLLING FOR PARTY IDENTIFICATION AND TURNOUT

Respondent's Placement of Challenger	Respondent's Position: Government Insurance Plan	(2)	(3)	(4)	(5)	(6)	Private Insurance Plan	Total	
				Party I.D.: SAME AS INCUMBENT					
Govt. Insur.	39%	36%	27%	46%	...	53%	44%	41%	[47]
(4)	18	36	27	46	...	5	28	25	[29]
Priv. Insur.	43	27	46	9	...	42	28	33	[38]
[N]	[28]	[11]	[11]	[11]	[9]	[19]	[25]		[114]
				Party I.D.: R IS AN IND. INDEPENDENT					
Govt. Insur.	...	...	...	...	...	...	17%	29%	[10]
(4)	...	...	...	...	...	...	67	46	[16]
Priv. Insur.	...	...	...	...	...	...	17	26	[9]
[N]	[7]	[7]	[1]	[5]	[5]	[4]	[6]		[35]
				Party I.D.: DIFFERENT THAN INCUMBENT					
Govt. Insur.	38%	46%	64%	0%	...	21%	21%	32%	[37]
(4)	27	27	27	70	...	36	21	31	[36]
Priv. Insur.	35	27	9	30	...	43	58	37	[43]
[N]	[37]	[15]	[11]	[10]	[5]	[14]	[24]		[116]
				Turnout: VOTED					
Govt. Insur.	43%	50%	50%	32%	18%	38%	32%	38%	[62]
(4)	25	25	19	58	46	21	22	28	[46]
Priv. Insur.	33	25	31	11	36	42	46	34	[55]
[N]	[40]	[16]	[16]	[19]	[11]	[24]	[37]		[163]
				Turnout: DID NOT VOTE					
Govt. Insur.	31%	35%	...	...	...	31%	28%	32%	[32]
(4)	25	41	...	...	...	23	44	34	[34]
Priv. Insur.	44	24	...	...	...	46	28	35	[35]
[N]	[32]	[17]	[6]	[7]	[8]	[13]	[18]		[101]

TABLE 6-25

RESPONDENT'S POSITION ON THE ROLE FOR WOMEN SCALE
BY RESPONDENT'S PARTY IDENTIFICATION

Respondent's Position	Respondent's Party Identification								
	Str. Dem.	Weak Dem.	Ind. Dem.	Ind. Ind.	Ind. Rep.	Weak Rep.	Str. Rep.	Total	
Equal Role	44%	40%	53%	44%	40%	31%	28%	41%	[856]
(2)	9	10	12	13	15	11	12	11	[234]
(3)	9	8	6	9	9	11	8	8	[175]
(4)	12	20	17	16	14	21	20	17	[361]
(5)	5	7	6	6	10	8	10	7	[148]
(6)	4	6	3	5	5	7	7	5	[110]
In The Home	19	10	5	7	6	11	16	10	[218]
[N]	[314]	[517]	[315]	[295]	[208]	[282]	[171]		[2102]

TABLE 6-26

PARTY VOTE BY RESPONDENT'S POSITION ON THE ROLE FOR WOMEN
SCALE AND RESPONDENT'S PARTY IDENTIFICATION

Respondent's Position	Respondent's Party Identification								
	Str. Dem.	Weak Dem.	Ind. Dem.	Ind. Ind.	Ind. Rep.	Weak Rep.	Str. Rep.	Total	
Equal Role	88	84	66	56	41	27	15	61	[386]
(2)	91	76	56	67	55	29	39	62	[117]
(3)	88	82	50	67	11	19	14	53	[80]
(4)	73	64	56	31	17	33	28	48	[178]
(5)	...	93	0	75	33	39	17	58	[69]
(6)	...	91	100	...	...	55	11	53	[55]
In The Home	90	92	...	60	...	54	15	68	[83]
Total	86	80	61	58	36	33	20	58	
[N]	[160]	[196]	[122]	[95]	[107]	[145]	[113]		[968]

Cell entries are the proportion of voters who reported voting Democratic in the House race in their district.

TABLE 6-27

RESPONDENT'S PLACEMENT OF DEMOCRATIC CONGRESSIONAL CANDIDATE ON THE ROLE FOR WOMEN SCALE BY RESPONDENT'S OWN POSITION ON THE SCALE, CONTROLLING FOR PARTY IDENTIFICATION AND TURNOUT

Respondent's Placement of Democratic Candidate	Respondent's Position: Women Should Have Equal Role	(2)	(3)	(4)	(5)	(6)	Women's Place Is In The Home	Total	
Party I.D.: DEMOCRAT									
Equal Role	74%	57%	67%	42%	44%	39%	33%	59%	[274]
(4)	19	32	27	49	19	44	33	28	[129]
In The Home	8	11	6	9	37	17	35	13	[61]
[N]	[212]	[54]	[33]	[66]	[27]	[23]	[49]		[464]
Party I.D.: IND. INDEPENDENT									
Equal Role	62%	73%	...	...	...	...	...	56%	[45]
(4)	21	18	...	...	...	...	...	25	[20]
In The Home	17	9	...	...	...	...	...	19	[15]
[N]	[42]	[11]	[7]	[7]	[7]	[2]	[4]		[80]
Party I.D.: REPUBLICAN									
Equal Role	73%	81%	60%	41%	38%	43%	33%	58%	[135]
(4)	20	17	25	52	38	43	24	29	[68]
In The Home	7	2	15	7	25	14	43	13	[29]
[N]	[69]	[42]	[20]	[42]	[24]	[14]	[21]		[232]
Turnout: VOTED									
Equal Role	77%	75%	64%	41%	42%	54%	44%	63%	[284]
(4)	17	19	31	53	15	33	27	26	[117]
In The Home	6	6	6	7	42	13	29	11	[49]
[N]	[184]	[63]	[36]	[76]	[33]	[24]	[34]		[450]
Turnout: DID NOT VOTE									
Equal Role	65%	58%	61%	44%	36%	21%	27%	52%	[165]
(4)	22	33	26	46	40	50	27	30	[95]
In The Home	13	9	13	10	24	29	46	18	[57]
[N]	[132]	[43]	[23]	[39]	[25]	[14]	[41]		[317]

TABLE 6-28

RESPONDENT'S PLACEMENT OF REPUBLICAN CONGRESSIONAL CANDIDATE ON THE ROLE FOR WOMEN SCALE BY RESPONDENT'S OWN POSITION ON THE SCALE, CONTROLLING FOR PARTY IDENTIFICATION AND TURNOUT

Respondent's Placement of Republican Candidate	Respondent's Position: Women Should Have Equal Role	(2)	(3)	(4)	(5)	(6)	Women's Place Is In The Home	Total	
				Party I.D.: DEMOCRAT					
Equal Role	61%	63%	32%	34%	37%	...	39%	50%	[140]
(4)	18	26	53	43	32	...	36	29	[81]
In The Home	21	11	16	23	32	...	26	21	[59]
[N]	[124]	[35]	[19]	[44]	[19]	[8]	[31]		[280]
				Party I.D.: IND. INDEPENDENT					
Equal Role	62%	...	...	0%	...	...	...	44%	[27]
(4)	17	...	...	92	...	...	...	36	[22]
In The Home	21	...	...	9	...	...	...	21	[13]
[N]	[29]	[6]	[6]	[12]	[4]	[3]	[2]		[62]
				Party I.D.: REPUBLICAN					
Equal Role	74%	76%	62%	34%	27%	28%	22%	53%	[113]
(4)	14	12	29	63	41	22	14	28	[60]
In The Home	13	12	10	3	32	50	64	19	[40]
[N]	[72]	[25]	[21]	[41]	[22]	[18]	[14]		[213]
				Turnout: VOTED					
Equal Role	67%	67%	48%	27%	23%	20%	29%	49%	[171]
(4)	14	21	41	59	35	30	24	29	[99]
In The Home	19	13	10	14	42	50	48	22	[76]
[N]	[147]	[39]	[29]	[64]	[26]	[20]	[21]		[346]
				Turnout: DID NOT VOTE					
Equal Role	64%	68%	35%	34%	42%	...	41%	52%	[107]
(4)	20	25	47	56	37	...	30	31	[65]
In The Home	16	7	18	9	21	...	30	17	[35]
[N]	[75]	[28]	[17]	[32]	[19]	[9]	[27]		[207]

TABLE 6-29

RESPONDENT'S PLACEMENT OF INCUMBENT CONGRESSIONAL CANDIDATE ON THE ROLE FOR WOMEN SCALE BY RESPONDENT'S OWN POSITION ON THE SCALE, CONTROLLING FOR PARTY IDENTIFICATION AND TURNOUT

Respondent's Placement of Incumbent Candidate	Respondent's Position								
	Women Should Have Equal Role	(2)	(3)	(4)	(5)	(6)	Women's Place Is In The Home	Total	
	Party I.D.: SAME AS INCUMBENT								
Equal Role	76%	62%	68%	33%	34%	32%	27%	57%	[269]
(4)	16	30	27	64	31	32	34	30	[142]
In The Home	8	9	5	3	34	36	39	13	[62]
[N]	[203]	[47]	[41]	[78]	[32]	[31]	[41]		[473]
	Party I.D.: R IS AN IND. INDEPENDENT								
Equal Role	63%	75%	...	8%	...	...	...	50%	[47]
(4)	19	17	...	85	...	...	...	31	[29]
In The Home	19	8	...	8	...	...	...	19	[18]
[N]	[48]	[12]	[8]	[13]	[7]	[2]	[4]		[94]
	Party I.D.: DIFFERENT THAN INCUMBENT								
Equal Role	64%	77%	48%	34%	40%	30%	37%	54%	[164]
(4)	22	17	38	49	28	50	33	30	[89]
In The Home	14	6	14	17	32	20	30	16	[49]
[N]	[113]	[53]	[21]	[53]	[25]	[10]	[27]		[302]
	Turnout: VOTED								
Equal Role	73%	73%	56%	32%	32%	40%	39%	57%	[297]
(4)	17	21	39	61	26	28	30	29	[152]
In The Home	10	6	5	7	42	32	30	14	[70]
[N]	[222]	[66]	[41]	[94]	[38]	[25]	[33]		[519]
	Turnout: DID NOT VOTE								
Equal Role	67%	67%	54%	31%	42%	18%	30%	52%	[175]
(4)	20	24	32	59	35	41	30	31	[104]
In The Home	13	9	14	10	23	41	40	18	[59]
[N]	[133]	[45]	[28]	[49]	[26]	[17]	[40]		[338]

TABLE 6-30

RESPONDENT'S PLACEMENT OF INCUMBENT CHALLENGER ON THE ROLE FOR WOMEN SCALE BY RESPONDENT'S OWN POSITION ON THE SCALE, CONTROLLING FOR PARTY IDENTIFICATION AND TURNOUT

Respondent's Placement of Challenger	Respondent's Position: Women Should Have Equal Role	(2)	(3)	(4)	(5)	(6)	Women's Place Is In The Home	Total	
Party I.D.: SAME AS INCUMBENT									
Equal Role	62%	53%	50%	46%	33%	...	44%	52%	[81]
(4)	16	35	36	42	40	...	25	28	[43]
In The Home	22	12	14	12	27	...	31	20	[31]
[N]	[58]	[17]	[14]	[26]	[15]	[9]	[16]		[155]
Party I.D.: R IS AN IND. INDEPENDENT									
Equal Role	55%	...	...	...	...	...	...	45%	[18]
(4)	25	...	...	...	...	...	...	33	[13]
In The Home	20	...	...	...	...	...	...	23	[9]
[N]	[20]	[5]	[3]	[6]	[4]	[1]	[1]		[40]
Party I.D.: DIFFERENT THAN INCUMBENT									
Equal Role	65%	71%	50%	57%	39%	...	25%	58%	[80]
(4)	22	8	30	30	23	...	17	22	[30]
In The Home	14	21	20	13	39	...	58	21	[29]
[N]	[51]	[24]	[10]	[23]	[13]	[6]	[12]		[139]
Turnout: VOTED									
Equal Role	65%	63%	56%	41%	33%	50%	35%	54%	[110]
(4)	18	19	31	46	22	20	18	24	[50]
In The Home	18	19	13	14	44	30	47	22	[45]
[N]	[80]	[27]	[16]	[37]	[18]	[10]	[17]		[205]
Turnout: DID NOT VOTE									
Equal Role	58%	60%	46%	61%	36%	...	39%	54%	[70]
(4)	21	30	36	33	36	...	23	28	[36]
In The Home	21	10	18	6	29	...	39	19	[24]
[N]	[48]	[20]	[11]	[18]	[14]	[6]	[13]		[130]

TABLE 6-31

RESPONDENT'S POSITION ON SEGREGRATION/DESEGREGRATION
BY RESPONDENT'S PARTY IDENTIFICATION

Respondent's Position	Str. Dem.	Weak Dem.	Ind. Dem.	Ind. Ind.	Ind. Rep.	Weak Rep.	Str. Rep.	Total	
Favor Desegregation	47%	36%	43%	34%	31%	30%	32%	37%	[763]
Something In Between	44	59	53	61	67	66	63	58	[1208]
Strict Segregration	9	5	4	5	3	5	5	5	[110]
[N]	[319]	[518]	[306]	[286]	[206]	[277]	[169]		[2081]

TABLE 6-32

PARTY VOTE
RESPONDENT'S POSITION ON SEGREGRATION/DESEGREGRATION
AND RESPONDENT'S PARTY IDENTIFICATION

Respondent's Position	Str. Dem.	Weak Dem.	Ind. Dem.	Ind. Ind.	Ind. Rep.	Weak Rep.	Str. Rep.	Total	
Favor Desegregation	91	78	70	55	32	38	15	62	[359]
Something In Between	83	80	52	59	42	33	24	56	[570]
Strict Segregration	92	75	100	57	...	40	...	68	[34]
Total	87	79	60	58	38	35	21	58	
[N]	[190]	[200]	[120]	[96]	[106]	[141]	[110]		[963]

Cell entries are the proportion of voters who reported voting Democratic in the House race in their district.

TABLE 6-33

RESPONDENT'S POSITION ON WHETHER FEDERAL TAXES ARE TOO HIGH CONSIDERING THE SERVICES THE GOVERNMENT PROVIDES BY RESPONDENT'S PARTY IDENTIFICATION

Respondent's Position	Respondent's Party Identification: Str. Dem.	Weak Dem.	Ind. Dem.	Ind. Ind.	Ind. Rep.	Weak Rep.	Str. Rep.	Total	
Taxes Not Too High	41%	36%	38%	34%	32%	30%	38%	36%	[731]
Taxes Are Too High	59	64	62	66	68	70	62	64	[1301]
[N]	[297]	[505]	[313]	[279]	[204]	[268]	[166]		[2032]

TABLE 6-34

PARTY VOTE BY RESPONDENT'S POSITION ON WHETHER FEDERAL TAXES ARE TOO HIGH CONSIDERING THE SERVICES THE GOVERNMENT PROVIDES AND RESPONDENT'S PARTY IDENTIFICATION

Respondent's Position	Respondent's Party Identification: Str. Dem.	Weak Dem.	Ind. Dem.	Ind. Ind.	Ind. Rep.	Weak Rep.	Str. Rep.	Total	
Taxes Not Too High	93	84	66	64	47	30	27	66	[351]
Taxes Are Too High	80	76	59	54	34	35	17	53	[587]
Total	86	79	62	57	38	34	21	58	
[N]	[176]	[197]	[121]	[95]	[103]	[136]	[110]		[938]

Cell entries are the proportion of voters who reported voting Democratic in the House race in their district.

TABLE 6-35

RESPONDENT'S POSITION ON ABORTION
BY RESPONDENT'S PARTY IDENTIFICATION

Respondent's Position	Str. Dem.	Weak Dem.	Ind. Dem.	Ind. Ind.	Ind. Rep.	Weak Rep.	Str. Rep.	Total	
Should Never Be Permitted	17%	10%	9%	10%	9%	8%	9%	11%	[223]
Only If Life Is In Danger	51	49	34	45	41	44	50	45	[954]
Care For Child Would Be Difficult	13	18	19	17	21	18	11	17	[359]
Should Never Be Forbidden	20	23	38	28	30	31	30	28	[586]
[N]	[325]	[534]	[309]	[294]	[213]	[280]	[167]		[2122]

TABLE 6-36

PARTY VOTE BY RESPONDENT'S POSITION ON ABORTION
AND RESPONDENT'S PARTY IDENTIFICATION

Respondent's Position	Str. Dem.	Weak Dem.	Ind. Dem.	Ind. Ind.	Ind. Rep.	Weak Rep.	Str. Rep.	Total	
Should Never Be Permitted	88	90	50	20	50	60	43	70	[94]
Only If Life Is In Danger	87	77	57	56	33	33	23	59	[432]
Care For Child Would Be Difficult	88	93	64	71	25	32	15	59	[158]
Should Never Be Forbidden	83	76	68	48	46	30	11	54	[277]
Total	87	80	62	55	37	34	19	58	
[N]	[193]	[201]	[119]	[92]	[108]	[140]	[108]		[961]

Cell entries are the proportion of voters who reported voting Democratic in the House race in their district.

TABLE 6-37

RESPONDENT'S POSITION ON THE PREFERENTIAL TREATMENT SCALE
BY RESPONDENT'S PARTY IDENTIFICATION

Respondent's Position	Respondent's Party Identification								
	Str. Dem.	Weak Dem.	Ind. Dem.	Ind. Ind.	Ind. Rep.	Weak Rep.	Str. Rep.	Total	
Give Prefer.	11%	6%	4%	3%	1%	1%	3%	5%	[87]
(2)	3	2	5	1	0	2	3	2	[43]
(3)	6	5	4	4	6	4	1	4	[84]
(4)	13	12	12	11	13	8	5	11	[213]
(5)	12	11	8	8	10	11	7	10	[184]
(6)	12	16	21	17	17	22	24	18	[347]
Ability Only	42	49	47	56	53	52	57	50	[957]
[N]	[278]	[458]	[299]	[267]	[193]	[259]	[161]		[1915]

TABLE 6-38

PARTY VOTE
RESPONDENT'S POSITION ON THE PREFERENTIAL TREATMENT SCALE
AND RESPONDENT'S PARTY IDENTIFICATION

Respondent's Position	Respondent's Party Identification								
	Str. Dem.	Weak Dem.	Ind. Dem.	Ind. Ind.	Ind. Rep.	Weak Rep.	Str. Rep.	Total	
Give Prefer.	93	88	...	...	...	...	...	81	[32]
(2)	...	...	...	...	...	...	...	79	[19]
(3)	89	...	...	...	...	...	...	66	[41]
(4)	95	79	72	50	57	27	...	69	[105]
(5)	91	62	46	33	10	47	...	53	[100]
(6)	78	85	50	75	29	40	19	52	[162]
Ability Only	82	80	61	55	36	31	17	53	[446]
Total	86	78	62	58	35	35	19	57	
[N]	[166]	[183]	[118]	[89]	[102]	[136]	[111]		[905]

Cell entries are the proportion of voters who reported voting Democratic in the House race in their district.

TABLE 6-39

RESPONDENT'S POSITION ON THE EQUAL RIGHTS AMENDMENT
BY RESPONDENT'S PARTY IDENTIFICATION

Respondent's Position	Respondent's Party Identification							
	Str. Dem.	Weak Dem.	Ind. Dem.	Ind. Ind.	Ind. Rep.	Weak Rep.	Str. Rep.	Total
Approve	72%	70%	78%	69%	56%	54%	46%	66% [1132]
Disapprove	28	30	22	31	44	46	54	34 [583]
[N]	[260]	[419]	[270]	[216]	[178]	[237]	[135]	[1715]

TABLE 6-40

PARTY VOTE
RESPONDENT'S POSITION ON THE EQUAL RIGHTS AMENDMENT
AND RESPONDENT'S PARTY IDENTIFICATION

Respondent's Position	Respondent's Party Identification							
	Str. Dem.	Weak Dem.	Ind. Dem.	Ind. Ind.	Ind. Rep.	Weak Rep.	Str. Rep.	Total
Approve	85	79	65	52	43	30	17	62 [521]
Disapprove	84	83	56	45	32	41	22	51 [305]
Total	85	80	63	49	37	35	20	58
[N]	[161]	[167]	[113]	[75]	[91]	[122]	[97]	[826]

Cell entries are the proportion of voters who reported voting Democratic in the House race in their district.

two tables use the matrix of citizens' Ideological Positions with Party Identification to present Turnout (Table 7-2) and Vote for Incumbent (Table 7-4).

The tables presented as Parts III and IV are intended to serve as a final introduction and guide to the articles which follow. The table in Part III lists all of the variables discussed in this section and identifies where they are to be found in the dataset. Finally, the table in Part IV should be helpful to those scholars interested in comparing the use of the dataset by the authors whose articles appear in Chapters 2 to 6. In that table the list of variables is repeated and their location in the substantive chapters, if any, is indicated.

TABLE 7-1

RESPONDENT'S POSITION ON THE IDEOLOGY SCALE BY RESPONDENT'S PARTY IDENTIFICATION

Respondent's Position	Respondent's Party Identification								
	Str. Dem.	Weak Dem.	Ind. Dem.	Ind. Ind.	Ind. Rep.	Weak Rep.	Str. Rep.	Total	
Ex. Liberal	4%	1%	5%	4%	0%	1%	1%	2%	[38]
Liberal	17	12	18	11	4	3	3	11	[178]
Sl. Liberal	17	18	21	11	12	5	1	13	[322]
Moderate	39	41	40	44	30	31	21	36	[602]
Sl. Conserv.	10	17	11	16	29	32	20	19	[307]
Conservative	10	8	4	13	22	24	45	15	[255]
Ex. Conserv.	3	2	1	2	3	4	10	3	[51]
[N]	[232]	[380]	[265]	[210]	[182]	[237]	[147]		[1653]

TABLE 7-2

TURNOUT BY RESPONDENT'S POSITION ON THE IDEOLOGY SCALE AND RESPONDENT'S PARTY IDENTIFICATION

Respondent's Position	Respondent's Party Identification								
	Str. Dem.	Weak Dem.	Ind. Dem.	Ind. Ind.	Ind. Rep.	Weak Rep.	Str. Rep.	Total	
Ex. Liberal	70	...	46	...	...	...	...	49	[37]
Liberal	77	35	41	13	...	...	...	47	[174]
Sl. Liberal	62	51	45	30	57	25	...	48	[211]
Moderate	66	41	50	49	49	58	85	53	[570]
Sl. Conserv.	70	54	55	47	67	55	82	60	[294]
Conservative	57	53	27	37	62	67	77	61	[240]
Ex. Conserv.	...	...	...	...	...	78	79	56	[48]
Total	66	45	47	40	58	59	78	54	
[N]	[218]	[360]	[253]	[206]	[180]	[222]	[135]		[1574]

Cell entries are the proportion of respondents who reported voting in the House race in their district.

TABLE 7-3

PARTY VOTE BY RESPONDENT'S POSITION ON THE IDEOLOGY SCALE AND RESPONDENT'S PARTY IDENTIFICATION

Respondent's Position	Respondent's Party Identification								
	Str. Dem.	Weak Dem.	Ind. Dem.	Ind. Ind.	Ind. Rep.	Weak Rep.	Str. Rep.	Total	
Ex. Liberal	...	...	...	...	...	...	...	100	[17]
Liberal	90	79	63	33	...	...	...	68	[75]
Sl. Liberal	88	80	50	57	40	...	...	66	[97]
Moderate	81	80	59	46	48	41	27	60	[282]
Sl. Conserv.	86	79	56	57	30	36	27	50	[172]
Conservative	67	73	33	44	30	32	15	35	[142]
Ex. Conserv.	...	...	...	...	0	50	9	39	[23]
Total	85	80	59	51	35	35	20	55	
[N]	[142]	[155]	[106]	[76]	[97]	[128]	[104]		[808]

Cell entries are the proportion of voters who reported voting Democratic in the House race in their district.

TABLE 7-4

INCUMBENCY VOTE BY RESPONDENT'S POSITION ON THE IDEOLOGY SCALE AND RESPONDENT'S PARTY IDENTIFICATION AND INCUMBENT'S PARTY

Respondent's Position	Respondent's Party Identification and Incumbent's Party				
	Same	Resp. is Ind. Ind.	Different	Total	
Ex. Liberal	100	...	0	69	[16]
Liberal	97	...	44	80	[59]
Sl. Liberal	96	...	68	85	[75]
Moderate	91	90	57	78	[207]
Sl. Conserv.	97	73	59	78	[129]
Conservative	100	67	45	73	[109]
Ex. Conserv.	82	...	33	71	[14]
Total	95	83	53	78	
[N]	[318]	[57]	[234]		[609]

Cell entries are the proportion of voters who reported voting for the Incumbent in districts where the Incumbent was opposed.

TABLE 7-5

RESPONDENT'S PLACEMENT OF DEMOCRATIC CONGRESSIONAL CANDIDATE ON THE IDEOLOGY SCALE BY RESPONDENT'S OWN POSITION ON THE SCALE, CONTROLLING FOR PARTY IDENTIFICATION AND TURNOUT

Respondent's Placement of Democratic Candidate	Respondent's Position								
	Extreme Liberal	Liberal	Slight Liberal	Mod-erate	Slight Conserv	Conser-vative	Extreme Conserv	Total	
Party I.D.: DEMOCRAT									
Liberal	53%	49%	44%	40%	32%	20%	...	40%	[173]
Moderate	27	27	37	40	36	37	...	35	[151]
Conservative	20	25	19	20	32	43	...	24	[104]
[N]	[15]	[68]	[90]	[154]	[62]	[30]	[9]		[428]
Party I.D.: IND. INDEPENDENT									
Liberal	...	...	...	14%	44%	8%	....	28%	[25]
Moderate	...	...	...	57	33	58	....	47	[41]
Conservative	...	...	...	29	22	33	....	25	[22]
[N]	[5]	[9]	[9]	[35]	[18]	[12]	[0]		[88]
Party I.D.: REPUBLICAN									
Liberal	...	...	90%	34%	49%	54%	50%	49%	[129]
Moderate	...	...	0	43	30	26	25	31	[81]
Conservative	...	...	10	24	21	20	25	21	[55]
[N]	[2]	[6]	[10]	[68]	[83]	[80]	[16]		[265]
Turnout: VOTED									
Liberal	64%	58%	54%	39%	41%	46%	65%	46%	[219]
Moderate	9	27	33	45	33	35	18	35	[168]
Conservative	27	16	13	16	26	19	18	19	[89]
[N]	[11]	[45]	[63]	[147]	[109]	[84]	[17]		[476]
Turnout: DID NOT VOTE									
Liberal	36%	42%	41%	31%	46%	31%	...	36%	[106]
Moderate	46	29	32	39	30	31	...	34	[99]
Conservative	18	29	27	30	24	39	...	30	[87]
[N]	[11]	[38]	[44]	[106]	[50]	[36]	[7]		[292]

TABLE 7-6

RESPONDENT'S PLACEMENT OF REPUBLICAN CONGRESSIONAL CANDIDATE ON THE IDEOLOGY SCALE BY RESPONDENT'S OWN POSITION ON THE SCALE, CONTROLLING FOR PARTY IDENTIFICATION AND TURNOUT

Respondent's Placement of Republican Candidate	Respondent's Position: Extreme Liberal	Liberal	Slight Liberal	Moderate	Slight Conserv	Conservative	Extreme Conserv	Total	
Party I.D.: DEMOCRAT									
Liberal	9%	24%	20%	21%	28%	14%	...	21%	[59]
Moderate	9	21	31	32	30	36	...	30	[82]
Conservative	82	55	49	47	43	50	...	49	[137]
[N]	[11]	[38]	[55]	[100]	[40]	[22]	[2]		[278]
Party I.D.: IND. INDEPENDENT									
Liberal	...	...	...	13%	18%	...	...	20%	[14]
Moderate	...	...	...	52	55	...	...	41	[28]
Conservative	...	...	...	36	27	...	...	39	[27]
[N]	[3]	[8]	[7]	[31]	[11]	[8]	[1]		[69]
Party I.D.: REPUBLICAN									
Liberal	...	50%	64%	21%	14%	5%	0%	15%	[40]
Moderate	...	20	18	36	26	20	11	24	[64]
Conservative	...	30	18	43	60	76	90	61	[159]
[N]	[1]	[10]	[11]	[58]	[77]	[87]	[19]		[263]
Turnout: VOTED									
Liberal	...	34%	24%	19%	13%	2%	0%	15%	[60]
Moderate	...	17	28	37	26	22	18	27	[109]
Conservative	...	49	48	44	61	76	82	58	[233]
[N]	[9]	[35]	[46]	[124]	[85]	[86]	[17]		[402]
Turnout: DID NOT VOTE									
Liberal	...	17%	42%	19%	32%	20%	...	26%	[51]
Moderate	...	28	27	36	34	33	...	32	[64]
Conservative	...	56	31	44	34	47	...	42	[83]
[N]	[6]	[18]	[26]	[72]	[41]	[30]	[5]		[198]

TABLE 7-7

RESPONDENT'S PLACEMENT OF INCUMBENT CONGRESSIONAL CANDIDATE ON THE IDEOLOGY SCALE BY RESPONDENT'S OWN POSITION ON THE SCALE, CONTROLLING FOR PARTY IDENTIFICATION AND TURNOUT

Respondent's Placement of Incumbent Candidate	Respondent's Position								
	Extreme Liberal	Liberal	Slight Liberal	Moderate	Slight Conserv	Conservative	Extreme Conserv	Total	
	Party I.D.: SAME AS INCUMBENT								
Liberal	75%	52%	48%	30%	17%	11%	22%	30%	[147]
Moderate	17	22	39	42	30	21	17	32	[156]
Conservative	8	26	13	28	52	68	61	37	[181]
[N]	[12]	[54]	[71]	[156]	[92]	[81]	[18]		[484]
	Party I.D.: R IS AN IND. INDEPENDENT								
Liberal	...	50%	50%	14%	35%	8%	...	26%	[26]
Moderate	...	20	25	57	41	58	...	46	[46]
Conservative	...	30	25	30	24	33	...	28	[28]
[N]	[4]	[10]	[12]	[44]	[17]	[12]	[1]		[100]
	Party I.D.: DIFFERENT THAN INCUMBENT								
Liberal	...	37%	34%	25%	36%	39%	...	32%	[108]
Moderate	...	27	26	35	30	25	...	30	[99]
Conservative	...	37	40	40	34	36	...	38	[127]
[N]	[7]	[30]	[35]	[109]	[80]	[67]	[6]		[334]
	Turnout: VOTED								
Liberal	46%	53%	42%	27%	24%	21%	29%	30%	[172]
Moderate	0	21	38	43	30	28	24	33	[191]
Conservative	54	26	20	30	47	51	47	37	[213]
[N]	[13]	[53]	[76]	[185]	[122]	[110]	[17]		[576]
	Turnout: DID NOT VOTE								
Liberal	60%	40%	49%	26%	34%	30%	...	33%	[105]
Moderate	30	26	26	39	32	23	...	32	[101]
Conservative	10	34	26	35	34	48	...	35	[111]
[N]	[10]	[38]	[39]	[117]	[62]	[44]	[7]		[317]

TABLE 7-8

RESPONDENT'S PLACEMENT OF INCUMBENT CHALLENGER ON THE IDEOLOGY SCALE BY RESPONDENT'S OWN POSITION ON THE SCALE, CONTROLLING FOR PARTY IDENTIFICATION AND TURNOUT

Respondent's Placement of Challenger	Respondent's Position								
	Extreme Liberal	Liberal	Slight Liberal	Moderate	Slight Conserv	Conservative	Extreme Conserv	Total	
Party I.D.: SAME AS INCUMBENT									
Liberal	...	...	28%	26%	65%	56%	...	40%	[56]
Moderate	...	...	22	35	23	33	...	26	[37]
Conservative	...	...	50	39	13	11	...	34	[48]
[N]	[5]	[8]	[18]	[46]	[31]	[27]	[6]		[141]
Party I.D.: R IS AN IND. INDEPENDENT									
Liberal	...	...	...	11%	...	...	...	21%	[10]
Moderate	...	...	...	61	...	...	...	41	[19]
Conservative	...	...	...	28	...	...	...	37	[17]
[N]	[3]	[6]	[4]	[18]	[9]	[6]	[0]		[46]
Party I.D.: DIFFERENT THAN INCUMBENT									
Liberal	...	23%	44%	49%	30%	4%	...	30%	[38]
Moderate	...	54	25	23	33	32	...	31	[40]
Conservative	...	23	31	29	36	64	...	40	[51]
[N]	[4]	[13]	[16]	[35]	[33]	[25]	[3]		[129]
Turnout: VOTED									
Liberal	...	13%	39%	39%	39%	29%	...	34%	[38]
Moderate	...	47	17	35	29	31	...	30	[60]
Conservative	...	40	44	27	33	40	...	37	[75]
[N]	[6]	[15]	[23]	[57]	[49]	[45]	[8]		[203]
Turnout: DID NOT VOTE									
Liberal	...	17%	33%	21%	65%	21%	...	32%	[36]
Moderate	...	25	33	36	26	36	...	32	[36]
Conservative	...	58	33	43	9	43	...	36	[41]
[N]	[6]	[12]	[15]	[42]	[23]	[14]	[1]		[113]

III: Guide to Location of Variables in Tabular Form, Sourcebook Section

	Subsection Table Numbers								
Variable	*1-1 to 1-12*	*2-1 to 2-21*	*3-1 to 3-23*	*4-1 to 4-16*	*5-1 to 5-28*	*5-29 to 5-55*	*6-1 to 6-30*	*6-31 to 6-40*	*7-1 to 7-8*
Type of Race	x	x	x		x	x			
Party Identification of Constituents	x	x	x	x	x		x	x	x
Party Identification: Used as Control							x		x
Congruency of Candidate's Party and Constituent's Party Identification		x	x			x			
Party of Candidate				x					
Party Vote as Democratic Proportion	x	x	x		x		x	x	x
Turnout: Distribution	x	x	x						x
Turnout: Used as Control							x		x
Vote for Incumbent Candidate	x	x	x	x		x			x
Interest in Election Campaign		x							
Care Which Party Wins Election		x							
Follows What Goes On In Government and Public Affairs		x							
Recognition of Candidate				x	x	x			
Recall of Candidate's Name					x	x			
Likes Candidate					x	x			
Dislikes Candidate					x	x			
Feeling Thermometer Rating of Candidate				x	x	x			
Incumbent's Job Performance				x					
Candidate's Service to Congressional District				x					
Contacted *by* Candidate				x	x	x			
Contacted Candidate				x					

III: Guide to Location of Variables in Tabular Form, Sourcebook Section

	Subsection Table Numbers								
Variable	*1-1 to 1-12*	*2-1 to 2-21*	*3-1 to 3-23*	*4-1 to 4-16*	*5-1 to 5-28*	*5-29 to 5-55*	*6-1 to 6-30*	*6-31 to 6-40*	*7-1 to 7-8*
Incumbent Would be Helpful If Asked				x					
Agree With Incumbent's Voting Record				x					
Rating of Carter's Job Performance			x						
Feeling Thermometer Rating of Carter			x						
Rating of Congresses Job Performance			x						
Constituents Position on Issues							x	x	x
Constituent Perception of Candidate's Position on Issues							x		x

IV: Guide to Location of Variables by Chapter

Variable	*Abramowitz*	*Hinckley*	*Jacobson*	*Mann and Wolfinger*	*Parker*
Type of Race	x	x	x	x	x
Party Identification of Constituents	x	x			x
Party Identification: Used as Control		x		x	
Congruency of Candidate's Party and Constituents Party Identification		x		x	
Party of Candidate			x		x
Party Vote as Democratic Proportion	x		x	x	
Turnout: Distribution		x			
Turnout: Used as Control		x			
Vote for Incumbent Candidate	x	x	x	x	
Interest in Election Campaign			x		
Care Which Party Wins Election					
Follows What Goes On In Government and Public Affairs					
Recognition of Candidate		x	x	x	
Recall of Candidate's Name			x		
Likes Candidate			x	x	x
Dislikes Candidate			x	x	x
Feeling Thermometer Rating of Candidate	x	x	x	x	
Incumbent's Job Performance				x	x
Candidate's Service to Congressional District		x		x	x
Contacted *by* Candidate	x	x	x	x	x
Contacted Candidate	x	x	x	x	x
Incumbent Would Be Helpful If Asked				x	
Agree With Incumbent's Voting Record				x	x
Rating of Carter's Job Performance	x			x	x

IV: Guide to Location of Variables by Chapter

Variable	*Abramowitz*	*Hinckley*	*Jacobson*	*Mann and Wolfinger*	*Parker*
Feeling Thermometer Rating of Carter					
Rating of Congresses Job Performance					x
Constituents Position On Issues	x			x	x
Constituent Perception of Candidate's Position on Issues	x			x	x

NOTE

1. The full set of data collected in connection with the CPS/NES study of the 1978 congressional election is available for public use. Persons affiliated with institutions that are members of the consortium can obtain the data and documentation through normal channels. Others should write to Ms. Janet Vavra, Director of Services, ICPSR, P.O. Box 1248, Ann Arbor, Michigan 48106 for further details.

REFERENCES

Board of Overseers (1979) Annual Report for the National Election Studies, Center for Political Studies of the University of Michigan, submitted to the Institute for Social Research, University of Michigan (June 1).

Miller, W. E. et al. (1980) The American National Elections Studies Data Sourcebook, 1952–1978. Cambridge, MA: Harvard University Press.

2

CANDIDATES AND PARTIES IN CONGRESSIONAL ELECTIONS

THOMAS E. MANN

RAYMOND E. WOLFINGER

During the first generation of research on voting behavior, scant attention was paid to congressional elections. In the 1970s scholars interested in congressional elections quickly exhausted the analytic possibilities of data from the principal source of nationwide sample surveys, the biennial National Election Studies of the University of Michigan Center for Political Studies (CPS). Their research provided **some interesting findings but also pointed to a need for more and better survey items to explain the gaps and contradictions in the existing state of scholarly understanding.**

The Michigan CPS study of the 1978 elections included a number of new questions about public perceptions of congressional candidates and incumbent members of Congress; for the first time scholars

---

Reprinted from the *American Political Science Review*, September 1980.

The data used in this article were made available by the Inter-university Consortium for Political and Social Research and were originally collected by the Center for Political Studies of the University of Michigan. Neither the ICPSR nor the CPS has any responsibility for our analyses or interpretations.

have data with which to find valid answers to some of the fundamental questions about how members of Congress are elected. In this article we will exploit the new data source to provide answers to these questions: What do voters know about congressional candidates? How do voters decide between candidates? Why are House incumbents so successful at getting reelected by wide margins? Why do Senate incumbents fare less well? How are elections won or lost?

I
THE 1978 NATIONAL ELECTION STUDY

The unusually widespread scholarly interest in the 1978 congressional elections stems from the availability of a distinctly new dataset rather than from any unusual features of the results. The outcome of the election can be briefly summarized. The Democratic party maintained the majority status in both houses that it has enjoyed without interruption for over two decades. The national net Republican gain in the House of Representatives of 2.8% of the votes and 3.4% of the seats was modest by midterm election standards, but not wholly unexpected, given several mitigating factors: the absence of presidential coattails in 1976 (Jimmy Carter ran behind 270 of the 292 Democrats elected to the House in that year); Carter's partial and temporary recovery in the opinion polls following his Middle East Camp David summit meeting; and the electoral advantage of incumbency. Twenty-four House incumbents seeking reelection were defeated—5 in the primaries and 19 in the general election—leaving 94% successful. Incumbency was a less obvious advantage in the Senate, where 10 of the 25 senators seeking reelection were defeated—3 in the primaries and 7 in the general election.[1]

The 1978 elections witnessed the continuation of three additional trends that have been present for several successive elections. First, turnout declined to a postwar low of 35.1 %. Second, David Mayhew's (1974a) vanishing marginals vanished even further. In 1978, 76% of all House races contested by an incumbent were won by a margin of 60% or more. Third, the growing insulation of House incumbents from defeat has not led to stability in membership. To the contrary, 18% of the House were replaced following the 1978 elections. When added to the shifts following the 1974 and 1976 elections, this means that half the members of the 96th Congress were not in office when Richard Nixon resigned from the presidency. This is equally true for the Senate, where 20 new members entered following the 1978 election and where 49 are in their first term. The answer to this seeming paradox is obvious: Retirement has replaced defeat as the primary source of turnover and the number of retirements has been rising since 1972. Once again, 1978 was no exception to this pattern—49 representatives and 10 senators declined to seek reelection. Both figures are as high as any in modern times.

The 1978 National Election Study is the first nationwide survey in 20 years to include more than the most basic questions concerning congressional elections. A substantial portion of the questionnaire was devoted to congressional matters. At the same time, the primary sampling units were changed from counties to congressional districts, which produced a more even distribution of respondents across districts than was the case for the Miller-Stokes 1958 study (Stokes and Miller, 1962). The addition of a substantial body of contextual data permits analysis with the district as well as the individual as the unit of analysis.

A better sense of the opportunities as well as the limitations of working with this new dataset can be gained by looking at Table 1, which presents the number of respondents, voters, districts, and states in the 1978 sample. In the House the major constraint is the total number of respondents in districts with contested races who reported voting for one of the major party candidates—757 where the incumbent ran and 116 where there was an open-seat contest.[2] There are enough voters in incumbent-contested races for most analytic purposes, but it should be remembered that there is an average of fewer than 10 voters per district. The small number of voters in elections without incumbents prevents all but the most straightforward presentation of frequencies.

If one has a special interest in races where the outcome is not a foregone conclusion, the sample's limitations are more pronounced. As we indicated above, 24% of all House incumbents seeking reelec-

Table 1. Respondents, Voters, Districts and States in the 1978 National Election Study, by Type of Election

	Districts or States	Total Respondents	Total Voters*	Democratic Voters	Republican Voters
House of Representatives					
Total	108	2304	1027	590	419
Contested races	88	1803	885	479	394
Democratic incumbent	47	917	432	342	88
Republican incumbent	30	651	334	74	253
Open seat	11	235	119	63	53
Uncontested races	20	501	142	111	25
Democratic incumbent	13	335	103	99	–
Republican incumbent	5	126	26	–	25
Open seat	2	40	13	12	–
Senate					
Total	39	2304	556	284	273
No race	13	1092	–	–	–
Contested races	24	1116	550	272	273
Democratic incumbent	8	256	122	82	39
Republican incumbent	8	558	274	116	157
Open seat	8	302	154	73	77
Uncontested races	2	96	16	12	0
Democratic incumbent	1	37	–	–	–
Republican incumbent	0	–	–	–	–
Open seat	1	59	16	12	0

Source: 1978 National Election Study, Center for Political Studies, University of Michigan.

*Includes all respondents who identified the candidate for whom they voted, not just major-party voters.

tion won with margins of less than 60%, which is matched almost perfectly in the sample with 18 "marginal" races out of 77 incumbent-contested races. Although the sample was right on target in this respect, the number of voting respondents in these districts is small for most analytic purposes (178, of whom 170 are major-party voters). Moreover, there is a clear incumbent bias in the voting reports of these respondents. While challengers in all marginal districts averaged 46% of the actual vote, less than 35% of all the respondents in the sample of these districts reported a vote for the challenger. Any interpretation of the public's view of challengers in competitive districts must take this discrepancy into account.

Actually, an overreport of the vote for incumbents in the sample is not limited to marginal districts. In the universe of districts in which they faced opposition, incumbents won 66% of the major-party vote; yet in the CPS sample of these districts 79% of the vote was reportedly cast for incumbents.

Only 1 of the 19 districts in which incumbents were defeated fell within the sample; by chance, we would have expected 4 or 5. We cannot expect the sample to represent such districts; nor would their inclusion have altered substantially the figures for the entire sample. Nonetheless, it is worth observing that a politically and analytically important type of district is underrepresented in the sample.

The Senate sample poses much more serious problems. There is no purposive sample of Senate races; what we have is a by-product of designing a national sample of noninstitutionalized adults and of congressional districts. Roughly half the respondents were in states without a 1978 Senate contest. Moreover, the remaining respondents are distributed *very unevenly* across states with Senate elections, ranging from 19 in Iowa to 152 in Texas. There are two major limitations in the data on states where an incumbent senator sought reelection: (1) Fewer than 400 respondents reported casting a vote for a major-party candidate. (2) Most of these respondents lived in Illinois, Michigan, or Texas, states in which senior Republican senators were engaged in expensive battles for survival. There are not enough cases for study of any of these three races, and at the same time we feel uneasy about using respondents from these three states as the principal basis for generalizations about Senate elections. We think it best to use the Senate figures for only the simplest comparisons with the House. This article primarily concerns voting in House elections.

II
THE IMPORTANCE OF PARTY

Because members of Congress are less familiar than the president to most voters, it is easy to accept the proposition that party identification is a far more important determinant of congressional than of presidential voting. This notion can be evaluated by examining Table 2, which displays the proportion of voters in every House and presidential election from 1956 through 1978 who were pure Independents, people who identified with a party and voted for that party's candidate, and people who identified with one party and voted for the candidate of the other party.[3]

The first observation to be made is the marked increase in defection in presidential elections in 1968 and 1972, and then the equally sharp return in 1976 to the same modest levels of defection that were found during the 1950s. The trend toward weakening party lines that was so widely discussed in literature based on the 1968 and 1972 elections may well have reflected the candidacies of George Wallace and George McGovern rather than any secular movement in the strength of party loyalties (Nie et al., 1976).

Second, and more interesting for our present purposes, is the continuous increase in the proportion of congressional voters who defect. In 1956, just 9% of all those people casting a ballot in a House contest voted for the other party's candidate, compared with 15% of presidential voters. The proportion of House defectors crept up slowly and steadily in virtually every election since 1956. Until the most recent elections, however, defection was always lower than in presidential races, and so the contrast between presidential and House voting remained consistent with the proposition that ignorance about House candidates led to greater party-line voting than in presidential balloting, where public familiarity with the candidates produced more

Table 2. The Composition of the Vote in Presidential and House Elections, 1956–1978 (Percent)

	House Elections			Presidential Elections		
	Party-Line Voters[a]	Defectors[b]	Pure Independents	Party-Line Voters[a]	Defectors[b]	Pure Independents
1956	82	9	9	76	15	9
1958	84	11	5			
1960	80	12	8	79	13	8
1962	83	12	6			
1964	79	15	5	79	15	5
1966	76	16	8			
1968	74	19	7	69	23	9
1970	76	16	8			
1972	75	17	8	67	25	8
1974	74	18	8			
1976	72	19	9	74	15	11
1978	69	22	9			

Source: National Election Studies, Center for Political Studies, University of Michigan.

[a]Party identifiers who vote for the candidate of their party.

[b]Party identifiers who vote for the candidate of the other party.

Table 3. Vote for House and Senate, by Party Identification and Incumbency, 1978 (Percent)

	Party Identification of Voter		
	Incumbent's Party	Independent	Challenger's Party
Vote for House			
Incumbent	95	79	54
Challenger	5	21	46
n =	(407)	(72)	(277)
Vote for Senate			
Incumbent	89	64	31
Challenger	11	36	69
n =	(179)	(36)	(179)

Source: 1978 National Election Study, Center for Political Studies, University of Michigan.

defection. But more recently the continued increase in House defection combined with a return to party-line presidential voting to reverse the previous relationship. In 1976, just 15% of presidential voters defected; by 1978, a substantially larger number of House voters—22%—identified with one party and voted for the other party's candidate. This reversal, whether temporary or permanent, is sufficiently damaging to the conventional wisdom to require further investigation.

III
INCUMBENCY AS AN ELECTORAL FORCE

Defection has not increased in a politically neutral manner. Cover and Mayhew (1977) found that the proportion of defections in favor of House incumbents rose substantially after 1970 and accounted for over three-quarters of all votes cast against party lines in House races. Even in 1974, when national tides ran strongly against the Republican party and 36 Republican representatives were defeated, 74% of all defections favored the incumbent. By 1978, challengers received only 11% of the defections; two decades earlier the comparable number was 43%.[4] These findings suggest that the secular decline in party-line voting observed in Table 2 reflects the greater ability of incumbents to attract votes from people who identify with the other party.

The relationship between party, incumbency, and vote choice in the 1978 elections can be seen more directly in Table 3. Party and incumbency together appear to be an almost unbeatable combination in House elections. Only 5% of the voters (19 respondents) who belonged to the same party as their incumbent representative (hereafter called "incumbent partisans") voted for the challenger. When party and incumbency are in conflict, the latter appears as the more powerful electoral force. By contrast, incumbency has a somewhat weaker influence in Senate voting.

Before exploring the source of this incumbency advantage, we believe it is worth introducing here a theme to which we return later.

The figures reported in the last paragraph are national averages, and they reflect the overwhelming advantage incumbents enjoy nationally. Yet House elections are held in individual congressional districts and the relative influence of party and incumbency may vary from one district to another. One study based on surveys in a number of congressional districts (most of which were in the "marginal" range at one point or another during the last six years) found that some challengers attracted as many as 20% of the votes of incumbent partisans, while some incumbents received only 14% of the support of challenger partisans (Mann, 1978). Of course, these examples are not representative of districts generally, but no discussion of voting in congressional elections is complete without a consideration of when and how challengers make the best showing against incumbents. Without this understanding, we are in no position to learn the conditions under which change might occur. But with only 19 incumbent partisans voting for challengers in the 1978 dataset, there is no variance to investigate. Nonetheless, this need not prevent us from looking for processes of individual decision making that, when certain conditions change, might produce very different results.

The source of the increased incumbency advantage that was registered in the 1960s has been a puzzle to scholars. David Mayhew (1974b) originally suggested three possible explanations: (1) incumbents benefited from favorable redistricting that increased the number of majority partisans in their districts; (2) incumbents gained political support by becoming more adept at advertising, credit-taking, and position-taking; and (3) incumbents benefited fortuitously from the erosion of party loyalties—incumbency replaced party as a voting cue. Mayhew did not explicitly mention a fourth possibility, not unrelated to his third, that the visibility and attractiveness of challengers decreased during this time.

Cover (1977) and Ferejohn (1977) have shown that redistricting does not account for the increased advantage of incumbency, although doubtless there are particular cases where redrawing district lines made incumbents safer. Investigation of the second and third explanations has been constrained by the lack of adequate data on public perceptions of congressional candidates. Cover (1977), Ferejohn (1977), and Nelson (1978) all show that the increase in incumbents' electoral advantages was not accompanied by any increase in the proportion of the population who could recall their names, which suggested that incumbency provided a voting cue unmediated by public awareness of the incumbent. The same conclusion came more directly from Nelson's finding that many voters defected to incumbents whose names they could not recall. This implausible possibility can now be safely dismissed, as we will soon see. But unraveling the other two possibilities—that incumbents are better known and/or better liked now than before or that the advantage in visibility and reputation long held by incumbents, although not increased, now translates more profitably into votes because party ties are weaker—has been frustrated by the lack of appropriate recognition and reputation measures during the decade when the advantage increased. While we can never adequately investigate this period of change, we can begin to describe more accurately what the public knows about incumbents and challengers today.

IV
CANDIDATE FAMILIARITY

Incumbents are better known than their opponents. Scholars have generally said that incumbents enjoy more "name recognition," and point to repeated findings that incumbents are known to about twice as many people as challengers. What the surveys invariably measure, however, is not name *recognition* but name *recall*. The Michigan CPS (1975: 124) question in 1974 was: "Do you happen to remember the names of the candidates for Congress—that is, for the House of Representatives in Washington—that ran in this district last November?" Of course, it is far more difficult to recall someone's name without help than it is to recognize a name when it is encountered. Many voters unable to recall the names of their representatives or challengers can nevertheless recognize the names when presented with them, which is the situation they face in the voting booth (Mann, 1978). It seems reasonable to expect, then, that the apparent existence of an incumbent electoral advantage without public knowledge

Table 4. Candidate Recognition Among Voters in Contested Races, House and Senate, 1978 (Percent)

	Recognize and Rate	Recognize, but not Rate	Don't Recognize
House			
Incumbents (n = 754)	93	4	3
Challengers (n = 754)	44	19	37
Open seat candidates (n = 116)	72	20	8
Senate			
Incumbents (n = 408)	96	3	1
Challengers (n = 408)	86	7	7
Open seat candidates (n = 158)	88	8	5

Source: 1978 National Election Study, Center for Political Studies, University of Michigan.

of the incumbent reflects a faulty measure of knowledge, not an ability to impress voters without their conscious awareness.

The 1978 Michigan study for the first time included a true measure of name recognition, one that resembled (although not exactly) the situation voters face in the polling place. This was done with the "candidate thermometer," which elicited responses to a number of public figures, including all major party congressional candidates as well as several national political celebrities. For each person on the list of more than 20 names, the respondents could indicate they did not recognize the name, that they recognized but could not rate the person, or that they recognized and rated the person (see appendix). The thermometer thus measures both name recognition and affect toward the person. Table 4 shows the percentage of voters in contested races who recognized and rated the House and Senate candidates, those who claimed to recognize but could not rate the candidate, and those who confessed they could not recognize the candidate.

We see that House incumbents are almost universally recognized by voters in their districts, while the names of challengers are familiar to just under two-thirds of the voters. The lead of incumbents over challengers is more pronounced when we use a more stringent standard of recognition—both recognizing and rating the candidate. Open-seat candidates are substantially more visible than those who challenge incumbents, confirming the general view that open seats are more hotly contested than incumbent-held seats. The contrast with the Senate is instructive, with a caveat for the peculiar nature of the Senate sample. Senate challengers are almost as visible to the electorate as Senate incumbents, probably reflecting both more serious efforts by the opposition and the publicity that comes automatically to a statewide challenger.

Although most voters know the names of challengers and almost all are familiar with the incumbent, this discrepancy alone does not explain the incumbent advantage. Incumbents' very high victory rate is not fully explained by their greater name familiarity. Challengers have an uphill fight even when the voters know them. This is revealed in Table 5, which displays defection by incumbency, party identifica-

Table 5. Party Defection by Incumbency and Candidate Recognition, 1978 House Elections (Percent)*

	Voter Recognizes**			
	Incumbent		Challenger	
Party Identification	Yes	No	Yes	No
Incumbent's party	4	14	7	3
n =	(366)	(29)	(161)	(243)
Challenger's party	57	15	46	63
n =	(257)	(20)	(145)	(132)

Source: 1978 National Election Study, Center for Political Studies, University of Michigan.

*The entry in each cell is the percentage of voters with the indicated characteristics who defected.

**Defined as able to rate candidates on thermometer from 0–100.

tion, and name recognition. Voters who belong to the incumbent's party are almost sure to vote for the incumbent. Even the handful who do not recognize their representative's name have only a one-in-seven chance of defecting. By the same token, the challenger whose name is known to the incumbent's partisans wins only 7% of their voters—and loses fully 46% of his or her own partisans. The challenger is better off being recognized, but visibility alone is not enough. Thus we must move beyond simple name recognition in order to understand the advantages of incumbency and the opportunities for challengers.

V
CANDIDATE REPUTATION

The 1978 National Election Study interview schedule gave respondents several opportunities to evaluate the congressional candidates in their district and state. Responses to these questions are all consistent with the proposition that, as a class, incumbents are well regarded by their constituents. Table 6 shows the percentage of voters who rated the candidates on the feeling thermometer as positive, neutral, negative, or unknown. Almost three-fourths rated the incumbent positively, while less than a fifth made similar evaluations of the challenger.

One can better understand the advantage of incumbency in House elections by contrasting these figures with those for candidates in open House seats and for Senate incumbents and challengers. In the latter cases, the standing of the nonincumbents is relatively high and the gap between the two candidates is relatively narrow.

In addition to thinking highly of incumbents' personal qualities, most voters also feel that their representative is doing a good job. The two sorts of assessment are not always similar. (Sometimes the public combines generalized admiration for a political figure and a low assessment of performance. Jimmy Carter and Gerald Ford come immediately to mind.) Table 7 presents the job ratings of House members by party identification and the amount of defection at each

Table 6. Voters' Feelings About Candidates, 1978 (Percent)

	Feeling Thermometer Evaluation			
	Positive	Neutral	Negative	Can't Rate; Don't Recognize
House				
Incumbents (n = 754)	73	10	9	7
Challengers (n = 754)	17	18	9	56
Open-seat candidates (n = 116)	50	13	9	28
Senate				
Incumbents (n = 408)	61	15	20	4
Challengers (n = 408)	48	17	20	15
Open-seat candidates (n = 158)	58	16	14	12

Source: 1978 National Election Study, Center for Political Studies, University of Michigan.

Table 7. Incumbent Job Ratings, and Defection by Voters in House Elections, 1978 (Percent)

	Rating of Incumbent's Performance					
	Very Good	Good	Fair	Poor	Very Poor	Don't Know
Percent of all voters rating incumbent	20	44	22	3	1	10
Percent defecting from:						
Incumbent's party	0	4	12	–	–	8
n =	(113)	(180)	(68)	(3)	(2)	(38)
Challenger's party	89	75	35	11	–	21
n =	(28)	(114)	(83)	(19)	(4)	(29)
Percent of Independents voting for challenger	0	11	27	–	–	30
n =	(7)	(36)	(15)	(3)	(1)	(10)

Source: 1978 National Election Study, Center for Political Studies, University of Michigan.

category of performance assessment. These figures confirm the well-known point that individual members are highly esteemed despite the public's critical view of Congress as an institution (Fenno, 1975). Nearly two-thirds of all voters think their representative is doing a "good" or "very good" job, and a mere 4% have a distinctly unfavorable view. As we would expect, these assessments are affected by party identification; the incumbent's partisans are more enthusiastic than members of the other party. The more important finding, however, is that half the challenger's partisans have a favorable view of the incumbent's performance, and only 8% say the incumbent is doing a "poor" or "very poor" job.

The relationship between job assessment and defection is about as strong as we could expect, particularly in light of the handful of incumbent partisans who defected. Incumbents lost no votes at all from members of their own party who say they are doing a "very good" job, and very few from those who rate them "good" or "fair." The numbers are much more striking among challenger partisans, whose support for the incumbent ranges from 89% to 11%, depending on their evaluation of his performance. Support for the challenger among pure Independents is similarly related to the incumbent's job rating.

A final measure of candidate affect comes from the open-ended questions asking respondents if there is anything they like and dislike about the Democratic and Republican House candidates. Predictably, voters' party affiliations shape their answers. Whether incumbents or challengers are the object of the query, the incidence of favorable comments is about 15 percentage points higher among their own partisans. This modest difference is overshadowed by the far stronger relationship of incumbency to favorable assessment, as Table 8 shows. Only a fifth of the voters in the challenger's party had anything good to say about the challenger, while three times as many of them expressed favorable opinions about the incumbent in the other party.

The consequences of these assessments for the vote can be seen in the bottom line of Table 8. This shows both the importance of candidate image in congressional voting decisions and incumbents' vastly greater success in creating favorable impressions. Differences in de-

Table 8. Favorable Comments About House Candidates, Party Identification, Incumbency, and Defection, 1978 (Percent)

	Incumbent				Challenger			
	Same Party		Other Party		Same Party		Other Party	
Percent liking something about the candidate	71		56		20		6	
n =	(407)		(277)		(277)		(407)	
	Yes	No	Yes	No	Yes	No	Yes	No
Percent defecting	2	12	72	30	16	63	20	3

Source: 1978 National Election Study, Center for Political Studies, University of Michigan.

Note: "Yes" and "No" refer to whether the respondent likes anything about the candidate in the given category.

fection rates in this table are more pronounced, especially for challengers, than those associated with simple name recognition (Table 5). Thus the advantage of incumbents reflects more than just their ability to get their names before the public. It seems likely, moreover, that defection rates would be less loaded toward incumbents if more challengers could make themselves favorably known to voters.

Two final notes on the open-ended comments about the candidates. First, the number of respondents who disliked something about the incumbent or the challenger was relatively small—18% for the former, 12% for the latter—but higher, particularly for the incumbent, than appeared on either the feeling thermometer or the job rating. Second, the content of the open-ended remarks was highly personalized, with very few references to party, ideology, or issues. Voters appear to judge candidates, and incumbents in particular, on the basis of their perceived character, experience, and ties to the local community. Issues and ideology are subordinated to these personal and particularistic concerns.

VI
CANDIDATE PREFERENCE

The evidence presented above makes clear that voting in congressional elections is strongly associated with evaluations of the candidates. Yet up to this point we have analyzed vote choice only as it relates to the assessment of a single candidate. A more likely decision process is for the voters to evaluate both candidates at the same time and to choose the more attractive one. It is possible that a number of voters who rate the challenger positively have an even higher opinion of the incumbent. The reverse is less likely in view of the challenger's lower visibility, but it is possible. In order to deal with this possibility, we must include comparative candidate preferences, not just individual candidate ratings.

Table 9 displays the vote for incumbent and challenger by party identification and candidate preference, following a format developed by Richard Brody (1976) for the study of presidential elections. Candidate preference is determined by the relative ranking of the incumbent and challenger on the feeling thermometer. "Don't recognize" and "can't rate" responses are treated as neutral; in cases where one candidate is not recognized or rated, feelings toward the other candidates are decisive. A respondent who does not recognize the challenger but who rates the incumbent negatively is coded as preferring the challenger.

The figures in Table 9 confirm the appropriateness of the candidate preference model for congressional voting: 94% of all respondents who prefer the incumbent vote for the incumbent; 88% of all respondents who prefer the challenger vote for the challenger. In cases where neither candidate is preferred, party identification is the best predictor of the vote, although incumbents fare better among challenger partisans in this situation than we might expect. This is probably best explained by our coding conventions—incumbents who were recognized but rated as neutral on the thermometer were treated the same as challengers who were not recognized, although the former have an edge in recognition.

With the data in Table 9 we can divide the vote for incumbents and for challengers into four categories: votes consistent with both party identification and candidate preference, those consistent with candidate preference only, those consistent with party identification only, and those consistent with neither. The results of this exercise, displayed in Table 10, demonstrate that routine party support not backed up by express preference for the party's candidate provides a small part of incumbents' total support (22%), and a substantially larger part for that of challengers (43%). This reflects the failure of most challengers to build a substantial personal following. Yet, overall, most party-line votes are accompanied by a preference for the party's candidate; when partisanship and candidate preference conflict, voters are likely to defect from their party.

This analysis of candidate preference is, of course, colored by the relatively low visibility and standing of challengers in our national sample. The 17 cases in the lower left-hand cell of Table 9—where incumbent partisans prefer the challenger—are not sufficient to produce confidence in our finding that candidate preference for challengers will override partisanship to the detriment of incumbents. As

Table 9. Vote in 1978 House Election by Party Identification and Candidate Preference

	Party Identification							
Candidate Preference* and Vote	Incumbent's Party		Independent		Challenger's Party		Total	
	N	%	N	%	N	%	N	%
Prefer incumbent								
Incumbent	258	99	31	91	103	84	392	94
Challenger	2	1	3	9	20	16	25	6
Prefer neither								
Incumbent	123	95	25	81	45	47	193	75
Challenger	7	5	6	19	50	53	63	25
Prefer challenger								
Incumbent	7	41	1	14	2	3	10	12
Challenger	10	59	6	86	58	97	74	88
Total								
Incumbent	388	95	57	79	150	54	595	79
Challenger	19	5	15	21	128	46	162	21

Source: 1978 National Election Study, Center for Political Studies, University of Michigan.

*Determined by the relative ranking of the incumbent and challenger on the feeling thermometer.

Table 10. Relationship of Party Identification and Candidate Preference to Each Candidate's Total Vote, House, 1978 (Percent)

Vote Consistent With:	Incumbent	Challenger
Party ID and candidate preference	44	36
Candidate preference only	23	10
Party ID only	22	43
Neither*	12	11
	100	100
n =	(595)	(162)

Source: 1978 National Election Study, Center for Political Studies, University of Michigan.

*Vote is consistent with neither party identification nor candidate preference.

additional support for our conclusion, therefore, we refer readers to a similar investigation based on surveys in a sample of generally competitive districts (Mann, 1978). That study confirms the ability of more visible and attractive challengers to garner the support of substantial numbers of incumbent partisans.

VII
WHY INCUMBENTS ARE WELL-KNOWN AND WELL-LIKED

We have argued that voting in a congressional election primarily involves choosing between competing candidates; party plays an important role for some voters in determining whether a candidate is attractive and in providing guidance for voters who lack information about the candidate, but it is secondary to the images of the candidates themselves. Incumbents have an enormous advantage over challengers, not because the voters' decision rules are rigged in their favor, but rather because they are more visible and more attractive. Why are members of Congress in such a desirable position?

Table 11. Voter Contact with House and Senate Candidates, 1978 (Percent)

Form of Contact	House			Senate		
	Incumbent	Challenger	Open Seat	Incumbent	Challenger	Open Seat
Any type	90	44	73	94	82	88
Met personally	23	4	14	9	5	9
Saw at meeting	20	3	13	10	5	13
Talked to staff	12	2	13	6	4	9
Received mail	71	16	43	53	32	47
Read about in newspaper, magazine	71	32	57	73	63	78
Heard on radio	34	15	28	45	37	49
Saw on TV	50	24	48	80	70	78
Family or friend had contact	39	11	26	–	–	–
n =	(756)	(756)	(121)	(409)	(409)	(158)

Source: 1978 National Election Study, Center for Political Studies, University of Michigan.

The data in Table 11 move us a long way toward an explanation. Each entry in this table represents the percentage of all voters who had the designated form of contact with incumbents, challengers, or open-seat candidates, in the House and Senate. When contrasted with the image of relative anonymity that appeared in the 1958 study of congressional elections (Stokes and Miller, 1962), the figures in this table, especially for incumbents, are staggering. Only 10% of all voters had no form of contact with the House incumbent. Almost a fourth met their representative personally, while nearly three-fourths had seen press coverage about him or her via the print media and/or television. By contrast, only 44% of these voters had any type of contact with the challenger. The gap between incumbent and challenger is greatest in mail contacts, which probably reflects the enormous advantage members of the House enjoy in blanketing their districts with mass and specialized mailings. The prohibition on franked (free) mass mailing by representatives for 60 days before an election evidently does not erase the effects of this perquisite of office.

The more one examines Table 11, however, the less impressive one finds the argument that the inherent advantages of office adequately explain incumbents' greater visibility. Candidates for open House seats reached a far larger share of voters than challengers did, and in many types of contact were nearly as successful as incumbents. One way or another, open-seat candidates reached 73% of the voters, compared to 90% for incumbents and 44% for challengers. The putative advantages of office are even less evident in Senate races, where voters have nearly as much contact with challengers and open-seat candidates as with incumbents. (Amount of contact is measured by numbers of voters reached, not the number of separate interactions.)

We believe that House incumbents benefit more from the scarcity of serious challenges than from the perquisites of office. Evidence on this point can be found in the data on House and Senate campaign expenditures displayed in Table 12. We assume that budgets are a reliable index of total campaign effort, particularly for nonincum-

Table 12. Mean Campaign Expenditures in House and Senate Races, 1978

All Races	House	Senate
Open-seat candidates	$201,049	$ 820,787
n =	(111)	(25)
Incumbents	111,557[a]	1,341,942[b]
n =	(377)	(22)
Challengers	72,373	697,766
n =	(309)	(21)

Incumbent-Contested Races by Election Outcome	House		Senate	
	Incumbent	Challenger	Incumbent	Challenger
Incumbent won with 60% or more of vote	$ 93,218	$ 32,564	$ 453,772	$ 47,346
n =	(287)	(219)	(7)	(6)
Incumbent won with less than 60% of vote	161,856	156,445	2,496,484[c]	992,831
n =	(71)	(71)	(8)	(8)
Incumbent lost to the challenger	200,607	217,083	908,348	918,054
n =	(19)	(19)	(7)	(7)

Source: Computed by authors from Federal Election Commission data presented in *Congressional Quarterly Weekly Report*, September 29, 1979.

[a]Includes 68 uncontested races.

[b]Includes 1 uncontested race.

[c]Without the $7.5 million spent in Jesse Helms' narrowly successful reelection campaign in North Carolina, this figure would be $1.8 million.

bents who must pay for many services that are free to sitting members. The generous spending of candidates for open House and Senate seats helps explain our earlier findings about their visibility to the electorate. In races contested by incumbents, however, the campaign effort and consequently, we believe, the visibility of challengers vary enormously. Just over 70% of these elections were won by an incumbent with more than 60% of the vote. These campaigns were low-budget productions on both sides. The spending was even more lopsided than the voting, with challengers being outspent three-to-one by the victorious incumbents. Budgets were far larger in the 90 House races decided by smaller margins, particularly for the challengers, who spent on average five to six times as much as their counterparts in noncompetitive races.

The pattern is similar in Senate contests—challengers in the closer races spend vastly more than challengers who are defeated decisively—but the frequencies are quite different. Most Senate challengers are big spenders and run competitive races, while the vast majority of House challengers have small budgets and even smaller chances of winning.

The absence of serious challenges to most House incumbents surely owes something to their public standing and their resourcefulness in exploiting the advantages inherent in their office. We suspect that many decisions not to wage a major challenge involve other factors as well, including the vitality of the local opposition party, the high cost of a serious campaign, the difficulty of raising enough money, and some degree of satisfaction with the incumbent among local interests. Moreover, some House districts have such a lopsided division of Republicans and Democrats that members of the minority party have little chance of winning under any circumstances. This is seldom true of Senate races because statewide constituencies generally are more evenly balanced between the two parties.

Table 11 also confirms other bits of conventional wisdom about House-Senate differences. Senators and those aspiring to the office are much more likely than their House counterparts to communicate with the electorate via broadcast media, especially television. Doubt-

Table 13. Defection in 1978 House Elections, by Contact with Incumbent and Challenger (Percent)

	Contact with:			
Defection from:	Both Candidates	Incumbent Only	Challenger Only	Neither Candidate
Incumbent's party	8	2	–	8
n =	(155)	(213)	(0)	(38)
Challenger's party	46	72	–	32
n =	(145)	(103)	(1)	(28)
Support for challenger among Independents	29	7	–	–
n =	(34)	(30)	(1)	(6)

Source: 1978 National Election Study, Center for Political Studies, University of Michigan.

less this reflects the better fit between statewide constituencies and television audiences. In contrast, many congressional districts are such a small portion of a metropolitan television viewing area that their representatives' activities are not very newsworthy. And when the media audience is so large, advertising becomes prohibitively expensive for a candidate who wants to reach only a fraction of it. Also, senators are bigger celebrities than representatives, a result of their smaller number and differences between the impersonal House and the Senate's star system.

The electoral payoff of contact with the voters can be seen from Table 13. Among voters who had contact only with incumbents, challengers lose 72% of their partisans and attract but 2% of the incumbent's partisans. Defection among challenger partisans is 26% lower among voters who have had contact with both candidates and 40% lower among the handful of respondents who have had contact with neither candidate. These latter results point to the importance of efforts by both incumbent and challenger.

In the face of these striking findings on the extent of candidate contact with voters, the increased advantage of incumbency clearly is not a result only of the errand boy or ombudsman activities of House members (Fiorina, 1977). Responses to a battery of questions on citizen-initiated contact with representatives let us assess more directly the electoral consequences of these activities. One-fifth of the voting respondents said that they had contacted their representative or someone in the representative's office—to express an opinion, to seek information, or to seek help with a problem, in roughly equal proportions. Virtually everyone received a response, and the vast majority were very satisfied with that response. Yet defection rates between those who contacted their representative's office and those who did not are almost identical. (Actually, the absence of a difference for all voters masks a partisan difference: Democratic incumbents do slightly better among those voters who *have not* contacted their office, while Republican incumbents do slightly better with those who *have* contacted their office.) If we look at just those respondents who wrote to seek help with a problem, we find that a large majority are incumbent partisans; and of the 19 challenger partisans who fell into this category, 11 voted for the incumbent, producing a defection rate identical to that of all challenger partisans in the sample. In other words, responding to constituent requests paid no special vote dividend for House members in 1978.

While the direct payoff for constituent service may have been limited, a reputation for service appears to have been more valuable. Many voters who have not themselves made requests of their congressmen know others who have, and this latter phenomenon is more strongly related to the vote. Moreover, a third of the voters believe their representative would be "very helpful" if asked to help with a problem, and this reputation for service garners the vote of almost 80% of the challenger partisans. It is very likely that congressmen build a reputation for service in a variety of ways, exploiting vehicles for mass publicity without limiting themselves to direct servicing of constituent requests. In any case, the reach of other forms of contact with voters extends considerably beyond the constituent service domain.

One final note on additional ingredients in the positive image of incumbents. Richard Fenno (1978) has demonstrated that House members adopt a diversity of "home styles" in presenting themselves in their districts. Some members are highly issue-oriented in their discussions with constituents while others stress their personal identification with the district and make few references to substantive issues. In either case, however, Fenno believes that the result of such encounters with House members is an impression of their personal qualities rather than specific information on their issue positions or voting record. This proposition is confirmed by responses to items in the 1978 study that deal with the member's voting record or positions on issues. Only 15% of all voters remembered how their representative voted on any bill in the past couple of years. Fewer than half could say whether they generally agreed or disagreed with the way that representative voted in Washington. In either case, there was very little disagreement with the representative's actions, and the consequent loss in votes was trivial. These data strike a heavy blow at the argument that House members are likely to accumulate enemies because they must take visible stands on many controversial issues. Indeed, only a fraction of all comments about incumbents concern their positions on issues, and the vast majority of these are favorable.

There is somewhat wider awareness of the general ideological posture of representatives—80% of voters could place themselves on a liberal-conservative scale and 63% could place their congressman. However, only 26% were able to classify the challenger. Most ideological descriptions are accurate; Democrats are seen as predominately liberal, Republicans as conservative. We can gauge the importance of ideological proximity voting by looking at those voters who could place themselves and the two candidates on the scale—roughly a fourth of all voters. Table 14 displays the level of defection in House elections by the ideological distance of voters from the incumbent and challenger. The entries confirm the presence of proximity voting, but the sparse number of cases in each cell, particularly those where party and proximity conflict, demonstrate how minimal its effect is.

It would be a mistake, however, to conclude that issues and roll-call voting have no importance for congressional elections. The low salience of issues may reflect in part the efforts of the incumbent to avoid being dramatically out of step with district sentiment. In order to preserve a favorable public image, incumbents may act to forestall vociferous criticism on policy grounds. Incumbents must state positions on issues to satisfy local groups that are important for endorsements, campaign contributions, and volunteers. House members realize that the best way of ensuring their continued reelection is to discourage serious opposition. This requires making peace with those in the district who might otherwise underwrite a vigorous challenge. Finally, most politicians operate at the margin, not at the base. A loss of 2% or 3% of the vote as a result of a vote or a position taken on an issue will give them pause. Thus the small numbers of cases in Table 14 are not conclusive evidence against the proposition that taking positions on issues could affect the outcome of some House elections, and that the prospect of such an influence may well constrain members of Congress.

Table 14. Party Defection, by Ideological Distance of Voters from House Candidates (Percent)*

	Voter's Ideological Position		
Party Identification	Closer to Incumbent	Equidistant from Candidates	Closer to Challenger
Incumbent's party	2	6	50
n =	(54)	(18)	(10)
Challenger's party	58	57	15
n =	(12)	(21)	(40)

Source: 1978 National Election Study, Center for Political Studies, University of Michigan.

*Includes only voters who classified their own ideological position and that of the two candidates.

VII
MIDTERM ELECTIONS AS REFERENDUMS ON PRESIDENTIAL PERFORMANCE

Several scholars have presented evidence that voting in congressional elections is affected by public assessment of the president's performance. Members of the president's party who like the job the president is doing are less likely to vote for a House candidate of the other party. By the same token, people in the other party who like the way the president is behaving in office are more likely than their fellow-partisans to vote for a congressional candidate in the president's party (Arseneau and Wolfinger, 1973; Kernell, 1977). Using aggregate data, Tufte (1975, 1978) argues that the size of the losses sustained by the president's party in midterm elections depends on his popularity and how the economy is faring. Actually, this latter theory predicts only changes in the partisan division of the national vote for the House of Representatives, either from the preceding presidential year or from some standardized measure of the normal midterm vote. Consequently, at the individual level, we should expect to see its effects only at the margin. And in a year like 1978, when the national swing was less than 3%, we should find little evidence of voting in reaction to the president's performance. Moreover, since incumbency seems to insulate House members of the president's party somewhat from adverse judgments of the president's performance (Nelson, 1978), we might expect that the rising electoral effects of incumbency would reduce the referendum effect.

Table 15 shows how voting for the House varied according to respondents' judgments of President Carter's performance. Twenty-six percent of Democrats who disapproved of his performance defected, compared to 22% of those Democrats who liked his White House record. Republicans who liked the job Carter was doing voted for Democratic House contenders at a rate of 29%, compared to 21% for Republicans who disapproved. While these differences are miniscule compared to those based on the relative attractiveness of the congressional candidates discussed earlier, they are sufficient to account for the national shift that was observed in 1978. The bottom

Table 15. Two Measures of Carter's Job Performance and Voting in House Elections (Percent)

	Democrats		Independents		Republicans	
House Vote	Approve	Disapprove	Approve	Disapprove	Approve	Disapprove
Democrat	78	74	51	47	29	21
Republican	22	26	49	53	71	79
	100	100	100	100	100	100
n =	336	98	45	19	106	185

	Democrats*				Republicans*			
House Vote	Very Good	Good	Fair	Poor	Good	Fair	Poor	Very Poor
Democrat	87	78	73	72	24	27	20	14
Republican	13	22	27	28	76	73	80	86
	100	100	100	100	100	100	100	100
n =	45	168	214	24	41	169	75	28

Source: 1978 National Election Study, Center for Political Studies, University of Michigan.

*There were too few Democrats giving "very poor" and Republicans giving "very good" ratings to be included in the table.

half of Table 15 demonstrates that differences in defection rates are somewhat larger when more refined measures of presidential performance are used.

This finding in no way contradicts a major conclusion of this article—that in deciding how to cast their ballots, most voters are influenced primarily by the choice of local candidates. But if we want to explain changes in the national division of the vote from one election to another, especially when those shifts are substantial, we must turn our attention to national forces. How the national swing then translates into swing at the district level and swing in the number of seats, and how important these national forces seem to candidates contesting in local districts, are other questions entirely.

IX
CONCLUSION

Recent congressional elections can no more be accurately viewed as reflecting standing party decisions than can presidential elections. Most voters have sufficient information about at least one and often both of the candidates to base their decision on something other than party loyalty. Scholars have underestimated the level of public awareness of congressional candidates primarily because of faulty measures. Voters are often able to recognize and evaluate individual candidates without being able to recall their names from memory. At the same time, the content of these evaluations is both thin and highly personalized, with little apparent ideological or issue content.

Incumbents are both better known and better liked than challengers, which accounts for their obvious electoral advantage. No one activity of incumbents—such as the much-heralded ombudsman role on behalf of their constituents—is solely responsible for their popularity. A variety of activities that bring them to the attention of the voters in their districts pay handsome electoral dividends. Yet it is inaccurate to portray congressional voting as simply favorable or unfavorable (but mostly favorable) decisions on the incumbent. Equally important are the public visibility and reputation of the challenger. Most voters make their decision between candidates by judging which one they like better, not by pulling the party lever or turning automatically to the incumbent. In most districts the challenge to incumbents is so inconsequential that the largely favorable images of incumbents prevail. In a much smaller number of districts, challengers stage a strong enough campaign to make the task of choosing between candidates a meaningful exercise. The advantage of incumbency in House elections—in contrast to Senate elections—is enhanced by the absence of a serious challenge and the greater likelihood of a lopsided partisan balance in the smaller and more homogeneous House constituency. The explosion of congressional perquisites has enabled House members to communicate with their constituents far more frequently and directly; and the absence of meaningful party competition at the district level coupled with traditional patterns of local press reporting (Robinson, 1981) works against alternative sources of (negative) information about the incumbent.

Finally, public assessments of the president provide a national dynamic to congressional voting, but the effect is modest compared to the salience of the local choices.

These findings raise as many new questions as they answer old ones. One of us has begun to explore how the conditions of election and reelection outlined here influence the way members of Congress behave in Washington (Mann, 1978, 1981). We will not repeat those arguments. Instead, we conclude with a comment on the research agenda of those who study congressional elections.

If most elections to the House are won for lack of a contest, and the evidence for this is impressive, then we need to know much more about the conditions under which a serious challenge is waged. Incumbent popularity among the voters is certainly an important deterrent to potential opponents and to those who might underwrite their campaign. When an incumbent looks popular, the most attractive candidates are unlikely to waste their time and credibility in a challenge against apparently heavy odds. The same consideration probably keeps contributors' checkbooks closed. Yet local leaders are likely to take other factors into consideration as well, such as the incumbent's record on legislative matters of great interest to them. Fenno reports that incumbents consciously strive to forestall serious opposition. We need to know more about what they do to accomplish that objective, and how these efforts are reflected, if at all, among the voters. These and other questions relating to the recruitment of candidates and the mobilization of resources should lead us to supplement national samples with surveys of individual districts as well as studies of leaders and of contribution patterns at the district level. If most incumbents win reelection before the campaign begins, we should start to find out what happens between elections.

APPENDIX

This is the candidate thermometer (or "feeling thermometer") question (A16) used in the 1978 Michigan study:

I'd like to get your feelings toward some of our political leaders and other people who are in the news these days.

I will use something we call the feeling thermometer, and here is how it works:

I'll read the name of a person and I'd like you to rate that person using the feeling thermometer. Ratings between 50 degrees and 100 degrees mean that you feel favorable and warm toward the person. Ratings between 0 degrees and 50 degrees mean that you don't feel favorable toward the person and that you don't care too much for that person.

If we come to a person whose name *you don't recognize,* you don't need to rate that person. Just tell me and we'll move on to the next one.

If you do recognize the name, but you *don't feel particularly warm or cold* toward the person, you would rate the person at the 50 degree mark.

NOTE

1. Two of the three senators defeated in the primaries were short-term appointees filling vacant seats, as was one of the seven who lost their seats in the November election.

2. Nine respondents voted for third-party candidates in incumbent-contested elections, as did three respondents in districts with open-seat races.

3. People who initially call themselves Independents and then (in response to the follow-up question) admit that they lean toward one or the other party think and vote like outright identifiers with that party rather than like people who insist that they are Independents (Keith et al., 1977). Therefore we have classified these Independent Democrats and Independent Republicans with the relevant party here and throughout this article.

4. Because the 1978 CPS sample overreported the national vote for incumbents, defections favoring challengers probably were somewhat higher in 1978.

REFERENCES

ABRAMOWITZ, A. I. (1975) "Name, familiarity, reputation, and the incumbent effect in a congressional election." Western Political Quarterly 27: 668–684.

ARSENEAU, R. B. and R. E. WOLFINGER (1973) "Voting behavior in congressional elections." Presented at the annual meeting of the American Political Science Association.

BRODY, R. A. (1976) "Communication." American Political Science Review 70: 924–926.

COVER, A. D. (1977) "One good term deserves another: The advantage of incumbency in congressional elections." American Journal of Political Science 21: 532–542.

______ and D. R. MAYHEW (1977) "Congressional dynamics and the decline of competitive congressional elections," in L. C. Dodd and B. I. Oppenheimer (eds.) Congress Reconsidered. New York: Praeger.

CPS 1974 American National Election Study (1975). Ann Arbor: Universtiy of Michigan, Center for Political Studies.

FENNO, R. F., Jr. (1978) Home Style: House Members in Their Districts. Boston: Little, Brown.

______ (1975) "If, as Ralph Nader says, Congress is 'the broken branch' how come we love our Congressmen so much?", pp. 275–287 in N. J. Ornstein (ed.) Congress in Change: Evolution and Reform. New York: Praeger.

FEREJOHN, J. A. (1977) "On the decline of competition in congressional elections." American Political Science Review 71: 166–176.

FIORINA, M. P. (1977) Congress, Keystone of the Washington Establishment. New Haven, CT: Yale University Press.

JACOBSON, G. C. (1978) "The effects of campaign spending in congressional elections." American Political Science Review 72: 469–491.

KEITH, B. E. et al. (1977) "The myth of the independent voter." Presented at the annual meeting of the American Political Science Association.

KERNELL, S. H. (1977) "Presidential popularity and negative voting: An alternative explanation of midterm congressional decline in the president's party." American Political Science Review 71: 44–66.

MANN, T. E. (1981) "Congressional elections," in T. E. Mann and N. J. Ornstein (eds.) The New Congress. Washington, DC: American Enterprise Institute.

______ (1978) Unsafe at any Margin: Interpreting Congressional Elections. Washington, DC: American Enterprise Institute.

MAYHEW, D. R. (1974a) "Congressional elections: The case of the vanishing marginals." Polity 6: 295–317.

______ (1974b) Congress: The Electoral Connection. New Haven, CT: Yale University Press.

NELSON, C. J. (1978) "The effect of incumbency on voting in congressional elections, 1964–1974." Political Science Quarterly 93: 665–678.

NIE, N. H. et al. (1976) The Changing American Voter. Cambridge, MA: Harvard University Press.

ROBINSON, M. (1981) "The three faces of congressional media," in T. E. Mann and N. J. Ornstein (eds.) The New Congress. Washington, DC: American Enterprise Institute.

STOKES, D. E. and W. E. MILLER (1962) "Party government and the saliency of Congress." Public Opinion Quarterly 26: 531–546.

TUFTE, E. R. (1978) Political Control of the Economy. Princeton, NJ: Princeton University Press.

______ (1975) "Determinants of the outcome of midterm congressional elections." American Political Science Review 69: 812–826.

PARTY AND INDIVIDUAL ACCOUNTABILITY IN THE 1978 CONGRESSIONAL ELECTION

ALAN I. ABRAMOWITZ

Electoral accountability is generally regarded as essential to the well-being of a representative democracy. By holding elected officials accountable for their performance, voters provide an incentive for these officials to govern in accordance with the wishes of the electorate. Thus, electoral accountability links governmental performance with public opinion. However, this linkage depends upon the ability of the electorate to reward or punish officeholders at the polls for their performance. Voters must judge the individual or collective performance of public officials and cast their ballots accordingly. However, previous research has raised serious questions about the competence of the electorate in American congressional elections. In the first place, voters may not possess the information needed to render a positive or negative judgment on the individual or collective performance of members of Congress. In their path-breaking and highly influential study of voting in the 1958 midterm election, Stokes and Miller (1962) found that voters knew almost nothing about the performance of either the parties or individual members of Congress. In fact, about half of the electorate did not even know which was the majority party in Congress and most could not even recall the name of

AUTHOR'S NOTE: The data used in this article were provided by the Inter-university Consortium for Political and Social Research. The author accepts all responsibility for the analyses and interpretations presented in this article.

their own congressman. In the absence of any information about the performance of the parties or individual members of Congress, the large majority of voters simply cast their ballots according to party affiliation. In contrast to presidential elections, midterm elections were seen as characterized by very weak short-term forces and high levels of partisan voting (Campbell, 1960).

In the last 10 years, however, new evidence has led to a reassessment of the nature of voting in congressional elections. Tufte (1975) has demonstrated that the outcomes of midterm elections are influenced by the popularity of the incumbent president and the state of the economy. Thus, an element of party accountability may be present in midterm elections, with voters holding the president's party responsible for the performance of his administration. In addition, several recent studies have suggested that the growing advantage of incumbency in elections for the House of Representatives is due to more than simple name recognition (Abramowitz, 1975; Ferejohn, 1977; Mann, 1978). Incumbency may be an advantage because voters are generally satisfied with the performance of their elected representatives.

This study will assess accountability in congressional elections by analyzing voting for U.S. Senator and Representative in the 1978 midterm election. Since the actions of the President are far more visible to the public than those of Congress, we will explore the possibility that voters hold the President's party accountable for his performance by voting for or against his party's candidates for the Senate and House of Representatives. This does not require that voters know anything about the legislative records of the parties in Congress or even which party has a majority of seats in Congress.

Advocates of responsible party government have long recognized the serious obstacles presented to party accountability by American political institutions. The separation of presidential and congressional elections tends to insulate the latter from the national issues which frequently influence presidential contests. The weakening of party loyalties in the electorate and the growth of split-ticket voting may accentuate this separation. We shall therefore consider individual accountability as an alternative to party accountability in congressional elections. Individual accountability requires voters to judge the performance of the incumbent Senator or Representative and vote accordingly. The incumbent is evaluated on the basis of her individual performance rather than as a member of a party team. This model of accountability appears to be more realistic than one based on party accountability, given the high degree of policy individualism and the weakness of party discipline in Congress. However, individual accountability also increases voters' information requirements. They must know enough about their Senator or Representative to judge his performance. The quality of that judgment will therefore depend upon the quality of the information available to the electorate.

Recent elections have produced a wide disparity between the outcomes of House and Senate races involving incumbents. While House incumbents have continued to enjoy overwhelming success, incumbent Senators have been highly vulnerable. In both 1976 and 1978, less than 5% of incumbents seeking reelection to the House were defeated while close to a third of the incumbent Senators seeking reelection lost their races. Despite having only a third of its seats at stake, the Senate has actually had proportionately greater turnover in its total membership than the House in the past two elections.

Several factors may help to explain the difference between House and Senate election results. There are fewer one-party states than one-party House districts. In addition, Senate challengers generally wage more visible and effective campaigns than House challengers. Electoral accountability depends upon effective competition. Even if the voters are less than completely satisfied with an incumbent, they may not be willing to vote for an unknown quantity. Finally, voters may have different criteria for evaluating the performance of Senators and Representatives. Senators are associated more often with controversial national issues than Representatives, whose positions on such issues do not generally receive as much publicity. Their greater prominence in the media may also result in Senators' having less control over the information which voters receive about their performance. Thus, voters may receive more objective, or even critical information about Senators than about Representatives. Most of the information which voters receive about their Representative probably comes from their contacts with the incumbent.

I
DATA

The data used in this study come from the Center for Political Studies 1978 National Election Study. Postelection interviews were conducted with 2304 eligible voters in 108 congressional districts throughout the United States. For the first time since 1958, the survey instrument was designed primarily for the purpose of analyzing voting in congressional elections. Many questions concerning perceptions and evaluations of individual House and Senate candidates were included in addition to more traditional items concerning the parties, issues, and national political figures. Therefore the 1978 Election Study is particularly well-suited to our purpose.[1]

II
FINDINGS

As Stokes and Miller argued in their study of the 1958 midterm election, partisan voting is not equivalent to party accountability. Party loyalties are generally established early in life and are not very responsive to emerging issues or events. To the extent that voters in House and Senate elections simply follow traditional party loyalties, evaluations of the performance of the administration or of individual incumbents cannot influence the outcomes of House and Senate elections. In 1958, according to Stokes and Miller, 84% of all votes for the House of Representatives were cast by party identifiers supporting their parties. Since 1958, however, partisan voting in House elections has declined steadily, reaching a low of 72% in 1976 (Mann, 1978).

The results of the 1978 Election Study reveal a continuation of the decline in partisan voting. According to Table 1, only 69% of all votes for the House of Representatives in 1978 were cast by party identifiers supporting their parties while 21% were cast by party defectors and 9% by voters with no party loyalties. The Senate results are very similar, with 71% of the votes cast by party loyalists, 20% by

TABLE 1 1978 House and Senate Vote by Party Identification

	House Vote (Percentage Democratic) Party Identification[a]			
Vote	*Democrats*	*Independents*	*Republicans*	*Total*
Democratic	41	5	9	55
Republican	12	4	28	44
Total	53	9	37	99[b]
	Senate Vote (Percentage Democratic)			
Vote	*Democrats*	*Independents*	*Republicans*	*Total*
Democratic	40	4	7	51
Republican	13	5	31	49
Total	53	9	38	100

[a]The Democratic and Republican categories include all persons who classified themselves as having some degree of party loyalty, including independent leaners.
[b]Rounding error.

defectors, and 9% by independents.[2] Thus, deviations from partisan voting were fairly common in 1978. The question these findings raise is what explains these deviations—were they produced by national or local forces, or some combination of the two? Since the rates of partisan defection were about equal for Democrats and Republicans, it is difficult to discern any national pattern in these findings. Strong short-term national forces generally favor one party disproportionately. However, we cannot dismiss the possibility that counterbalancing national forces were at work in 1978. To test this hypothesis, we must directly examine the impact of voter evaluations of the Carter administration.

If there is an element of party accountability in midterm elections, it is probably based on voters' evaluations of the President's performance.[3] The President's actions are both more visible and more easily understandable to the electorate than those of Congress with its complex internal structure and rules. Furthermore, the President's party affiliation is almost universally known while many voters are unaware of which party controls Congress. Tufte's (1975) analysis of aggregate election results revealed a close relationship between marginal fluctuations in the outcomes of midterm elections over time and two independent variables: the popularity of the incumbent President and changes in real personal income. Using survey data, Kernell (1977) uncovered evidence of negative voting in midterm elections. Voters who were dissatisfied with the President's performance were more likely to vote against his party's congressional candidates. While such voting may not be "programmatic" in the strict sense required by Stokes and Miller, it clearly does constitute a judgment about the performance of the party in power. Outside of presidential elections, this is probably as close an approximation to party accountability as can be expected, given the diffusion of party responsibility in the American political system.

We have used four questions to measure voter evaluations of the performance of the Carter administration. One is simply a rating of Carter's overall performance as President. The remaining three questions asked voters to assess the government's performance in handling the problems of inflation, unemployment, and whatever they felt was the most important problem facing the country. Table 2 shows that evaluations of the performance of the Carter administration in these areas had very little impact on voting for Senator or Representative in 1978, after controlling for party identification. Only 4 out of 24 relationships shown are statistically significant, and even these are rather weak. Evaluations of the Carter administration's performance explain no more than a small fraction of deviations from partisanship in 1978.[4]

The absence of strong national forces in 1978 raises the possibility that deviations from partisanship were due largely to local factors, the most prominent being the House and Senate candidates. This of course would depend upon voters being aware of, and having opinions about, individual House and Senate candidates. Such a requirement runs contrary to the traditional view, based largely on name recall data, that "members of Congress, and their opponents at election time, remain largely unknown to most of their constituents" (Miller and Levitin, 1976: 33). Some recent studies, however, have found that many voters who cannot recall a candidate's name in an interview situation can express a meaningful opinion about the candidate when the name is presented to them (Abramowitz, 1975; Mann,

TABLE 2 1978 House and Senate Vote by Evaluation of Government Performance

	House Vote (Percentage Democratic)				
	Performance Rating				
	Good	*Fair*	*Poor*	*Tau*	*(Sig.)*
CARTER JOB PERFORMANCE					
Democrats	82	82	78	.01	(N.S.)
Independents	58	45	40	.15	(.05)
Republicans	28	23	16	.09	(N.S.)
MOST IMPORTANT PROBLEM					
Democrats	85	80	83	−.02	(N.S.)
Independents	73	50	44	.10	(N.S.)
Republicans	a	25	18	.08	(N.S.)
INFLATION					
Democrats	90	80	84	−.02	(N.S.)
Independents	69	52	43	.11	(.05)
Republicans	a	25	17	.09	(.05)
UNEMPLOYMENT					
Democrats	83	79	90	−.04	(N.S.)
Independents	51	59	43	.06	(N.S.)
Republicans	18	23	22	−.02	(N.S.)
	Senate Vote (Percentage Democratic)				
	Good	*Fair*	*Poor*	*Tau*	*(Sig.)*
CARTER JOB PERFORMANCE					
Democrats	86	71	67	.18	(.01)
Independents	51	36	35	.12	(N.S.)
Republicans	21	21	18	.01	(N.S.)
MOST IMPORTANT PROBLEM					
Democrats	82	82	74	.08	(N.S.)
Independents	36	43	41	.01	(N.S.)
Republicans	a	14	22	−.09	(N.S.)
INFLATION					
Democrats	93	77	75	.06	(N.S.)
Independents	50	40	41	.01	(N.S.)
Republicans	a	17	21	−.05	(N.S.)
UNEMPLOYMENT					
Democrats	84	78	75	.07	(N.S.)
Independents	42	43	39	.03	(N.S.)
Republicans	22	17	31	−.08	(N.S.)

[a]Less than 10 cases.

1978). In the 1978 Election Study, most respondents were unable to recall the name of either House candidate while barely half could recall the name of either Senate candidate. Nevertheless, 72% of

Path Analysis of Voting for House and Senate in 1978

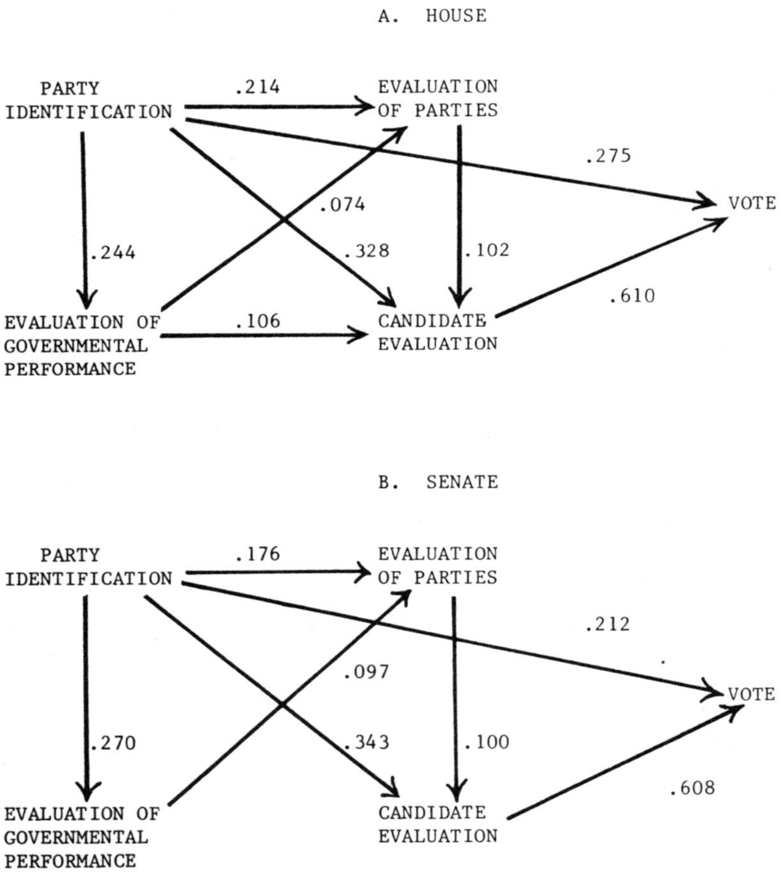

Note: All non-significant paths omitted. Weights shown are standardized regression coefficients.

Figure 1

respondents were willing to rate the job performance of the incumbent Representative from their district (no such question was asked about incumbent Senators). Furthermore, 57% of the voters in contested House races gave a positive or negative evaluation of the Democratic House candidate on the feeling thermometer and 52% gave a positive or negative evaluation of the Republican candidate. Among those voting in contested Senate races, 74% gave a positive or negative evaluation of the Democratic Senate candidate and 73% gave a positive or negative evaluation of the Republican Senate candidate. These findings suggest that large numbers of voters do have meaningful opinions about individual House and Senate candidates even if they cannot recall their names. We would like to know what impact these opinions have on voting decisions.

Figure 1 presents the results of a path analysis of voting for Representative and Senator in 1978. The dependent variable in this analysis is the party direction of the vote. The independent variables are party identification, evaluation of overall government performance (a summary scale based on the four questions used in Table 2), party evaluation (a summary scale based on three questions which asked voters which party they thought would better handle inflation, unemployment, and the most important problem facing the country), and candidate evaluation (measured by the relative evaluation of the Democratic and Republican candidates on the feeling thermometer).[5] The results of the path analysis indicate that candidate evaluation was by far the most important direct influence on the vote for Senator and Representative. Moreover, voters' appraisals of House and Senate candidates, although clearly influenced by party identification, were far from being simply a partisan reflex. We need to consider other factors which may influence evaluations of House and Senate candidates.

As might be expected, incumbents were generally better known and more positively evaluated than challengers. There was, however, a substantial difference between House and Senate races with regard to evaluations of incumbents and challengers. Table 3 shows that incumbency had a much greater impact on candidate evaluations and voting decisions in House races than in Senate races. In House contests, incumbents were evaluated more favorably than challengers by all groups of voters, including those who identified with the challenger's party, and almost half of the supporters of the challenger's party voted for the incumbent. Senate challengers generally fared much better than their House counterparts, especially among their own party's voters and independents. Altogether, 78% of the votes in contested House races favored the incumbent while only 60% of the votes in contested Senate races favored the incumbent.[6]

Why did House incumbents do so much better than Senate incumbents? There are two answers to this question. First, House incumbents are evaluated more positively than Senate incumbents. Among all respondents, 56% gave their Representative a positive rating on the feeling thermometer while only 8% gave the incumbent a nega-

TABLE 3 Incumbency, Candidate Evaluation and Voting for House and Senate in 1978

	A. HOUSE				
	Democratic Incumbent	*Open Seat*	*Republican Incumbent*	*Tau*	*(Sig.)*
CANDIDATE EVALUATION[a]					
Democrats	+56	+29	−37	.45	(.001)
Independents	+41	− 6	−41	.44	(.001)
Republicans	+14	−34	−65	.43	(.001)
VOTE[b]					
Democrats	95	81	53	.35	(.001)
Independents	79	38	18	.60	(.001)
Republicans	45	16	3	.41	(.01)
	B. SENATE				
CANDIDATE EVALUATION					
Democrats	+37	+38	+ 9	.15	(.001)
Independents	+ 4	+ 4	−26	.16	(.001)
Republicans	−18	−23	−48	.16	(.01)
VOTE					
Democrats	85	81	74	.10	(.05)
Independents	64	47	30	.27	(.001)
Republicans	35	22	10	.20	(.01)

[a]Percentage more favorable toward Democratic candidate minus percentage more favorable toward Republican candidate on feeling thermometer.
[b]Percentage voting Democratic.

tive rating. Among respondents in states with Senate contests, 53% gave the Senate incumbent a positive rating while 16% gave the incumbent a negative rating. Even more striking, however, was the difference between House and Senate challengers. Only 14% of respondents gave a positive rating to the House challenger while 7% gave the challenger a negative rating. The vast majority of respondents (79%) had not formed any opinion about the House challenger. In contrast, 40% of respondents gave the Senate challenger a positive rating while 16% gave the challenger a negative rating and 44% had no opinion. Thus, House incumbents were doubly advantaged. Not only did they receive overwhelmingly positive evaluations from their constituents but also their opponents were almost invisible. In contrast, Senate incumbents faced a larger proportion of dissatisfied voters and much more vigorous opposition.

We have seen that most voters did have opinions about candidates for the House and Senate, except for House challengers, and these opinions had a powerful impact on voting decisions. The candidates, rather than the parties, were the most salient objects to voters in House and Senate elections. The implications of this for electoral accountability, however, depend upon on what evaluations of incumbent Senators and Representatives were based. Mayhew (1974) has argued that the popularity of House incumbents is a function of their ability to control the information which constituents receive about their performance through such activities as advertising, credit claiming, and position taking. If this is the case, we should find that evaluations of House incumbents are based largely on voters' contacts with their Representative, rather than ideology or party affiliation. The more contact voters have had with their Representative, the more positive their evaluation should be. If, as hypothesized, Senators have less control over information voters receive about their performance, contact may not have as positive an impact on evaluations of Senate incumbents.

The 1978 Election Study included questions about various types of contact with candidates for the House and Senate. Table 4 shows high levels of voter contact with House incumbents. High levels of contact were also reported with Senate incumbents, although these contacts followed a somewhat different pattern, with more media contact and less personal contact. Once again, there is a large discrepancy between House and Senate challengers. Largely due to the influence of the mass media, respondents reported fairly high levels of exposure to Senate challengers. In contrast, the large majority of respondents reported having had no contact with the House challenger in their district.

In order to assess the impact of party affiliation, ideology, and contact on evaluations of House and Senate candidates, we conducted a path analysis using relative ratings of incumbents and challengers on the feeling thermometer as the dependent variable. The independent variables were overall incumbent contact, overall challenger contact, party identification, and ideological proximity to the incumbent.[7] The results shown in Figure 2 indicate that evaluations of House and Senate candidates were based on somewhat different criteria. Contact with the incumbent was by far the most important influence on evaluations of House candidates. The more voters had seen or heard about the incumbent, the more they liked him. Ideology had no discernible effect on evaluations of House candidates. Contact with

TABLE 4 Contact with Incumbents and Challengers (%)

Type of Contact	*House Incumbent*	*House Challenger*	*Senate Incumbent*	*Senate Challenger*
Personal Meeting	14	3	7	4
Group Meeting	12	2	8	3
Staff	8	2	5	3
Mailing	52	13	41	22
Radio	27	11	40	30
Television	43	20	72	61
Newspaper	52	24	60	49
Indirect[c]	28	8	b	b
Self-initiated	15	a	b	a
Other-initiated[d]	19	a	b	a
Total Reporting Any Contact	77	37	84	70

[a]Not relevant for challenger.
[b]Not asked about Senate candidates.
[c]Does respondent know of anyone else who has had any contact with candidate.
[d]Does respondent know of anyone else who has initiated any contact with candidate.

Path Analysis of Candidate Evaluation in House and Senate Elections Involving Incumbents

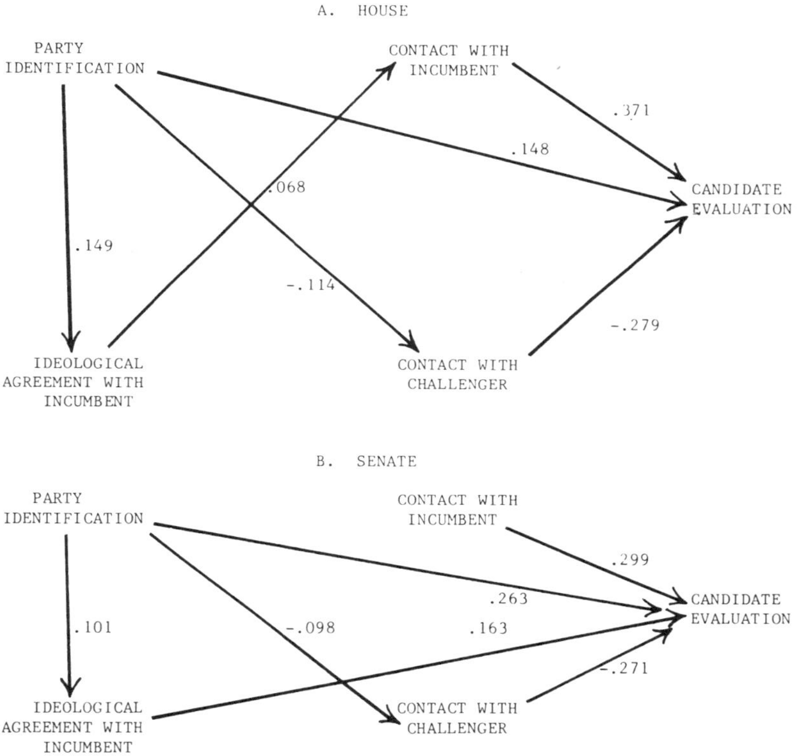

Note: All non-significant paths omitted. Weights shown are standardized regression coefficients. Analysis assumes no causal connection between incumbent and challenger contact.

Figure 2

the incumbent had a somewhat weaker impact on evaluations of Senate candidates, but party identification and ideology were both more important.

Different types of contact may have different effects on voters' evaluations of candidates. Table 5 presents the results of a multiple

TABLE 5 The Impact of Contact on Evaluations of House and Senate Candidates

Type of Contact	*B (S.E.)*	*Frequency*	*Net Effect*
	A. HOUSE INCUMBENTS		
Personal Meeting	+5.3 (1.4)	.14	+0.74
Group Meeting	+4.2 (1.5)	.12	+0.50
Staff	+2.9 (1.7)	.08	+0.23
Mailing	+5.2 (0.9)	.52	+2.70
Radio	+0.9 (1.0)	.27	+0.24
Television	+3.6 (0.9)	.43	+1.55
Newspaper	+3.2 (1.0)	.52	+1.66
Indirect	+3.5 (1.1)	.28	+0.98
Self-initiated	+3.5 (1.3)	.15	+0.52
Other-initiated	+3.1 (1.2)	.19	+0.59
Intercept (54.00) + Total Effect (+9.71) = Average Rating (63.71)			
	B. HOUSE CHALLENGERS		
Personal Meeting	+9.5 (1.9)	.03	+0.23
Group Meeting	−2.4 (2.5)	.02	−0.05
Staff	+7.1 (2.7)	.02	+0.14
Mailing	+2.6 (0.9)	.13	+0.34
Radio	+1.6 (1.0)	.11	+0.18
Television	+1.8 (0.8)	.20	+0.36
Newspaper	−0.6 (0.8)	.24	−0.14
Indirect	+0.3 (1.2)	.08	+0.02
Intercept (50.05) + Total Effect (+1.13) = Average Rating (51.18)			
	C. SENATE INCUMBENTS		
Personal Meeting	+7.7 (3.4)	.07	+0.54
Group Meeting	+5.0 (3.2)	.08	+0.40
Staff	+5.7 (3.7)	.05	+0.28
Mailing	+1.8 (1.7)	.41	+0.74
Radio	+2.4 (1.8)	.40	+0.96
Television	+3.7 (1.9)	.72	+2.66
Newspaper	−1.4 (1.8)	.60	−0.84
Intercept (55.42) + Total Effect (+4.74) = Average Rating (60.16)			
	D. SENATE CHALLENGERS		
Personal Meeting	+16.4 (3.8)	.04	+0.66
Group Meeting	+ 8.7 (4.1)	.03	+0.26
Staff	+ 7.2 (4.2)	.03	+0.22
Mailing	+ 0.8 (1.7)	.22	+0.18
Radio	+ 2.8 (1.6)	.30	+0.84
Television	+ 6.5 (1.6)	.61	+3.96
Newspaper	− 3.3 (1.6)	.49	−1.62
Intercept (51.30) + Total Effect (+4.50) = Average Rating (55.80)			

regression analysis of the effects of contact on evaluations of incumbents and challengers. Since the dependent variable is the feeling thermometer rating, each unstandardized regression coefficient (B) can be interpreted as the average change in degrees on the feeling thermometer produced by each type of contact, controlling for all other types of contact. Multiplying this figure by the frequency of each type of contact indicates the net effect of each type of contact on the average voter's evaluation of each type of candidate. These effects can then be summed to estimate the net effect of all types of contact.

The results presented in Table 5 indicate that House incumbents derived considerably greater benefit from contact (a net gain of almost 10 degrees on the feeling thermometer) than any other type of candidate. Mailings (presumably newsletters and questionnaires as well as campaign literature) had the largest positive effect followed by television and newspaper coverage. It is striking that every type of contact had a positive impact on evaluations of House incumbents, even after controlling for all other types of contact. In contrast, the overall impact of contact on evaluations of House challengers was negligible (a gain of only 1 degree on the feeling thermometer). The effects of contact on evaluations of Senate incumbents and challengers were almost identical, with television coverage having by far the largest positive impact for both. Presumably much of this television coverage consisted of paid advertising which has become a prominent feature of most Senate campaigns. More than two-thirds of the difference between ratings of House incumbents and challengers on the feeling thermometer can be attributed to the effects of contact. Moreover, if we remove the effects of contact, the advantage of incumbency was almost identical in House and Senate elections.

Our findings thus far indicate that House incumbents enjoy a much larger advantage over their challengers than Senate incumbents due largely to the fact that Senate challengers are far more visible to the electorate than House challengers. Unless they are aware of the challenger, voters who are dissatisfied with an incumbent may still prefer a known quantity to an unknown quantity. Table 6 lends support to this hypothesis. The relationship between evaluation of the incumbent and candidate choice in House and Senate elections is much stronger among voters who had been exposed to the challenger than among voters who had not been exposed to the challenger. Among voters who gave a positive evaluation of the incumbent, exposure to the challenger had very little effect on candidate choice. However, among voters who were negative or neutral toward the incumbent, contact with the challenger greatly increased the likelihood of voting against the incumbent. The large majority of voters who were negative or neutral toward the incumbent, but unaware of the challenger, voted for the known quantity.

The findings presented in Table 6 underline the crucial role played by the challenger in the process of electoral accountability. Among voters in Senate races involving an incumbent and challenger, 83% reported having had some contact with the challenger. In contrast, only 44% of the voters in House contests between an incumbent and challenger had been exposed to the challenger. Thus, the advantage of incumbency in House contests is largely due to the weakness of House challengers. The absence of a visible alternative to the incumbent is a serious obstacle to electoral accountability.

The higher visibility of Senate challengers is not the only difference between House and Senate elections, however. In addition, House and Senate candidates seem to be evaluated according to different criteria. Evaluations of House incumbents were based largely on voters' contacts with their Representative, which were overwhelmingly positive in nature. Contacts with Senate incumbents did not have as large a net positive impact, suggesting that voters are less

TABLE 6 Percentage Voting for Incumbent in House and Senate Elections by Evaluation of Incumbent and Exposure to Challenger

	A. HOUSE		
	EVALUATION OF INCUMBENT		
Exposure to Challenger	*Positive*	*Neutral or Negative*	*Tau (Sig.)*
Yes	84	29	.43 (.001)
No	93	65	.24 (.001)
	B. SENATE		
Yes	78	22	.59 (.001)
No	83	72	.15 (N.S.)

dependent on such contacts for information about Senators. Party affiliation and ideology had a greater impact on evaluations of Senate candidates than on evaluations of House candidates. The result of this is shown in Table 7. While ideological proximity to the incumbent had a negligible impact on candidate choice in House elections, it had a substantial impact on candidate choice in Senate elections among two groups of voters: independents and supporters of the challenger's party. The success of Senate incumbents in gaining support from voters of the opposing party depended largely on their ideological position. Whereas House incumbents were favored by an overwhelming 66% of the voters whose ideological position was opposite to their own, Senate incumbents received only 30% of the vote from this group. Thus, it appears that voters were much more likely to hold Senators accountable for their ideological position than Representatives.

The evidence from the 1978 Election Study does not provide a satisfactory answer to the question of why Senators are more likely to be held accountable for their overall voting record than Representatives. It does appear that voters were more likely to know something about their Senator's voting record than about their Representative's voting record. Whereas 51% of respondents were able to place their Senate incumbent on a seven-point liberal-conservative scale, only 37% were able to place their Representative on the same scale. In addition, perceptions of Senators' positions on the liberal-conservative scale appear to have been somewhat more accurate than perceptions of Representatives' positions.[8] We can only speculate that this may be a function of differences between the types of information available to voters about Senators and Representatives, and particularly the greater ability of House incumbents to control the flow of information about their own performance to constituents. House incumbents may stress noncontroversial activities such as casework and constituency service in their communications with constituents, rather than positions on controversial national issues. Due to greater media interest in members of the upper chamber, Senators may have less control over the information voters receive about their performance. These findings may also reflect greater activity by ideological or single-issue interest groups in Senate campaigns. Whatever the explanation, the result is an important difference in the extent of ideological voting between House and Senate elections.

III
Summary and Conclusions

Our findings support the conclusion of Stokes and Miller, based on their analysis of the 1958 midterm election, that evaluations of the performance of the national parties have only a slight impact on voting decisions at midterm. Voters' evaluations of the Carter administration apparently had little or no bearing on how they cast their ballots for Senator or Representative in 1978. The American political system is not well-suited to party accountability. The electoral and institutional separation of the executive and legislative branches discourages voters from connecting the two when they cast their ballots. The recent decline in party loyalties in the electorate has probably widened the separation in the minds of the voters between the President and members of his party in Congress. Furthermore, in 1978, as in most midterm elections, there were no strong national forces

TABLE 7 Percentage Voting for Incumbent in House and Senate Elections by Party Identification and Ideology

	A. HOUSE			
	IDEOLOGICAL PROXIMITY TO INCUMBENT			
Party Identification	*Closest*	*In-Between*	*Farthest*	*Tau (Sig.)*
Same Party	96	94	100	−.00 (N.S.)
Independent	87	81	69	.13 (.05)
Other Party	52	46	40	.11 (N.S.)
	B. SENATE			
Same Party	87	90	a	−.02 (N.S.)
Independent	83	62	39	.33 (.001)
Other Party	39	15	7	.30 (.01)

[a]Less than 10 cases.

favoring one party or the other. Most voters were neither thrilled nor dismayed by the performance of the Carter White House. In the absence of any such overriding national concerns, most voters apparently cast their ballots on the basis of their opinions about the candidates for House and Senate seats.

Our findings depart significantly from those of Stokes and Miller with regard to the impact of candidate evaluation on voting in congressional elections. Not only did large numbers of voters have opinions about individual House and Senate candidates but also these opinions were by far the strongest direct influence on voting decisions. Partisan voting in congressional elections has declined substantially since 1958. About one party identifier in five voted for a candidate of the opposing party for House and Senate in 1978 (a proportion very similar to the average rate of partisan defection in recent presidential elections). Almost all of these defections were attributable to voters' evaluations of House and Senate candidates.

If they do not hold members of the President's party in Congress accountable for the performance of his administration, voters may hold individual members of Congress accountable for their own performance. Indeed, this would seem to be a reasonable strategy, given the wide variation in support for administration policies generally found among members of the President's party in Congress. However, our findings have revealed a serious problem with individual accountability as an alternative to party accountability. Individual accountability depends upon the ability of House and Senate challengers to present voters with an alternative to the incumbent. This condition is not met in most House races. House challengers appear to be almost invisible to the electorate. Without a visible alternative, even voters who are unhappy with the incumbent generally prefer a known quantity to an unknown quantity.

The lack of effective competition in most House races is a serious obstacle to electoral accountability, but it could be removed by recruiting more aggressive challengers and providing them with greater resources to communicate with the electorate.[9] Even if this were done, however, most House incumbents would probably remain secure in their positions because the large majority of their constituents are very satisfied with their performance. When asked to rate the job performance of their own Representative, 72% of all respondents expressed an opinion, and 65% of this group gave the incumbent a rating of "very good" or "good" while 31% gave a rating of "fair" and only 5% gave a rating of "poor" or "very poor." In marked contrast, among the 80% of respondents expressing an opinion about the performance of Congress, only 20% rated its performance as "very good" or "good" while 52% gave Congress a "fair" rating and 28% rated its performance as "poor" or "very poor."[10] These findings lend strong quantitative backing to Fenno's (1975) conclusion, based on his observation of 10 House members in their districts, that voters love their congressman but dislike Congress. However, comparison of the feeling thermometer ratings of Representatives and Senators (since the job performance question was not asked about Senate incumbents) indicates that voters do not love their Senator quite as much as they love their Representative.

What we conclude about individual accountability in House and Senate elections depends on for what we think members of Congress should be held accountable. If we expect our elected representatives to communicate frequently with their constituents, provide assistance with individual problems, and obtain federal projects for their districts, it need not concern us that House incumbents' ideological positions have very little bearing on their popularity. It is often suggested that members of Congress can use noncontroversial activities such as casework and constituency service to earn political support from the voters and thereby gain freedom of action on important national issues. Voters, according to this view, are tolerant about a member's positions on national issues as long as he "brings home the bacon." The findings presented here suggest, however, that voters are much more tolerant toward their Representative than toward their Senator.

NOTES

1. The exact wording of the questions used in this article can be found in the codebook for the 1978 Election Study available from the Inter-university Consortium for Political and Social Research (ICPSR, 1979). Because the 1978 Election Study was designed primarily for the purpose of studying voting for the House of Representatives, some questions asked about House candidates were not asked about Senate candidates. In addition, the sample of respondents in states with Senate races is smaller than would be desirable and is concentrated in a relatively small number of heavily populated states. However, the author does not believe that these deficiencies jeopardize the validity of the findings presented in this article.

2. These data are based on races with two major-party contestants.

3. Most respondents did express opinions about the collective performance of Congress (which were predominantly negative). However, these opinions appear to have had little or no impact on voting for House or Senate candidates. Seventy-five percent of voters who gave a "poor" or "very poor" rating to Congress still cast their ballots for the incumbent in their own House race. Likewise, how voters rated Congress had very little impact on the partisan direction of their vote.

4. In the remainder of this article, leaning independents are classified as independents; and strong and weak partisans, as partisans. This classification is based on an attempt to control for the long-term component of party identification. While some independent leaners are undoubtedly "closet partisans," this group as a whole shows much less partisan consistency in its voting behavior than weak party identifiers. This classification also has the advantage of providing sufficient numbers of independents to permit separate analysis of their attitudes and behavior. All of the analyses presented here were done with only pure independents classified as independents. This produced almost no change in the results.

5. In order to avoid large quantities of missing data, all respondents who did not recognize a candidate were placed at the neutral point (50 degrees) on the feeling thermometer. The relative position of the two candidates on the feeling thermometer was an excellent predictor of the vote for House and Senate.

6. There appears to have been some overreporting of voting for the incumbent as well as turnout in the 1978 Election Study. The actual vote for House incumbents in the districts included in the survey with contested races was about 69%. Some of this discrepancy may be due to nonvoters' disproportionately reporting having voted for the incumbent.

7. The measure of ideological proximity is based on Senators' and Representatives' (ADA) ratings and respondents' positions on a seven-point liberal-conservative scale (1 = most liberal, 7 = most conservative). ADA ratings were used because of the well-established liberal identity of this organization and the wide range of issues on which the ratings were based. ADA ratings also correlate very highly with ratings of other ideological groups. Since the distributions of Senators and Representatives on ADA ratings differed (and different issues were included in the two sets of ratings), slightly different procedures were used to calculate ideological proximity scores in order to produce similar distributions for voters in House and Senate elections. Ideological proximity was measured as follows (1 = closest to incumbent, 3 = farthest from incumbent):

A. Senate

ADA Rating	*Respondent's Position*	*Proximity Score*
0–19	1–3	3
0–19	4	2
0–19	5–7	1
20–39	1–3	2
20–39	4–7	1
50–59	1–4	1
50–59	5–7	2
60+	1–3	1
60+	4	2
60+	5–7	3

(Note: No running Senate incumbent had an ADA rating between 40 and 49)

B. House

ADA Rating	*Respondent's Position*	*Proximity Score*
0–39	1–3	3
0–39	4	2
0–39	5–7	1
40–59	1–3	2
40–59	4	1
40–59	5–7	2
60+	1–3	1
60+	4	2
60+	5–7	3

8. The correlation (Tau) between ideological proximity and subjective ideological distance was .26 for Senate incumbents and .15 for House incumbents.

9. Two recent studies of campaign spending in congressional elections have concluded that higher spending by challengers significantly improves their performance while spending by incumbents has little effect (Glantz et al. 1976; Jacobson, 1978).

10. By comparison, 34% of respondents with an opinion gave President Carter a "very good" or "good" rating while 49% rates his performance as "fair" and 16% gave him a rating of "poor" or "very poor."

REFERENCES

ABRAMOWITZ, A. (1975) "Name familiarity, reputation, and the incumbency effect in a congressional election." Western Political Quarterly 27: 668–684.

CAMPBELL, A. (1960) "Surge and decline: A study of electoral change." Public Opinion Quarterly 24 (Fall).

FENNO, R. (1975) "If as Ralph Nader says, Congress is the 'broken branch,' how come we love our Congressmen so much?", in N.J. Ornstein (ed.) Congress in Change. New York: Praeger.

FEREJOHN, J. (1977) "On the decline of competition in congressional elections." American Political Science Review 71: 166–176.

GLANTZ, S., A. ABRAMOWITZ, and M. BURKART (1976) "Election outcomes: Whose money matters?" Journal of Politics 38: 1033–1038.

Inter-university Consortium for Political and Social Research (1979) The American National Election Study, 1978. Ann Arbor, MI: Author.

JACOBSON, G. (1978) "The effects of campaign spending in congressional elections." American Political Science Review 72: 469–491.

KERNELL, S. (1977) "Presidential popularity and negative voting: An alternative explanation of the midterm congressional decline of the President's party." American Political Science Review 71: 44–66.

MANN, T. (1978) Unsafe at Any Margin: Interpreting Congressional Elections. Washington, DC: American Enterprise Institute.

MAYHEW, D. (1974) Congress: The Electoral Connection. New Haven, CT: Yale University Press.

MILLER, W. and T. LEVITIN (1976) Leadership and Change: Presidential Elections from 1952 to 1976. Cambridge, MA: Winthrop.

STOKES, D. and W. MILLER (1962) "Party government and the saliency of Congress." Public Opinion Quarterly 26 (Winter).

TUFTE, E. (1975) "Determinants of the outcomes of midterm congressional elections." American Political Science Review 69: 312–326.

HOUSE REELECTIONS AND SENATE DEFEATS: THE ROLE OF THE CHALLENGER

BARBARA HINCKLEY

The advantage of incumbency has long intrigued students of congressional elections research. Whether measured at individual or aggregate levels, by reelection rates or voting margins, the advantage has been striking: Simply knowing that there is an incumbent in the contest supplies a major predictor of the vote. The person in office—the incumbent—is overwhelmingly likely to win reelection and to win by larger margins than victorious nonincumbents.

Studies of the subject point to a complex of factors explaining incumbents' success including visibility, office support, and a general positive reputation. Within this complex, however, two factors have been given varying explanatory emphasis: those of voter information and incumbent activity. In studies emphasizing voter information, incumbency—like party—supplies an easy voting cue in the gener-

Reprinted from the *British Journal of Political Science* October 1980, pp. 441–460.

AUTHOR'S NOTE: The data from the 1978 American National Election Study used in this study were made available by the Inter-university Consortium for Political and Social Research and originally collected by the Center for Political Studies, ISPR, the University of Michigan, under a grant from the National Science Foundation. Neither the original collectors of the data nor the consortium bears any responsibility for the analysis or interpretations presented here.

An earlier draft of this article was presented at the annual meeting of the American Political Science Association, Washington, D.C., September 1979. My thanks to Diane Kaiser, Scott Milliman, and Lyn Ragsdale for assistance on the project. My thanks also for the support provided by the Graduate Research Committee of the University of Wisconsin.

ally low-information context of congressional voting (see Stokes and Miller, 1962; Kostroski, 1973; Hinckley et al., 1974; Nelson, 1978/1979). Thus to be recognized, even in vague and general terms, when the challenger is not so recognized, is a decided electoral advantage. Other studies emphasize incumbent activity. Incumbents serve as bureaucratic errand runners, claim credit for federal projects in their districts, and perform other popular and noncontroversial service for constituents (see Mayhew, 1974, 1976; Fiorina, 1977). Even independently of these activities, incumbents work hard at creating a positive reputation in their "home style" and district activity (Fenno, 1978). Campaigning, in short, can be done on the job, between elections (Jones, 1966). Thus one can see, within the general agreement, a divergence in explanatory emphasis. In some studies, incumbents must do something *right* to win reelection. In others, incumbents might well be reelected no matter what activities (within reason) they pursue.

These various explanations, however, have focused primarily on House elections. This accords with the general emphasis on the House as opposed to the Senate in congressional research and with the limits of past survey data. Where congressional questions have been asked at all, they have concentrated on House contests.[1] Yet congressional arguments, like bills, must negotiate two chambers successfully, and Senate "incumbency" may be in the process of changing. Whereas in the past, Senate incumbents were nearly as safe as House incumbents, winning close to 90% of their contests, in recent elections the success rate has fallen sharply.[2] So in 1976, House incumbents won 97% of their bids for reelection and Senate incumbents won 64%. In 1978, House incumbents won 95% and Senate incumbents 68%. Something, then, appears to be happening in the Senate that is not happening in the House. Yet Senate incumbents enjoy the same institutional support and name recognition as their House and earlier Senate counterparts, nor is there reason to suppose they have stopped doing whatever House incumbents do or what Senate incumbents did before. Thus, while attention has focused on the "vanishing marginals" in the House, in the Senate it is not the marginals but the incumbents who are vanishing.

We may, in fact, be looking at the wrong end of the reelection contest. The advantage may be less a matter of what incumbents do right than of what challengers do wrong—or do not do at all. By a number of measures held to be important to the vote—visibility, campaign activity, positive reputation—Senate challengers may be competitive with their opponents and House challengers not competitive. We may find few differences between Senate and House incumbents, and these not important to the vote, and major differences between Senate and House challengers. Thus, to solve this mystery of electoral advantage, we need a four-fold design comparing incumbents and challengers in Senate and House elections.

For the first time, such a design appears possible through the 1978 postelection National Election Study. The survey asks a national sample of respondents a series of questions deliberately matched for both Senate and House races about incumbents, challengers (the candidates running against incumbents), and those nonincumbents contesting other nonincumbents. Note that it is not, and does not intend to be, a sample of either House or Senate races, but of people eligible to vote in the 1978 election. We cannot draw inferences about races in particular states or districts, only about voting behavior nationally.[3] The study also goes beyond past surveys in the range and depth of the congressional questions asked. It supplies new measures of voter information about candidates—through questions on name recognition and the kind of "contact" with candidates that voters report. The survey measures the extent of positive or negative evaluations for candidates and asks about the activities that voters feel Senators and Representatives should pursue. (These questions will be explained in detail in the following section.) Selecting these matched questions, then, for Senate and House, we can begin to evaluate the similarities and differences of voter response by types of races and types of candidates.

I
RESULTS

A summary of the House and Senate voting is presented in Tables 1 and 2. In the sample as in the actual voting results, House voters compared to Senate voters face a higher proportion of contests overall with incumbents running and a higher proportion of uncontested races with incumbents (see Table 1). While the following analysis

TABLE 1 House and Senate Voters by Type of Contest, 1978 National Election Study

	Number and Percent of Voters							
	Contests–Incumbents vs. Challengers		*No Contests–Incumbents Running*		*Contests Between Nonincumbents*[a]		*Total Voters*	
House	(757)	75%	(124)	12%	(128)	13%	(1009)	100%
Senate[b]	(395)	68%	(230)	4%	(162)	28%	(580)	100%

[a]The category includes 12 respondents in the House and 12 in the Senate voting in uncontested races with nonincumbents.
[b]The Senate questions were asked only of those respondents in the sample with a Senate race in their states.

TABLE 2 Voting in Contested Elections, Incumbents Vs. Challengers

		Percent Voting	
	N	*for Incumbent*	*for Challenger*
House			
Party Identifiers[a]	(501)	78	22
Independents	(256)	80	20
Total	(757)	79	21
Senate			
Party Identifiers	(255)	56	44
Independents	(140)	69	31
Total	(395)	61	39

[a] Party identifiers throughout the analysis are taken to be those Democrats and Republicans occupying the four extreme points on the traditional seven-part party ID scale, and Independents those occupying the three middle points.

concentrates only on voters in contested elections, it should be remembered that some House incumbents are advantaged to the extent that they face no opposition at all. Comparing the voting in contests between incumbents and challengers (Table 2), House incumbents are strongly preferred over challengers by both party identifiers and independents, Senate incumbents considerably less strongly preferred, particularly among party identifiers. Overall, 79% of the voters in contested elections voted for the House incumbent, 61% for the Senate incumbent. We ask, then, through a series of questions for Senate and House incumbents and challengers, what can help explain this difference in results.

RECOGNITION AND CONTACT: INCUMBENTS AND CHALLENGERS

One striking difference between House and Senate can be observed from the recognition and contact questions. Respondents were supplied the names of the candidates in their own states and districts along with a number of other names, of past and possibly future presidential candidates. They were then asked, if they recognized these people, to rate how they felt about them on a "feeling thermometer" scale from zero degree (most negative) to 100 degrees (most positive). Unlike the traditional memory-testing "recall" item,[4] the question taps the kind of cognitive activity demanded in the voting booth, that is, people are asked to recognize and rate the candidates. Respondents were also asked whether they had "come into contact with or learned anything about" the candidates and, if so, to check the kinds of contact, for example, by personal meeting, television or newspaper reporting, or newsletter or other mailing. Answers to these recognition and contact questions can be compared for incumbents, challengers, and those nonincumbents running against other nonincumbents. The results of the comparison are shown in Table 3.

As the table makes sharply clear, House challengers stand apart in comparison to other House candidates and all Senate candidates in their degree of visibility and contact with voters. Most voters could recognize and rate the incumbents and the Senate challengers; less than half could recognize and rate the House challengers.[5] Moreover, comparing challengers with other nonincumbents, Senate challengers are like the other candidates in recognition and House challengers are like the other candidates in recognition and House chal-

TABLE 3 Name Recognition and Contact in the Senate and House[a]

Voters who can Recognize and Rate the Candidates[b]

	Percent of Voters	
	House *N*	*Senate* *N*
Incumbents	(757) 92	(395) 95
Challengers	(757) 44	(395) 85
Nonincumbents D	(116) 78	(150) 92
Nonincumbents R	(116) 70	(150) 83

Voters who had contact with the Candidates[c]

	House					*Senate*				
	N	*Any*	*Met*	*Read About*	*TV*	*N*	*Any*	*Met*	*Read About*	*TV*
Incumbents	(757)	94	23	74	52	(395)	97	9	75	83
Challengers	(757)	46	4	34	22	(395)	85	5	65	73
Nonincumbents D	(116)	81	18	61	51	(150)	95	12	85	85
Nonincumbents R	(116)	72	11	58	50	(150)	91	7	79	79

a. These and all following results in the paper are based on voters in contested elections. The term incumbent includes only those running for re-election and nonincumbents refers only to those nonincumbents running against other nonincumbents. Challengers are the candidates running against incumbents.

b. Respondents were supplied with the names of candidates in their own states and districts and asked, if they recognized the names to rate them from zero to 100 degrees on the feeling thermometer. A small number who said yes they could recognize the candidates' names then said no they could not rate them. The measure reported here and throughout the analysis is based on those who could both recognize and rate.

c. Respondents were asked if they had had any contact with the candidates, had met them personally, read about them in newspapers or magazines, or seen them on television. For other contact questions, see note 6. The fact that the same percentages are given for nonincumbents in the last two columns of the table is apparently a coincidence of the data and not an inaccuracy in reporting.

lengers are not. While 78% and 70%, respectively, recognize House Democratic and House Republican nonincumbents, only 44% recognize the House challenger. The same pattern is seen in the contact questions.[6] In contrast to the frequencies for other House candidates and for all Senate candidates, less than half of the voters said that they had any contact with or learned anything about the challenger.

These results require one additional control. Party identification may increase the visibility of one's own-party candidates compared to the candidates of the opposing party. With more Democratic identifiers than Republicans in the sample and more Democratic House incumbents, this might explain some of the House challengers' situations. Nevertheless, controlling for party, challenger recognition and contact remain low even for those identifiers of the challenger's party:

	% Recognizing Challenger	% Any Contact
Voters of incumbent's party (318)	39	37
Independent voters (255)	45	47
Voters of challenger's party (183)	52	52

Visibility changes slightly with changes of party identification;[7] still, under the best of partisan conditions, only 52% of the voters could recognize or remember any contact with the challenger.

The relationship between recognition and contact and the vote is set forth in Table 4. In the House, simply recognizing the challenger or not makes a significant difference to the vote, within all categories of partisanship. Having contact with the challenger or not is significant for both categories of partisans, although not for independents. Perhaps the most striking difference, however, is found for voters of the challenger's party. Merely recognizing or remembering contact with the challenger or not changes the outcome from a tendency to vote for the challenger to a tendency to vote for the incumbent. The Senate pattern is provided for comparison, although the small number of cases on which some percentages are based should be treated with caution. Overall, however, the pattern is the same. Those at least recognizing the challenger are less likely to vote for the incumbent and significantly less likely for independents and party identifiers of the challenger's party.

TABLE 4 Name Recognition, Contact, and the Vote, Controlling for Party ID[a]

	Percent Voting for Incumbent					
	Party ID with Incumbent		*No Party ID*		*Party ID with Challenger*	
HOUSE						
Contact Challenger	N		N		N	
Yes	(118)	92	(121)	77	(96)	30
No	(199)	98*	(134)	84	(87)	60*
Recognize Challenger						
Yes	(124)	93	(115)	73	(95)	37
No	(194)	98*	(140)	86*	(88)	56*
SENATE[b]						
Contact Challenger						
Yes	(95)	84	(122)	66	(111)	23
No	(27)	96	(16)	88	(22)	50*
Recognize Challenger						
Yes	(103)	86	(122)	65	(112)	21
No	(19)	90	(17)	94*	(21)	62*

[a]The N's for the categories on which the percentages are based are provided in parenthesis. Thus of the 118 people whose party ID was the same as the incumbent, but who had contact with the challenger, 92 percent voted for the incumbent, whereas of the 199 people whose party ID was the same as the incumbent and who had no contact with the challenger, 98 percent voted for the incumbent. An asterisk indicates a tau b for the relationship significant at the .05 level.

[b]The Senate results are provided for comparison but because of the very small numbers of people not recognized or having contact with the challenger, the percentages should be interpreted with caution.

TABLE 5 House Incumbents' Personal Contact and the Vote, Controlling for Party ID[a]

	Percent Voting for Incumbent					
		Party ID with Incumbent	*No Party ID*		*Party ID with Challenger*	
Met Personally						
Yes	(81)	96	(62)	87	(33)	52
No	(237)	96	(193)	78	(150)	45
Attended Meeting						
Yes	(71)	97	(56)	86	(28)	64
No	(247)	96	(199)	79	(155)	43*

[a]The N's for the categories are given in parenthesis, following the format in Table 4. An asterisk indicates a tau b for the relationship significant at the .05 level. Five of the six crosstabulations reported in the table are not significant at this level.

PERSONAL CONTACTS: HOUSE INCUMBENTS

The one difference identified thus far favoring House over Senate incumbents is the former's higher degree of personal contact. Twenty-three percent of the voters said they had "met" House incumbents and 21% had attended meetings where they spoke. According to campaign wisdom, personal contacts have strongly positive effects: Thus, while the percentages are too low to explain much of the overall voting results, the relationship is worth examining (see Table 5). Controlling for party, however, there is no significant difference in the vote between those meeting incumbents personally and those not meeting them. Nor is there any significant difference found for attending meetings either for independents or partisans of the incumbent's party, although the 28 people of the challenger's party attending the meetings with incumbents are indeed more likely to vote for incumbents than the 155 people who did not. It is true that the percentages in Table 5 are in the expected direction: Those having personal contact are slightly more likely to vote for the incumbent than those without such contact, at least among independents and voters of the challenger's party. Nevertheless, there is little support overall for the likelihood that House incumbents' personal contact explains part of their voting advantage.

JOB EXPECTATIONS FOR SENATE AND HOUSE

We need to ask, however, whether different expectations about the job of Senator or Representative underlie both voting and visibility results. House expectations might be more easily satisfied than those for the Senate, reducing the need to look for alternative candidates. The survey asked people to rank the following list of congressional activities from most to least important:

(1) helping people in the district who have personal problems with government
(2) making sure the district gets its fair share of government money and projects
(3) keeping track of the way government agencies are carrying out laws passed by Congress

(4) keeping in touch with the people about what the government is doing
(5) working in Congress on bills concerning national issues.

If House expectations center on the district-related and the personal (thus categories 1, 2, and 4) and Senate expectations on the national and controversial (category 5 and possibly 3), this might help explain the difference in incumbents' support.

This possibility, however, is not supported by the data. While voters are dispersed widely in expectations, categories 4 and 5 are rated most important for both Senate and House: keeping in touch with the people and legislating in Congress. As the most important activity, House voters most frequently cite keeping in touch (category 4) and next most frequently legislating (category 5); Senate voters first cite legislating and next most frequently cite keeping in touch. Combining first and second preferences, both House and Senate voters most frequently cite keeping in touch. The least most important activity in both chambers (with the least frequent first mentions and the most frequent least important mentions) is category 1: helping individual constituents with government problems. Moreover, the differences in the most important activity cited by and large make no difference to the vote.

Table 6 reports the vote in terms of the most important activity cited. In the House, the percentages hold within five points of each other for all categories with the exception of category 2 voters, those emphasizing the district's "fair share." In the Senate, the percentages are in fact identical for four of the categories with the only marked exception category 3 voters, those emphasizing oversight of government agencies. Whether voters cite one category or another or all or none as most important, they are about equally likely to vote for the incumbent—at high rates in the House and substantially lower rates in the Senate. One cannot know at this point whether the two curious exceptions are merely products of particular issues in some 1978 campaigns or would hold upon further examination. The exceptions aside, the results are primarily important in eliminating differences in House and Senate job expectations as explanations of the difference in the vote.

CANDIDATE AFFECT: THERMOMETER RATINGS

The thermometer ratings provide us with a comparative evaluation of Senate and House candidates—overall how one "feels" about them, whatever the reasons or weighting of reasons contributing to the evaluation: whether partisanship, the incumbent's activity in office, issues in the campaign, or other influences. It is the only such comparative measure available from the survey: Open-ended questions asking why one liked or disliked the candidates and whether the incumbent had done "anything special" for the district were asked only for the House.[8] While the ratings supply a broad summary evaluation only, they should be useful in comparing candidates by type of contest and in separating negative from positive incumbency effects.

Table 7 reports thermometer ratings for the candidates, scoring the inability to recognize or rate as a neutral 50 degrees.[9] In candidate

TABLE 6 Job Expectations and the Vote: Senate and House[a]

	House			*Senate*		
	N	*%Rating*	*% Voting for Incumbent*	*N*	*%Rating*	*% Voting for Incumbent*
Helping people in the district	(73)	10%	82	(42)	11%	62
Making sure the district gets a fair share	(105)	14%	70	(61)	15%	62
Keeping track of government agencies	(131)	17%	79	(63)	16%	49
Keeping in touch with the people	(207)	27%	81	(84)	21%	62
Working in Congress on bills	(189)	25%	78	(116)	29%	62
All or None Important; DK	(52)	7%	83	(29)	7%	69
Total	757	100%		395	99%	

[a]The question supplied the list of congressional activities and asked respondents to rank them in order of importance: what they saw as the 'most important activity' Representatives or Senators should be pursuing and so on to the least important activity.

TABLE 7 Thermometer Ratings by Type of Candidate[a]

	Percent of Voters Rating				
Degrees on Thermometer	*House Incumbents*	*Senate Incumbents*	*Senate Challengers*	*House Challengers*	*(House Challengers II)*
100	15	10	5	1	2
90–99	1	0	0	0	1
80–89	22	19	12	3	7
70–79	19	17	15	5	12
60–69	16	15	15	8	17
50–59	18	20	33	74	41
40–49	3	7	9	4	8
30–39	2	4	4	2	4
20–29	0	0	0	0	0
10–19	1	4	4	2	3
0–9	2	5	4	2	4
Total	(99%)	(101%)	(101%)	(101%)	(99%)
N of Cases	757	395	395	757	334
Mean Degrees	68.9	61.3	56.5	51.3	52.9
Standard Deviation	21.7	25.1	21.6	12.6	18.8

[a]Based on scoring those who cannot recognize and rate as 50 degrees, for the first four columns of the table. See note 7. The final column, labelled House Challengers II, shows the distribution for those who can recognize and rate the challengers.

affect as in visibility, Senate challengers are more competitive with their opponents than House challengers. House incumbents edge Senate incumbents who in turn edge Senate challengers—all scoring positive average ratings—and House challengers bring up the rear. Only 27% of the House voters gave challengers anything other than a neutral 50 degree rating. Even discounting those voters who cannot recognize or rate the House challenger (and so looking at the final column in Table 7), this marked concentration at the 50 degree mark remains. We can note also the small proportion of clearly negative ratings for any candidates. Of the House voters, 5% and 6%, respectively, give incumbents and challengers ratings of less than 40 degrees; while in the Senate 13% and 12%, respectively, give these ratings. Incumbency, then, appears to have little negative effect nor one that disadvantages either set of incumbents in relation to their challengers.

What we do not know from the ratings is the interactive effect on evaluations as produced by a campaign. With two candidates seriously campaigning and contacting voters, the generally high affect for incumbents may be reduced as weak points are targeted and alternatives made known. If this is the case, the House incumbents' ratings might be reduced even closer to those for the Senate merely by increasing the competition. The same interactive effect might explain why both Senate candidates, incumbents and challengers, receive slightly more negative ratings than the House candidates. Competition, then, might decrease the frequency of positive ratings and increase the frequency of negative ratings. Further analysis distinguishing degrees of challenger competition—from the token race to the most hotly contested election—might provide more information on the question.

The relationship between candidate affect and the vote is reported in Table 8. While the proportions rating the challenger higher in both Senate and House change with changes in partisanship, a large number of party identifiers rate the two candidates counter to the expectations of party identification. Table 8 also makes clear that affect, while strongly and significantly related to the vote, is by no means tautological with it: It cannot be used as a surrogate measure of the

TABLE 8 Candidate Affect (by Thermometer Rating) and Vote, Controlling for Party ID[a]

	Percent Voting for Incumbent					
	Party ID with Incumbent		*No Party ID*		*Party ID with Challenger*	
HOUSE						
Challenger Affect						
Higher	(65)	83	(79)	51	(91)	13
Not Higher	(253)	99*	(176)	94*	(92)	78*
SENATE						
Challenger Affect						
Higher	(36)	64	(71)	45	(93)	11
Not Higher	(86)	97*	(68)	93*	(40)	68*

[a]The N's for the categories and significance levels follow the format of Tables 4 and 5. All of the cross tabulations in the table are significant at the .05 level.

vote. Many people rating the challenger higher still vote for the incumbent. The thermometer ratings, then, like the open-ended like-dislike questions typically used in voting studies, appear best understood as a summary but by no means determining influence on the vote, affected by but independent of party.[10] Thus in both Senate and House and for all categories of partisanship, the relative rating of candidates influences the vote for incumbent or challenger. House challengers, we saw, are given predominantly neutral ratings; but with the positive affect for congressional candidates generally, a neutral rating loses the election.

II
SUMMARY ANALYSIS

The variables identified separately can now be examined for their relative and combined influence on the vote. Treating the vote for incumbent or challenger as the dependent variable,[11] four independent variables may be specified as follows: party identification (in accord with the incumbent, no identification, in accord with the challenger); challenger recognition (whether one cannot even recognize the challenger or can do so); relative contact by candidates (the number of contacts cited for the incumbent minus the number cited for the challenger); and relative affect (the incumbent's degree rating on the thermometer minus the challenger's degree rating, scoring the inability to rate as 50 degrees). The measures of party, recognition, and affect are quite straightforward and follow from the preceding discussion.[12] The contact measure should be taken as more tentative. Ideally, we might wish to measure the relative advantage of one candidate having more contact with voters than another, but no questions in the survey directly measure amount of contact. The present measure taps range of contact and not amount directly, though a check on the data confirms that those having the least frequently reported kinds of contact have also had the more frequently reported kinds. We ask, then, the influence on the vote contributed first by party, then by recognition and a relative contact advantage, and finally by the relative affect for candidates. Note that by ordering the entry of variables in the equation, we ask about the *additional* effect of contacts by candidates after challenger recognition is controlled, and about the influence of candidate affect after all other variables are controlled. We thus avoid contamination between the affect and the recognition measures.

The results of the regression for Senate and House are reported in the top portion of Table 9. In the House, each of the variables contributes an independent and significant increment to the vote (and each of the variables, of course, strongly favors the incumbent). While, overall, the similarity of results for the House and Senate models should be noticed, the Senate recognition and contact variables appear less important. Party is strong and strikingly similar in effect in Senate and House voting; and independently of party, the relative affect for the candidates in the contests makes a substantial difference to the vote. Indeed, noting the standardized coefficients for both Senate and House, it is clear that candidate affect contributes the largest single influence to the vote even after the other influences are controlled. Altogether, the model explains 43% and 49%, respectively, of the variation in the vote for incumbents or challengers in Senate and House elections.

The same basic model can be generalized to all contests, whether incumbents face challengers or nonincumbents face each other. In

TABLE 9 Results of Regression Analysis for Senate and House Voting[a]

Voting in Contests Between Incumbents and Challengers:

	House				Senate			
	r	*R^2 change*	*B*	*beta*	*r*	*R^2 change*	*B*	*beta*
Party ID	.47	.22	.32**	.31	.49	.24	.34**	.28
Recognition	.19	.02	.15**	.09	.17	.03	.36*	.09
Contact	.30	.04	.04**	.08	.30	.03	.03	.04
Affect	.57	.15	.01**	.44	.64	.19	.01**	.50
	R^2 = .43					R^2 = .49		

Voting in All Contests:

	House				Senate			
	r	*R^2 change*	*B*	*beta*	*r*	*R^2 change*	*B*	*beta*
Party ID	.57	.27	.14**	.29	.54	.30	.15**	.32
Recognition	.51	.17	.17**	.12	.24	.04	.19*	.07
Contact	.57	.06	.04**	.11	.32	.03	.03	.05
Affect	.69	.10	.01**	.39	.67	.18	.01**	.49
Incumbency	.53	.01	.12**	.11	.19	.01	.13**	.10
	R^2 = .61					R^2 = .55		

[a]A double asterisk indicates coefficient significant at the .01 level, a single asterisk at .05.

this case, the dependent variable may be taken as the Democratic versus Republican vote (see Note 11), with recognition, contact, and affect measured for their expected advantage to Democratic or Republican candidates (thus recognition becomes whether one recognized the Democratic candidate only, both or neither candidates or the Republican candidate only). Party is measured by the conventional seven-part identification scale. Repeating the same order of variables entered into the regression, we can add the final variable of incumbency, that is, whether there was a Democratic incumbent, no incumbent, or a Republican incumbent in the contest. We thus ask the extent to which incumbency status in itself, separate from recognition, contact, and affect, exercises an additional influence on the vote beyond the effects of the other variables.

In the House in all contests, as in those where incumbents face challengers, all variables are significant at .01 levels—with affect strongest, as seen by the standardized coefficients, followed by party. While incumbency remains significant, even with the other variables controlled, it is reduced substantially in importance: Originally strongly correlated with the vote at .53, it contributes by its place in the model an addition to R^2 of only .01. In the Senate for all contests, as for those with incumbents and challengers, party and affect add separate and major influences to the vote. Incumbency, while only weakly related to the vote to start with, remains significant and contributes an addition to R^2 of .01. *So we have in effect, by controlling for the other variables, reduced House incumbency to an impact similar to Senate incumbency.* The R^2s for both House and Senate are impressive: The variables in combination explain 61% and 55%, respectively, of the variation in the House and Senate vote.[13]

Taken together, the four models support several more general statements of influence on congressional voting. Party is important, as expected, and appears fairly equally so in the Senate and House. However, the ratings of the candidates themselves are even more important, exhibiting the largest standardized coefficients in each of the four models. Congressional voting in this midterm 1978 election is more than a matter of party or the relative visibility of candidates. Incumbency—that is, the advantage to a candidate merely by being an incumbent—contributes a very small but significant impact in both Senate and House, once other influences are controlled. The major difference is found for recognition and contact. In the House these influences favor one candidate more than the other, with the advantage producing a significant impact on the vote. In the Senate, with recognition and contact more equally distributed between the candidates, these variables exhibit less impact. Under conditions of full competition, then, as found in some Senate and gubernatorial contests, we should expect these variables to cancel out in importance.

III
DISCUSSION

By this analysis, what is happening in the Senate and not in the House is that there are *two* candidates competing in the contests. Senate challengers were recognized by voters and remembered for contact with them in proportions only slightly smaller than Senate incumbents or other nonincumbents. While Senate incumbents retain some advantage from visibility, affect, and incumbency itself, the advantage is a fairly narrow one: So 61% of the voters in the sample voted for incumbents, and in the 1978 election incumbents won 68% of their contests. In the House by contrast, challenger visibility, in both recognition and contact, is markedly lower than for incumbents and other nonincumbents. Affect ratings converge toward a noncommittal 50 degrees. With all of these influences significantly related to the vote, and with incumbency itself retaining a small though significant additional influence, it is to be expected that challengers would be soundly defeated, as indeed they are: 79% of the voters in the sample supported incumbents, and incumbents won 95% of their bids for reelection. Studies of the effects of campaign spending find that it is the *challenger's* money, not the incumbent's that makes the difference (Jacobson, 1978; Glantz et al., 1976). The findings of this study are similar in targeting the challenger's, and not the incumbent's, recognition, contact, and affect as the key distinguishing factors in the House and Senate vote.

Several negative findings of the study are also important. No major differences were observed between Senate and House incumbents in visibility and contact measures. The greater personal contact of House incumbents was not found significantly related to the vote. No differences were found in Senate and House job expectations to suggest that one job might be more easily "filled," that is, less vulnerable to voter dissatisfaction, than the other. There was no substantial negative affect observed for either House or Senate incumbents nor were either disadvantaged overall in negative ratings compared to their challengers. House incumbents, it is true, were awarded higher ratings than Senate incumbents on the candidate thermometers, although the differences were small and might be further reduced through the interactive effects of serious campaigning.

This, of course, does not mean House incumbents do not need to do all the things they do nor that they do not do them well. What it does suggest is that House incumbents do little in terms of vote-getting activity that Senate incumbents do not also do. It is possible that some key Senate-House differences have been overlooked in the present study. The traditional seven-part issue scales can be analyzed. House open-ended questions can tell us more about why House incumbents are so positively perceived. Still, the explanatory performance of the models supports confidence in the variables presently identified. And explanations from House open-ended questions, like other incumbency hypotheses, must ultimately be tested against Senate results.

These findings have implications both for electoral competition and for representation in Congress. Attention directed only to House incumbents leads to speculations about what they must do right, being so enthusiastically reelected. Reelection becomes de facto the sign of successful representation. Voting is important, and the House is in good order. Focusing rather on House challengers and the Senate comparative results leads to very different conclusions. In the Senate, voters choose between two candidates they tend to recognize and remember contact with. Minimum conditions for competition between candidates are present. In the House by contrast, for any of a number of reasons which need to be investigated more fully, these conditions are not present.

Looking toward the future, then, the results suggest a shift in research attention from incumbents to challengers and to the conditions facilitating their election. What is the variation in challengers' qualifications and in the extent and kind of their campaign activity? To what extent does such variation affect their visibility with voters and success? As part of the 1978 study, a large amount of contextual data has been compiled, supplying information about the political context within which individual voting decisions are made. This includes biographical information on candidates, past election results, campaign spending information, and extensive coding of campaign materials. Hence questions about the challengers' background, campaigning, and electoral context—and their effects on the variables identified here—could be pursued with data already available.

More broadly, we need further refined analysis of that complex and reinforcing process of electoral success. The very safeness of incumbents can discourage strong challengers from entering the race, in turn resulting in the minimal campaigning and voter recognition of whoever is persuaded to run. One thus finds the situation, as reported earlier, where even voters of the challenger's party cannot recognize the candidate's name. Once an incumbent is perceived as vulnerable and/or a strong challenger decides to enter the race, the effects of campaign activity and recognition follow. A serious contest also attracts news media reporting, increasing visibility. A serious contest attracts—and spends—money. Clearly, one thing happening in the Senate and not in the House involves challengers' campaign spending. Yet money raising itself, as studies have pointed out, is part of the same circular process by which the very perception of "safeness" affects the kind of money challengers can raise. This vicious circle, apparently cut for the Senate, has not yet been cut for the House. The critical factors and processes, however, within this circle still need to be isolated; some may be more important than others.

In examining why incumbents are reelected, we ask about that voting decision that says, in effect, government should continue as it was before, and to what extent that decision is made by the voters or made by default. Pursuing that question beyond the present results would seem well worth doing.

NOTES

1. Two exceptions are the 1974 National Election Study and the 1968 Comparative State Election Project. Both include Senate questions but do not permit comparisons with the House.

2. For House and Senate reelection rates from 1960 to the present, see *Congressional Quarterly Weekly Report,* July 7, 1979, p. 1351.

3. Since the Senate, unlike the House, is proportioned by states and not by population, a disproportionate number of Senate respondents in the sample will fall in states of large population: in 1978, the states of Michigan, Illinois, and Texas. However, with only one exception, dichotomizing Senate respondents into those from the three largest population states and those from all other states showed no difference in results. The exception is reported in Note 5.

4. The traditional recall question asks, "Do you happen to remember the names of the candidates for Congress—that is, for the House of Representatives in Washington—that ran in the district this November?" It is asked in a postelection survey, typically conducted in December and January following the election.

5. The only potentially interesting difference in Senate results between those states (Michigan, Illinois, and Texas) largest in population and all others occurs with challenger recognition. While 91% of the voters in the three large-population states could recognize and rate the Senate challenger, 81% could do so in all other states. Incumbent recognition was virtually the same. This fact, of course, does not change the results of Table 3: Even at 81% rates, Senate challengers are quite competitive with other Senate candidates and quite distinct from House challengers. Nevertheless, the impact of state population size on Senate candidate visibility (whether from increased media attention, more money-raising capacity, the greater stakes perceived in the contest) might merit further attention.

6. The questions asked about seven different kinds of contact: had respondents met the candidates, attended meetings where they spoke, talked to their staff, received mail, read about them in newspapers or magazines, heard them on the radio, or seen them on television. The same pattern for Senate and House incumbents, challengers, and nonincumbents shown for the three kinds of contacts reported in Table 3 can be shown for the other questions. These three were selected to indicate the range of contact found for candidates and to differentiate personal contact from two different kinds of "mediated" contact opportunities.

7. This small effect of party identification on the visibility measures may explain the fact that Democratic nonincumbents in Table 3 are slightly but consistently more visible than Republican nonincumbents. There are more Democratic identifiers than Republicans in both the full sample and among voters in the sample.

8. Of all respondents asked the "anything special" question, 458 said yes there was something special and 1837 said no.

9. If one removes the small number of voters not able to recognize or rate the Senate candidates or House incumbents, the distributions for the first three columns in Table 8 would be very similar to those reported. Because of the large number not able to recognize or rate the House challenger, both distributions are reported in Table 7. It should also be noted that respondents placed in the 50–59 degree range are, with only a few exceptions, actually giving 50 degree ratings.

10. The zero-order correlations (Pearson's r) between affect and party identification and affect and the vote for incumbent or challenger are as follows, where affect is measured as thermometer degrees for the incumbent minus degrees for the challenger, and party ID is measured as in accord with, against, or in no relation to the incumbent: for the House, affect and

party = .31; affect and vote = .57; for the Senate, affect and party = .39, affect and vote = .64. For the independent effects of affect controlling for party identification, see Table 9 and corresponding discussion.

11. Formally, a dichotomous dependent variable violates the assumption of regression analysis that the error terms are normally distributed, and so may reduce confidence in the results. Therefore the regressions for all contests (see lower portion of Table 9) were checked by use of a probit procedure with no major difference in significance levels found for the coefficients in either the Senate or House.

12. Alternative affect measures were experimented with including incumbent affect alone, challenger affect, and a "collapsed" relative affect score assigning incumbents and challengers high, medium, and low ratings and measuring the difference. Incumbent and challenger affect alone were each strongly correlated with the vote, though as might be expected less strongly than the relative affect measure selected for the model. The collapsed measure, it should be noted, did considerably less well, possibly owing to the concentration of cases in the middle category. Alternative contact measures were also tried including a relative measure of some contact with the incumbent only, with both or neither candidates, or with the challenger only. For both affect and contact, the decision was to select the relative measure giving the most detail, which was also the one most strongly correlated with the vote.

13. Of the four models reported in Table 9, only the House all-contest model might be suspected of multicollinearity, with some independent variables intercorrelated at .5 and .6 levels. (By other rules of thumb, however, multicollinearity would not be said to be present; that is, the multiple R for the regression very considerably exceeds the intercorrelations between any of the independent variables; and the multiple R for the regression exceeds the multiple R when the other independent variables are regressed against incumbency, which is the most highly intercorrelated variable (see Lemieux, 1978). Nevertheless, for those following the first rule of thumb, it can be reported that all of the coefficients had very low standard errors and yielded extremely large F statistics with four of the coefficients significantly different from zero at the .001 level and the fifth just missing significance at .001.

REFERENCES

FENNO, R. (1978) Home Style. Boston: Little, Brown.

FIORINA, M. (1977) "The case of the vanishing marginals: The bureaucracy did it." American Political Science Review 71: 177–181.

GLANTZ, J. et al. (1976) "Election outcomes: Whose money matters." Journal of Politics 38: 1033–1041.

HINCKLEY, B. et al. (1974) "Information and the vote: A comparative election study." American Politics Quarterly 2: 131–158.

JACOBSON, G. (1978) "The effects of campaign spending on congressional elections." American Political Science Review 72: 469–491.

JONES, C. (1966) "The role of the campaign in congressional politics," p. 29 in K. Jennings and H. Ziegler (eds.) The Electoral Process. Englewood Cliffs, NJ: Prentice-Hall.

KOSTROSKI, W. (1973) "Party and incumbency in postwar Senate elections." American Political Science Review 67: 1213–1234.

LEMIEUX, P. (1978) "A note on the detection of multicollinearity." American Journal of Political Science 22: 183–196.

MAYHEW, D. (1976) "Congressional elections: The case of the vanishing marginals." Polity 6: 295–317.

______(1974) Congress: The Electoral Connection. New Haven, CT: Yale University Press.

NELSON, C. (1978/1979) "The effect of incumbency on voting in congressional elections." Political Science Quarterly 93: 655–678.

STOKES, D. and W. MILLER (1962) "Party government and the salience of Congress." Public Opinion Quarterly 26: 531–546.

5

CONGRESSIONAL ELECTIONS, 1978: THE CASE OF THE VANISHING CHALLENGERS

GARY C. JACOBSON

Scholars have only begun to exploit the wealth of information produced by the 1978 NES/CPS American National Election Study, but a thorough revision of accepted ideas about congressional electorates and elections is already in progress. This chapter is meant to be a technical and substantive contribution to that process. But it will also point out some important peculiarities in the sample as a caution against drawing overly general conclusions from the evidence of a single study which, as it happens, markedly exaggerates the strength of incumbents and the weakness of challengers.

The other substantive chapters in this volume make it clear that the image of the congressional voter arising from earlier survey studies (Stokes and Miller, 1966; Arseneau and Wolfinger, 1973) is no longer tenable. The notion that congressional voters rely on simple cues of party, incumbency, a familiar name, or their feelings about the president for their voting decisions conformed to the evidence at hand, but

AUTHOR'S NOTE: The data used in the article were made available in part by the Inter-university Consortium for Political and Social Research. The data for the American National Election Study, 1978, were originally collected by the Center for Political Studies of the Institute for Social Research, the University of Michigan, under a grant from the National Science Foundation. Neither the original collectors of the data nor the consortium bear any responsibility for the analyses or interpretations presented here. Warren Miller very kindly helped me acquire the data from the consortium, but he bears no responsibility for what I have done with it either.

the evidence was generated by survey instruments which did not tap other, more important influences on the vote.

The much more elaborate and extensive series of questions asked in the 1978 survey has done much to rectify this deficiency. Several of the new questions are used in the first section of this chapter to clear up a familiar puzzle concerning the electoral effects of incumbency and to establish that voters' evaluations of the candidates are the predominant influence on congressional voting. The 1978 study also includes an assortment of contextual data, some of which are used in the second section of this chapter to expose peculiar biases in the district and individual samples that must be recognized if the survey is to be used effectively.

Work with the study at this stage should still be considered exploratory. Choices must be made about how to use the data; large quantities of new material remain to be sifted. This chapter thus focuses on a few important variables, and the presentation is deliberately elaborate rather than parsimonious.

I

The most important challenge in congressional election research is to account for the enormous advantage now enjoyed by incumbent members of the House of Representatives. The value of incumbency has been thoroughly documented and variously explained (Erikson, 1971; Mayhew, 1974a, 1974b; Nelson, 1976; Cover, 1977; Cover and Mayhew, 1977; Ferejohn, 1977; Fiorina, 1977), but no firm conclusions could be reached without an adequate understanding of how incumbency affects individual voters. National surveys of congressional voters turned up some clues but also produced some puzzles. Stokes and Miller (1966) and Arseneau and Wolfinger (1973) showed that the incumbency advantage was somehow connected to an information advantage. Partisanship aside, voters were more likely to vote for a candidate whose name they could recall, and they were much more likely to recall the names of incumbents than of challengers. But careful analysis of these data indicated that more had to be involved than merely remembering a name. The incumbency advantage increased over time without any parallel increase in the incumbents' recall advantage; voters are more likely to vote for incumbents even when they cannot remember their names (Nelson, 1976; Ferejohn, 1977).

The solution to the mystery proposed by Abramowitz (1975) and Mann (1978) was fully confirmed by the first round of findings reported from the 1978 survey. A question which tapped the ability of respondents to *recognize* the names of candidates from a list (which is all they are required to do in the voting booth) was included along with the usual question about recalling their names.[1] The results are most enlightening. As the figures in Table 1 indicate, voters[2] recognize candidates' names much more readily than they recall them. And the recognition figures are deliberate underestimates. Those respondents who said they recognized the name but could not rate the candidate—and did not recall the name when asked earlier—are not included. If they were, the recognition frequencies for nonincumbents would read about 20 percentage points higher (Mann and Wolfinger, Ch. 2 above).

It is also clear from these figures that the advantage incumbents enjoy in recall is matched by an advantage in recognition. Nearly every voter recognizes the incumbent's name. The shift in focus from name recall to name recognition nicely resolves the apparent anomaly of voters' favoring incumbents without knowing who they are. But the latter does not simply replace the former. Each indicates a different level of familiarity with a candidate; combined, they form a three-point scale: remembering a candidate's name, recognizing it, or neither. The utility of such an index is evident from the data in Tables 2 and 3.

Table 2 is analogous to the tables offered by Stokes and Miller (1966) and Arseneau and Wolfinger (1973) which show the effects of

TABLE 1 Incumbency Status and Voter Familiarity with Candidates for the U.S. House of Representatives, 1978

	Percentage of voters who: *Recalled Name*	*Recognized Name*[a]	*Neither*	*N*
Incumbents	49.9	93.7	6.3	749
Challengers	16.6	45.9	54.1	749
Open-Seat Candidates	39.7	76.3	23.7	232

[a]Includes only respondents who reported voting and who could recognize and rate the candidate on the "feeling thermometer" or, if they could not rate the candidate, could recall the candidate's name.

Source: NES/CPS American National Election Study, 1978

name recall on partisan defections in House elections. The more familiar voters are with a candidate, the more likely they are to vote for him, with the effect also depending, in the same way, on the degree of familiarity with the other candidate. Defections are concentrated in the upper right-hand corner of the table; party loyalty predominates in the lower left-hand corner. Only 1.8% of the partisan voters defect to candidates less familiar than their own; 68.4% defect to candidates who are more familiar. Similarly, independent voters[3] favor more familiar candidates; 86.7% vote for the more familiar candidate when a difference exists.

Why is familiarity of so much benefit to congressional candidates? The answer proposed by Stokes and Miller, that "In the main, to be perceived at all is to be perceived favorably" (1966: 205), has not found much support in later work (Abramowitz, 1975; Jacobson, 1978; Mann, 1978). The issue is more complicated. Respondents were asked for the first time in 1978 what they liked and disliked about the House candidates.[4] As the figures in Table 3 indicate, the more familiar voters are with candidates, the more likely they are to

TABLE 2 Familiarity with Candidates and Voting Behavior in the 1978 House Elections (Percentage of Partisan Voters Defecting)

	Familiarity with own party's candidate:			
	Recalled Name	*Recognized Name*	*Neither*	*Marginal Totals*
Familiarity with other party's candidate:				
Recalled Name	17.6 (142)[a]	68.6 (35)	78.4 (51)	39.0 (228)
Recognized Name	4.1 (49)	25.3 (154)	60.9 (69)	30.5 (272)
Neither	1.7 (121)	0.9 (115)	16.0 (50)	3.8 (286)
Marginal Totals	9.3 (312)	21.1 (304)	52.9 (170)	23.3 (786)

[a]Number of cases from which percentages were computed.

Source: NES/CPS American National Election Study, 1978

find things they both like and dislike about them. Familiarity by no means breeds only favorable responses. Among incumbents and candidates for open seats, the ratio of favorable to unfavorable comments actually declines as familiarity increases, although in absolute terms the gap between them widens (among challengers little change is evident). Familiarity nonetheless remains very helpful at the polls; a suggestion of why this is so will be made later.

The benefits of incumbency obviously extend far beyond greater familiarity. Incumbents are better liked—by a wide margin—as well as better known than are challengers. At any level of familiarity, voters are more inclined to mention something they like, and less able

TABLE 3 Candidate Familiarity and Voters' Likes and Dislikes of House Candidates, 1978 (in percentages)

	Familiarity with candidate: *Recalled Name*	*Recognized Name*	*Neither*	*Total*
Incumbents				
Likes something about candidate	78.6	54.6	12.8	64.0
Dislikes something about candidate	26.9	10.8	2.0	18.2
N of cases	374	328	47	749
Challengers				
Likes something about candidate	38.7	14.6	1.7	11.6
Dislikes something about candidate	41.1	15.9	2.5	12.8
N of cases	124	220	405	749
Open-Seat Candidates				
Likes something about candidate	54.3	36.5	3.6	35.8
Dislikes something about candidate	30.4	14.1	0.0	17.3
N of cases	92	85	55	232

Source: NES/CPS American National Election Study, 1978

TABLE 4 Contact, Familiarity, and Evaluations of House Candidates, 1978 (in percentages)

	VOTER:						
Type of Contact	*Recalls Name*	*Recognizes Name*	*Neither*	*Likes Something*	*Dislikes Something*	*N*	*% of N*
Incumbents							
None	20.5	72.6	27.4	23.3	9.6	73	9.7
Any	53.1	96.0	4.0	68.3	19.2	676	90.3
Personal	67.3	99.6	0.4	85.4	26.5	260	34.7
Mail	58.0	97.8	2.2	71.0	20.5	538	71.8
Mass Media	53.9	96.4	3.6	69.9	20.3	605	80.8
Family & Friends	63.7	99.7	0.3	80.7	24.6	300	40.1
Challengers							
None	3.9	23.6	76.4	2.2	3.1	415	55.4
Any	32.3	73.7	26.3	23.4	24.9	334	44.6
Personal	47.9	91.7	8.3	50.0	47.9	48	6.4
Mail	43.2	80.0	20.0	34.4	29.6	125	16.7
Mass Media	34.7	76.1	23.9	42.7	26.2	305	40.7
Family & Friends	48.2	81.9	18.1	34.9	37.4	83	10.1
Open-Seat Candidates							
None	13.3	43.3	56.7	13.3	3.3	60	25.9
Any	48.8	87.8	12.2	43.6	22.1	176	74.1
Personal	61.5	96.2	3.8	71.2	28.8	52	22.0
Mail	51.0	90.2	9.8	52.0	25.5	102	43.2
Mass Media	50.3	88.8	11.2	45.3	21.7	161	69.4
Family & Friends	70.5	98.4	1.6	59.0	32.8	61	26.3

Source: NES/CPS American National Election Study, 1978

to think of something they do not like, about the incumbent than about the challenger. They mention at least one thing they like about the incumbent 3.5 times as often as they mention at least one thing they do not like; the same ratio for challengers is .91:1. On this, as on most other measures, candidates for open seats fall somewhere in between: 2.07:1.

Voters' likes and dislikes are to some degree a function of familiarity. What determines how well—and how favorably—voters know candidates? Another set of questions asked first in 1978 provides part of the answer. Voters were asked which, if any, of various possible ways they had come into contact with the candidates. I combined the possibilities into four basic modes of contact,[5] and the relationship between these and familiarity and evaluative comments are displayed in Table 4. This table is a rich source of information and merits careful inspection. It shows among other things that first, voters who report any kind of contact are substantially more familiar with the candidate and more likely to offer evaluative comments.

Second, some kinds of contact are more effective than others. Personal contact generally makes the most difference, particularly with regard to favorable comments (but some self-selection is no doubt involved; this kind of contact requires some effort on the part of the respondent, which is more likely if the respondent likes the candidate in the first place). Less effective is indirect "word-of-mouth" contact through experiences of family and friends. This supports the idea that the individual services congressmen perform for constituents have a valuable ripple effect extending beyond the direct beneficiary. Contact via the mails—letters and literature sent directly to individuals at home—appears to be slightly more effective than contact through the mass media.

Third, voters are much more likely to report contacts of all kinds with incumbents than with challengers, and incumbent contacts are more effective in generating a surplus of favorable over unfavorable responses.

Fourth, incumbents enjoy an especially pronounced advantage in mail contacts (compare the size of the gap between mass media and mail contacts for incumbents and nonincumbents), an unmistakable consequence of the frank.

TABLE 5 Candidate Contact and Vote for House Candidates, 1978

	Percentage voting for:		
Type of Contact	*Incumbents*	*Challengers*	*Open-Seat Candidates*
None	63.0	14.5	26.7
Any	80.2	30.2	58.1
Personal	84.2	45.8	73.1
Mail	80.7	38.4	62.8
Mass Media	81.5	30.2	57.8
Family & Friends	85.3	41.0	65.6

Source: NES/CPS American National Election Study, 1978

Contacts with the candidates are also—not surprisingly—related to the vote. The data showing this connection are reported in Table 5. Contacts are particularly important to nonincumbent candidates; voters are twice as likely to vote for them if they have come into contact with them in some way.

It is clear that contacts affect how well voters know and like candidates; that all of these factors are linked in some way to incumbency status; and that, together with incumbency and partisanship, they have a profound impact on the vote. Untangling these effects is no simple matter, but multivariate techniques are of some help. The three sets of multiple regression equations that follow thus provide some useful insights into how these processes work.[6] In particular, they unravel some of the sources of the incumbency advantage. Definitions of the variables in the regressions are listed in Table 6.

The first set of regression equations measures the relative impact of the four types of contact, plus two additional variables—the respondent's degree of interest in the election and the amount of money the candidate spent on the campaign—on the respondent's degree of familiarity with the candidate. The regression estimates for incumbents, challengers, and candidates for open seats, are found in Table 7.

First compare the intercepts. Notice that incumbents are much better known (remember that familiarity is on a scale of 0 to 2) than challengers or candidates for open seats even without taking the other

TABLE 6: Regression Equation Variables

Respondent's vote	1 if Democratic, 0 if Republican
Party identification	1 if strong, weak or independent Democrat, 0 if independent-independent, –1 if strong, weak, or independent Republican
Democrat is incumbent Republican is incumbent	1 if Democrat is incumbent, 0 otherwise, 1 if Republican, 0 otherwise
Familiarity with Democrat Familiarity with Republican	2 if respondent recalls candidate's name, 1 if name is recognized but not recalled, 0 if name is not recognized or recalled[a]
Likes something about Democrat Dislikes something about Democrat Likes something about Republican Dislikes something about Republican	For each variable, 1 if respondent mentions anything liked (or disliked) about the candidate, 0 otherwise
Democrat's thermometer rating Republican's thermometer rating	Respondent's feeling towards candidates on scale of 0 to 100; respondents who have no response or who do not know the candidate are placed at 50
Contact with Democrat Contact with Republican	1 if respondent reports having had any contact with candidate, 0 if not
Types of contact:	
Personal	1 if respondent has met candidate, attended a meeting where candidate spoke, or had contact with candidate's staff, 0 otherwise
Mail	1 if respondent received anything in the mail about the candidate, 0 if not
Mass Media	1 if respondent learned about candidate by reading newspapers and magazines, listening to the radio, or watching television, 0 otherwise
Family & Friends	1 if respondent's family or friends had any contact with the candidate, 0 if not
Identifies with candidate's party	1 if respondent's party identification and candidate's party coincide, 0 if not
Campaign expenditures	Candidate's campaign expenditures in $10,000's
Interest in the campaigns	1 if respondent was very much interested in the campaigns, 0 if not

[a]Familiarity can also be measured by a pair of dummy variables (one each for recall and recognition). The results differ by less than 5 percent from those using the three-point interval scale, indicating that the interval scale assumption is not unwarranted.

variables—in which they also usually have an advantage—into account.

The equations indicate that nonincumbent candidates benefit most from mass media contacts; other forms of contact generally add something to familiarity beyond that gained through mass media contact, but they are clearly less common and less critical. For in-

TABLE 7: Sources of Voters' Familiarity with House Candidates, 1978

	Regression Coefficient	*t-ratio*	*beta*	
Dependent Variable:				
Familiarity with Candidate				
Independent Variables:				
Incumbents (N=749)				
Intercept	.935			
Contact:				
Personal	.193	3.96	.15	
Mail	.284	5.73	.21	R^2=.17
Mass Media	.123	2.16	.08	
Family & Friends	.162	3.43	.13	
Interest in Campaigns	.112	2.54	.09	
Campaign Expenditures	.003	.93	.03	
Challengers (N=749)				
Intercept	.150			
Contact:				
Personal	.106	1.04	.03	
Mail	.182	2.71	.09	R^2=.38
Mass Media	.565	11.10	.37	
Family & Friends	.312	3.98	.13	
Interest in Campaigns	.184	3.93	.11	
Campaign Expenditures	.016	6.50	.21	
Open-Seat Candidates (N=232)				
Intercept	.525			
Contact:				
Personal	.028	.20	.01	
Mail	−.023	−.21	−.01	R^2=.29
Mass Media	.608	5.44	.36	
Family & Friends	.441	3.29	.25	
Interest in Campaigns	.195	2.01	.12	
Campaign Expenditures	.002	.38	.02	

cumbents, the most effective form of contact is through the mails; the benefits of the frank are again apparent. This is consistent with the notion that incumbents "campaign" most effectively by using their official resources before the formal campaign period begins. Nonincumbents must rely to a much greater extent on reaching voters through the mass media during the campaign; campaigns—and thus campaign resources—are therefore crucial to those not blessed with the benefits of incumbency (see Jacobson, 1980, for the full argument).

Voters interested in the campaigns are generally more familiar with the candidates, but not by a great amount. Other individual characteristics—attentiveness to the mass media, education, social class, whether the respondent shared the candidate's party affiliation—were not significantly related to familiarity with candidates and so were dropped from the analysis.

A campaign spending variable is included in this and the next set of equations because I found in previous work that campaign expendi-

TABLE 8: The Effects of Campaign Expenditures on Voters' Familiarity with 1978 House Candidates

	Regression Coefficient	*t-ratio*	*beta*	
Dependent Variable:				
Familiarity with Candidate				
Independent Variables:				
Incumbents (N=749)				
Intercept	1.384			
Campaign Expenditures	.005	1.52	.06	$r^2=.00$
Challengers (N=749)				
Intercept	.402			
Campaign Expenditures	.032	12.26	.41	$r^2=.17$
Open-Seat Candidates (N=232)				
Intercept	.836			
Campaign Expenditures	.016	3.77	.24	$r^2=.06$

tures help determine both how well voters know nonincumbent candidates and how frequently they vote for them (Jacobson, 1978, 1979, 1980). In these particular models, the effect of campaign spending is largely indirect. The more nonincumbents spend on the campaign, the more likely they are to have some kind of contact with voters, thus increasing their familiarity.

The simple relationship between expenditures and familiarity is, for nonincumbents, actually a good deal stronger. The regressions of familiarity on expenditures are reported in Table 8. Campaign spending had no significant effect of any kind on how well voters knew incumbents. This conforms to the patterns of previous years. The most plausible explanation is once again that members of Congress do most of their campaigning before the campaign period, putting the well-known resources that come with the office—notably the frank—to good use. Little additional familiarity is generated by the campaign itself.[7]

Campaign spending does have a substantial effect on how familiar voters are with nonincumbents, particularly challengers. A challenger would typically increase his familiarity by .314 on the scale for each $100,000 spent. *The average challenger would have to spend on the order of $320,000 to become as familiar to voters as the average incumbent.* (Notice that this figure is within the range of the commonly calculated monetary values of incumbency.)

Challengers' spending has direct as well as indirect effects; its regression coefficient is only halved when the contact variables are added to the equation. This is not true of spending by candidates for open seats; campaign spending enhances their familiarity only through its effects on contacts.

The second set of regressions, reported in Tables 9 and 10, assesses the impact of the contact variables—the respondent's degree of interest in the campaigns, the candidate's expenditures, the respondent's degree of familiarity with the candidate, and whether the respondent shares the candidate's party—on the probability that the voter will mention something liked or disliked about the candidate.

As we would expect, partisanship is not irrelevant. Voters are more inclined to mention things they like, and less inclined to men-

TABLE 9: Sources of Voters' "Likes" About 1978 House Candidates

	Regression Coefficient	*t-ratio*	*beta*	
Dependent Variable:				
Voter likes something about candidate				
Independent Variables:				
Incumbents (N=749)				
Intercept	.019			
Identifies with Candidate's Party	.134	4.29	.14	
Familiarity with Candidate	.179	6.44	.23	
Contact:				
Personal	.172	4.61	.17	
Mail	.067	1.74	.06	$R^2=.24$
Mass Media	.147	3.41	.12	
Family & Friends	.095	2.63	.10	
Interest in Campaigns	.035	1.09	.03	
Campaign Expenditures	.003	1.35	.05	
Challengers (N=749)				
Intercept	−.064			
Identifies with Candidate's Party	.086	4.03	.13	
Familiarity with Candidate	.092	5.38	.21	
Contact:				
Personal	.200	4.26	.15	$R^2=.27$
Mail	.091	2.92	.11	
Mass Media	.026	1.02	.04	
Family & Friends	.038	1.03	.04	
Interest in Campaigns	.059	2.68	.09	
Campaign Expenditures	.004	3.57	.13	
Open-Seat Candidates (N=232)				
Intercept	−.148			
Identifies with Candidate's Party	.244	4.54	.25	
Familiarity with Candidate	.156	3.90	.25	
Contact:				
Personal	.285	3.60	.25	$R^2=.34$
Mail	.078	1.23	.08	
Mass Media	.066	1.92	.07	
Family & Friends	−.113	−1.38	−.10	
Interest in Campaigns	.128	2.20	.13	
Campaign Expenditures	.003	1.01	.06	

TABLE 10: Sources of Voters' "Dislikes" About 1978 House Candidates

	Regression Coefficient	*t-ratio*	*beta*	
Dependent Variable:				
Voter dislikes something about candidate				
Independent Variables:				
Incumbents (N=749)				
Intercept	−.055			
Identifies with Candidate's Party	−.083	−3.14	−.11	
Familiarity with Candidate	.109	4.47	.17	
Contact:				
Personal	.066	2.02	.08	R^2=.09
Mail	−.021	−.61	−.02	
Mass Media	.038	1.00	.04	
Family & Friends	.040	1.27	.05	
Interest in Campaigns	.078	2.63	.09	
Campaign Expenditures	.044	2.15	.08	
Challengers (N=749)				
Intercept	−.023			
Identifies with Candidate's Party	−.050	−2.21	−.07	
Familiarity with Candidate	.102	5.62	.23	
Contact:				
Personal	.163	3.27	.12	R^2=.24
Mail	.001	.02	.00	
Mass Media	.076	2.78	.11	
Family & Friends	.081	2.08	.08	
Interest in Campaigns	.067	2.87	.09	
Campaign Expenditures	.005	3.72	.14	
Open-Seat Candidates (N=232)				
Intercept	−.002			
Identifies with Candidate's Party	−.132	−2.76	−.17	
Familiarity with Candidate	.124	3.51	.26	
Contact:				
Personal	.013	.18	.01	R^2=.16
Mail	.072	1.28	.10	
Mass Media	−.033	−.53	−.04	
Family & Friends	.071	.97	.08	
Interest in Campaigns	.008	.15	.01	
Campaign Expenditures	.004	1.83	.13	

tion things they do not like, about candidates of their preferred party. Notice, however, that partisan feelings make the most difference when incumbency is not involved. And partisanship is clearly not the only thing that matters. Familiarity is important in all six equations, affecting both likes and dislikes significantly. Personal contact stands out among the contact variables as having the strongest connection with positive comments about all candidates and, interestingly, negative comments about incumbents and challengers.

Since personal contact weighs more heavily on positive than on negative comments, we might be tempted to conclude that politicians' conventional faith in the personal touch is well-placed, but we should recall once more that voters who already favor the candidate are more likely to avail themselves of the opportunities for personal contact. Still, it is noteworthy that for nonincumbent candidates, personal contact does not significantly increase familiarity over and above the effects of mass media contact, but personal contacts are linked to favorable responses to them apart from the effects of familiarity, whereas mass media contacts are not.

Individuals interested in the campaigns are also more likely to report something they like (about nonincumbents) and dislike (about incumbents and challengers). Again, other individual characteristics were not significantly related to candidate evaluations.

Campaign spending has a small, though statistically significant, effect on the probability that voters like (or dislike) something about the challenger even apart from its effect on familiarity and contacts. The simple correlations reported in Table 11 offer an additional perspective on the connection between campaign spending and the other variables under study. Familiarity, contacts, and likes and dislikes are all much more strongly correlated with campaign spending by nonincumbents than they are with spending by incumbents. The vitality of the challenger's campaign (measured by how much is raised and spent) is especially important in this respect. The general importance of campaign spending to challengers shows itself in a variety of ways, a point emphasized here because it is central to the discussion in the second part of this article.

TABLE 11: Simple Correlations Between Campaign Expenditures and the Familiarity, Contacts, and Likes/Dislikes Variables

	Incumbents	*Challengers*	*Open-Seat Candidates*
Variables:			
Familiarity	.06	.41	.24
Contacts:			
Any	.09	.34	.34
Personal	−.03	.25	.33
Mail	.09	.34	.22
Mass Media	.12	.25	.36
Family & Friends	−.01	.35	.33
Likes something about candidate	.06	.32	.22
Dislikes something about candidate	.10	.32	.21

It is essential to recognize that these equations leave much of the variance in the dependent variables unexplained. And in light of the importance of voters' likes and dislikes about candidates to the voting decision—to be reviewed next—a crucial task for future work with the 1978 study and subsequent surveys is to provide a more thorough account of how voters develop their assessments of candidates.

Of course what finally counts is the effect these variables have on the vote. This is shown by the final set of regression equations reported in Table 12. Sets of variables are added incrementally to the model for a purpose that will become clear as we proceed.

The first equation in Table 12 looks on the vote as a function of party identification and incumbency status. All three variables have a very strong impact on the vote; together, they account for 45.8% of the variance. The multiple-partial correlation coefficient[8] for the incumbency variables, squared, indicates that, when party identification is taken into account, incumbency explains 38% of the variance in the vote.

The second equation adds the candidate familiarity variables to the regression. The impact of incumbency is thereby noticeably reduced;

TABLE 12 Regression Models of the Voting Decision in the 1978 House Elections

	Regression Coefficient	t-ratio	beta	r_p[a]	r_p^2
Dependent Variable:					
Respondent's Vote (N = 873)					
Independent Variables:					
Equation 1					
Intercept	.496				
Party Identification	.229	17.02	.43	.50	.25
Democrat is Incumbent	.235	6.11	.24	.62	.38
Republican is Incumbent	−.260	−6.53	−.25		
$R^2 = .458$					
Equation 2					
Intercept	.542				
Party Identification	.210	16.03	.40	.48	.23
Democrat is Incumbent	.142	3.67	.14	.28	.08
Republican is Incumbent	−.153	−3.76	−.15		
Familiarity with Democrat	.098	5.38	.15	.29	.09
Familiarity with Republican	−.151	−8.13	−.25		
$R^2 = .501$					
Equation 3					
Intercept	.578				
Party Identification	.156	13.04	.30	.41	.17
Democrat is Incumbent	.060	1.74	.06	.11	.01
Republican is Incumbent	−.055	−1.39	−.05		
Familiarity with Democrat	.073	4.09	.11	.22	.05
Familiarity with Republican	−.099	−5.55	−.16		
Likes something about Democrat	.199	7.49	.19	.55	.30
Dislikes something about Democrat	−.189	−6.18	−.14		
Likes something about Republican	−.316	−10.40	−.30		
Dislikes something about Republican	.157	4.81	.11		
$R^2 = .618$					
Equation 4					
Intercept	.533				
Party Identification	.137	11.50	.26	.37	.13
Democrat is Incumbent	.036	1.07	.04	.08	.01
Republican is Incumbent	−.041	−1.15	−.04		
Familiarity with Democrat	.055	3.17	.09	.18	.03
Familiarity with Republican	−.085	−4.89	−.14		
Likes something about Democrat	.112	3.81	.11		

TABLE 12 Regression Models of the Voting Decision in the 1978 House Elections

	Regression Coefficient	*t-ratio*	*beta*	r_p[a]	r_p^2
Dislikes something about Democrat	−.104	−3.21	−.08	.31	.09
Likes something about Republican	−.235	−7.35	−.23		
Dislikes something about Republican	.099	2.95	.07		
Democrat's Thermometer Rating	.0044	6.34	.18	.27	.07
Republican's Thermometer Rating	−.0038	−5.17	−.14		
R^2=.643					
Equation 5					
Intercept	.584				
Party Identification	.134	11.38	.25	.36	.13
Democrat is Incumbent	.012	.35	.01	.04	.00
Republican is Incumbent	−.026	−.73	−.03		
Familiarity with Democrat	.046	2.50	.07	.13	.02
Familiarity with Republican	−.063	−3.43	−.10		
Likes something about Democrat	.104	3.56	.10	.30	.09
Dislikes something about Democrat	−.106	−3.29	−.08		
Likes something about Republican	−.225	−7.06	−.22		
Dislikes something about Republican	.116	3.49	.08		
Democrat's Thermometer Rating	.0042	6.03	.17	.26	.07
Republican's Thermometer Rating	−.0037	−5.05	−.14		
Contact with Democrat	.054	1.90	.05	.14	.02
Contact with Republican	−.114	−4.00	−.11		
R^2=.650					

at this point it would appear that a major portion of the incumbency advantage derives from the greater familiarity incumbents enjoy—the old conventional hypothesis. But equation 3 suggests that the familiarity and, to an even greater extent, incumbency variables are surrogates for variables representing voters' evaluations of the candidates. Each of the four evaluative variables derived from the likes/dislikes questions has a strong impact on the vote; something liked or disliked changes the probability of voting for the Democrat by from .157 to .316 independently of other factors. Collectively, these variables account for an impressive 30% of the variance. The effects of incumbency per se are greatly diminished; the regression coefficients for the incumbency variables are less than one quarter as large as in equation 1, and they no longer differ significantly from zero. The impact of the familiarity variables is cut nearly in half.

The point is clear: *Voters are not attracted by incumbency itself, nor does the incumbency advantage arise merely from greater renown.* Of much greater importance are the very favorable public images members of Congress acquire and the much more negative images—if any—projected by their opponents (a point also emphasized by Mann and Wolfinger, 1979, and Hinckley, 1979). This no doubt reflects members' skill in presenting themselves to constituents (see Fenno, 1978) as well as the publicity resources at their disposal. But it also reflects the capacity of able incumbents to discourage serious opposition. And the incumbents sampled in 1978 were particularly able and so faced particularly lackluster opposition, a point argued more fully in the next section.

Observe, incidentally, that positive responses (likes) have a somewhat greater influence on the vote than do negative responses (dislikes). The general preponderance of likes over dislikes (challengers excepted) is also noteworthy. Contrary to conventional notions, congressional voters do not appear to be choosing the lesser of two evils; rather, they respond most strongly to what they like about the candidates. Even if familiarity generates unfavorable as well as favorable assessments, it helps candidates more than it hurts them if the favorable assessments weigh more heavily in the voting decision.

The fourth equation includes an additional measure of voters' responses to candidates, the "feeling thermometers" through which respondents indicate the degree of warmth or coldness they feel toward a candidate on a scale of 0 to 100. The ratings given on this dimension naturally overlap the likes and dislikes, but both sets of evaluative variables have a strong and separable impact on the vote. Taken together they account for a full 40% of the variance. The second most important variable, party identification, accounts for only 13% of the variance.

The likes/dislikes and feeling thermometer dimensions are not, by this evidence, interchangeable. The former are certainly more useful for probing the *content* of voters' evaluations of candidates, since the response requires that specific things liked and disliked be mentioned. Voters, in fact, evaluate candidates primarily in terms of personal characteristics, job performance, and competence, with relatively few references to general policy positions and even fewer to specific policy stands. It is not clear exactly how the feelings expressed on the thermometer scales ought to be interpreted; they do, however, suggest that phenomena are present that are not tapped by the likes/dislikes questions. If the thermometer instrument remains a standard weapon in the congressional election research arsenal, work needs to be done to ascertain what it actually measures in this context.

Equation 5 includes an additional pair of variables indicating whether the respondent had any kind of contact with either candidate. I had expected that contact with a candidate would influence the vote only indirectly, through its impact on familiarity and evaluations, but it evidently has direct effects as well, particularly for Republican candidates (indeed, most of the coefficients are larger for Republicans than for Democrats; no simple explanation comes to mind). All of the variables together explain 65% of the variance in the vote for Congress, a very satisfactory showing for individual-level data.

Evaluations of President Carter—measured by either the feeling thermometer or a question asking voters to rate his job performance[9]—had no significant impact on the vote when added to equations 4 and 5. Neither, from other evidence (Abramowitz, Ch. 3 above), did economic evaluations influence voters in 1978. This is only surprising if we assume that the robust impact of presidential popularity and economic conditions on aggregate congressional election results, shown most plainly by Tufte (1975, 1978), operates through simple, direct influence on the voters. Most probably it does not, but that argument cannot be pursued here (see Jacobson, 1979, 1980).

Some additional insight into the relationships between the variables in Table 12 can be gleaned from the matrix of simple correlations between each pair of variables, which is found in Table 13. The surprisingly small correlations between the evaluative variables and party identification are especially noteworthy. Evaluations are more strongly related to incumbency than to party affiliation. Their effect on the vote is by no means merely an indirect effect of partisanship.

Correlations among the likes and dislikes variables are low; the largest is –.28. These are evidently quite separable evaluative dimensions, a point reinforced by the substantively and statistically significant impact of all four variables in the regression equations. This is a strong argument for including the likes/dislikes battery of questions in future congressional election surveys. It is also a warning against building simpler indices by, for example, summing the positive and negative responses to both candidates as a general measure of a respondent's orientation to the candidates. Any technique which equates likes and dislikes—or even Democrats and Republicans—is probably unwise.

The evidence from the regressions, then, is that voters' evaluations of the candidates are the basic determinants of the vote. Incumbents prosper because they are well-known and well-liked, and their opponents are neither. The reknown and popularity incumbents enjoy can be traced to their success in reaching voters. Challengers suffer from obscurity and relatively unfavorable evaluations even when they emerge from it; most apparently do not mobilize sufficient campaign resources to overcome either problem. The picture for congressional challengers looks bleak indeed. But it would be a mistake to assume

TABLE 13 Simple Correlations Between Selected Regression Variables

	1	*2*	*3*	*4*	*5*	*6*	*7*	*8*	*9*
1. Respondent's Vote									
2. Party Identification	.50								
3. Democrat is Incumbent	.49	.13							
4. Republican is Incumbent	–.50	–.15	–.76						
5. Familiarity with Democrat	.28	.05	.37	–.42					
6. Familiarity with Republican	–.47	–.22	–.42	.47	.04				
7. Likes something about Democrat	.46	.22	.38	–.39	.49	–.12			
8. Dislikes something about Democrat	–.17	–.12	.03	–.07	.32	.24	.11		
9. Likes something about Republican	–.62	–.29	–.54	.58	–.16	.55	–.28	.13	
10. Dislikes something about Republican	.04	.00	–.06	.08	.15	.29	.16	.20	.12

that this depiction is universally appropriate. *For the 1978 study contains an unusually feeble group of challengers and a collection of voters inordinately hostile to them.* The peculiarities of the sample are the subject of the next section.

II

An immediate sign that something is odd about the 1978 sample is that only 21.5% of the voters surveyed reported voting for the challenger in contests between challengers and incumbents. The average proportion of votes won by challengers in all districts in 1978 was 34.2%. The mean percentage of votes won by challengers in the 75 districts that fell into the sample[10] was somewhat smaller, 31.7%, but is still more than 10 percentage points greater than that reported by the respondents.

One possible explanation is that survey respondents commonly overreport voting for winners, and incumbents almost always win (as did all but one in the 1978 sample). But it is not compatible with evidence from other years. The reported vote for challengers in the 1972 and 1974 surveys was practically identical to the average district-level figures for those years. The data are in Table 14. The figures for 1972 and 1974 are remarkably close; the faithful reflection of party differences is especially striking. Compared to voters surveyed in 1972 and 1974 and to the 1978 electorate in general, the people interviewed in 1978 were extraordinarily hostile to challengers, fond of incumbents, or both.

Some additional evidence suggests that the problem lay with the challengers. Table 15 contains figures comparing the percentage of voters who recalled the names of incumbents, challengers, and candidates for open seats in 1972, 1974, and 1978. Incumbents and candidates for open seats were remembered with about the same frequency in 1978 as in the earlier years. Challengers, on the other hand, were recalled much less frequently in 1978 than in the other years. Challengers from both parties were more obscure in 1978 than even were 1974 Republican challengers, who had been, in comparative terms, a

TABLE 14 The Vote for House Challengers, 1972, 1974 and 1978: District and Survey Data

	Mean district percentage of votes for challengers		*Reported vote for challengers in CPS surveys*		*Difference*
Year					
1972					
Democrats	34.9	(143)[a]	32.9	(222)[b]	−2.0
Republicans	33.9	(176)	35.5	(203)	1.6
Total	34.4	(319)	34.1	(425)	−0.3
1974					
Democrats	43.1	(162)	44.1	(399)	1.0
Republicans	28.6	(157)	27.9	(419)	−0.7
Total	36.0	(319)	35.8	(818)	−0.2
1978					
Democrats	34.2	(109)	22.9	(323)	−11.3
Republicans	34.2	(200)	20.4	(426)	−13.8
Total	34.2	(309)	21.5	(749)	−12.7

[a]Number of Districts
[b]Number of respondents

TABLE 15 Voter Recall of House Candidates 1972, 1974 and 1978

	Percent of voters recalling name of:					
	Incumbents		*Challengers*		*Open-Seat Candidates*	
1972						
Democrats	53.3	(229)[a]	29.1	(196)	42.6	(94)
Republicans	54.1	(196)	28.3	(229)	41.5	(94)
Total	53.6	(425)	28.7	(425)	42.0	(188)
1974						
Democrats	54.2	(419)	43.6	(399)	40.0	(160)
Republicans	63.2	(399)	20.3	(419)	38.1	(160)
Total	58.6	(818)	31.7	(818)	39.1	(320)
1978						
Democrats	48.1	(426)	18.6	(323)	43.1	(116)
Republicans	52.3	(323)	15.0	(426)	36.2	(116)
Total	49.9	(749)	16.6	(749)	39.6	(232)

[a]Number of cases from which percentages were computed.
Sources: CPS American National Election Studies, 1972, 1974 and 1978.

decidedly unimpressive lot (Jacobson, 1980). Since by the usual measures—campaign money, political experience—challengers as a group were no weaker than normal in 1978, something is amiss.

Voters sampled in 1978 do not accurately represent the voting population on at least some important dimensions. A similar problem—which partly if by no means completely explains the bias in the sample of voters—occurs in the district sample. Table 16 compares the districts in the sample to those not in the sample and to all congressional districts with major-party incumbents and challengers[11] across several district-level variables. All but one (of which more in a moment) indicate that unusually weak challengers—or unusually strong incumbents—were sampled. In fact, the Z score for the difference between the sample mean of the 1978 vote and either the population mean or the mean for challengers not in the sample is greater than 2.0; the difference is thus "statistically significant" at .05.

TABLE 16 Comparative Data on House Challengers In and Out of CPS/NES Sample

	In Sample	*Not in Sample*	*Total*
Number of Cases	75	234	309
Percent of Votes, 1978	31.7	35.0	34.3
Percent of Votes, 1976[a]	33.8	36.1	35.3
Campaign Expenditures	$63,061	$ 75,392	$ 72,304
Percent who have held elective office	21.3	18.8	19.4
Challengers who have held elective office			
Number of Cases	16	44	60
Percent of Votes, 1978	36.6	43.9	42.0
Campaign Expenditures	$83,241	$167,149	$144,774
Challengers who have not held elective office			
Number of Cases	59	190	249
Percent of Votes, 1978	30.4	32.9	32.3
Campaign Expenditures	$57,587	$ 54,743	$ 55,417

[a]Percent of votes for candidate of the challenger's party in the district in 1976.
Sources: NES/CPS American National Election Study; Federal Election Commission

The vote and expenditures variables are closely interrelated (Jacobson, 1980). Incumbents who win handily discourage future opposition. Potentially formidable challengers—and their financial backers—prefer to expend their political resources on more promising endeavors. The incumbents in the sample districts did better than average in 1976 and so were faced with weaker than average opposition in 1978. The weakness of the opposition is apparent from both the district and individual survey data. Only 1 of the 19 challengers who managed to win in 1978 was in a sampled district; a more fortunate sample would have included 4 or 5.

One piece of evidence does not fit this picture. Normally, challengers who have held elective office do much better than those who have not. In congressional elections from 1972 through 1978, the former received an average vote eight percentage points higher than the latter. An experienced challenger is normally a formidable challenger. In 1978, a higher proportion of these experienced challengers were found in the sample than out of it. But the challengers in the sample still turned out to be significantly weaker than those not in it. The reason is apparent in the lower part of table 16. Those candidates who usually mount the strongest challenges—ones who have previously won elections—do so because they are able to raise large campaign kitties. Their experience and prominence attract campaign contributions, which they then use to pursue popular reknown and affection and, ultimately, votes (Jacobson, 1980). But the experienced challengers in the 1978 sample raised and spent only half as much as those not in the sample. And so they scarcely benefited from their apparent advantage.

The evidence that campaign expenditures are crucial to challengers is extensive and now includes the data reported in the first section of this article. The challengers in the 1978 district sample—in particular those who had held elective office and thus would normally command the most extensive campaign resources—were, in relative terms, very poorly financed. From this it can be inferred that they conducted less vigorous campaigns, which helps explain why they were less successful than usual in making themselves familiar to voters. In 1972, challengers who had held elective office were recalled by 35.4% of the voters; the recall frequency for the rest was 27.5%. The equivalent figures for 1974 are 42.4% and 28.8%. In 1978, however, such challengers were slightly *less* familiar to voters. And so they did distinctly worse than would otherwise be anticipated on election day.

The 1978 sample is thus distorted in two mutually reinforcing ways. Districts in the sample differ in crucial respects from those not in the sample. But these differences do not fully account for the strong aversion to challengers shown by individual respondents. Both components affect the results (an extremely poor showing by challengers by a variety of measures), making caution in using this study doubly important.

It is plainly unwise to generalize too freely from the 1978 study about the relative strength of incumbents and challengers in House elections. The incumbents sampled in 1978 were politically stronger than average; their opponents were substantially less formidable than normal. The combination makes theoretical sense: Strong incumbents attract weak opposition. But the average incumbent is not so strong—and probably not so well-liked—and the average challenger is not so feeble, obscure, and unpopular. And this should be kept in mind by anyone using the 1978 survey to study congressional elections.

Several other lessons can be drawn from this discussion. One is the value of combining district-level contextual data with the national election surveys. The peculiarities of the sample would be impossible to pinpoint without these data. Another is that replication is particularly important in election research; some phenomena will be unique to a particular election year or sample, and it is necessary to sort them out before building a general theory of voting in congressional elections. Replication of the 1978 study in 1980 will not, however, eliminate all problems associated with the sample. The district sample will remain the same, and so most of the same incumbents will be involved once more. Having done so well in 1978, they can expect relatively feeble opposition once again. The sample of individuals will be different, however. And after 1980 a new district sample will be drawn (reapportionment and redistricting require it), so any sampling anomalies will not be repeated beyond the next election.

I do not mean to overstate the consequences of the sampling problem. The 1978 study remains an extraordinarily rich and useful source of information on congressional elections. The findings reported in the first section are by no means undermined by recognizing that we are dealing with unusually effective incumbents and ineffective challengers. Indeed, they help to explain why this is important. It will be fascinating to compare 1978 with later studies in which this condition no longer holds.

NOTES

1. The "feeling thermometer" was used to test whether the respondent recognized a candidate's name. Respondents were asked to indicate their degree of warmth or coldness toward a list of individuals on a scale of 0 to 100. If they did not recognize a name listed, they were to say so and proceed to the next without offering a "temperature."

2. Only survey respondents who reported voting are included in any of the analyses reported in this article.

3. Only independents leaning toward neither party are classified as independents in this article, since the independent leaners generally behave like weak partisans (see Brody, 1977).

4. The questions can be summarized as, "Was there anything in particular that you liked (disliked) about [name of candidate], the Democratic (Republican) candidate for the U.S. House of Representatives? What was that?"

5. For details on the classification, see Table 6.

6. Although probit is the preferred technique of analysis for dichotomous dependent variables (Áldrich and Cnudde, 1975), as some of these are, ordinary least squares regressions are better suited to our purposes at this stage because the results are much easier to interpret.

7. This holds unless the incumbent spends an extraordinary amount of money, as did some Republican incumbents coping with the effects of Watergate in 1974 (see Jacobson, 1980).

8. The multiple-partial correlation is defined as "a multiple correlation between a dependent variable and several independent variables, controlling for one or more independent variables" (Blalock, 1960: 350).

9. Respondents were asked how they would rate the job President Carter had been doing over the previous two years—very good, good, fair, poor, or very poor.

10. Only districts in which a Democratic incumbent faced a Republican challenger—or vice versa—are included; districts in which only minor-party candidates challenged the incumbent are omitted.

11. Campaign spending data were not available for four districts which met these other criteria, so they were excluded.

REFERENCES

ABRAMOWITZ, A. J. (1975) "Name familiarity, reputation, and the incumbency effect in a congressional election." Western Political Quarterly 28: 668–684.

ALDRICH, J. and C. F. CNUDDE (1975) "Probing the bounds of conventional wisdom: A comparison of regression, probit, and discriminant analysis." American Journal of Political Science 19: 571–608.

ARSENEAU, R. B. and R. E. WOLFINGER (1973) "Voting behavior in congressional elections." Presented at the 1973 annual meeting of the American Political Science Association, New Orleans, Louisiana, September 4–8.

BLALOCK, H. M. (1960) Social Statistics. New York: McGraw-Hill.

BRODY, R. A. (1977) "Stability and change in party identification: Presidential to off-years." Presented at the 1977 annual meeting of the American Political Science Association, Washington, D.C., September 1–4.

COVER, A. D. (1977) "One good term deserves another: The advantage of incumbency in congressional elections." American Journal of Political Science 21: 523–542.

______ and D. R. MAYHEW (1977) "Congressional dynamics and the decline of competitive congressional elections," in L. C. Dodd and B. I. Oppenheimer (eds.) Congress Reconsidered. New York: Praeger.

ERIKSON, R. S. (1971) "The advantage of incumbency in congressional elections." Polity 3: 395–405.

FENNO, R. F., Jr. (1978) Home Style: House Members in Their Districts. Boston: Little, Brown.

FEREJOHN, J. A. (1977) "On the decline in competition in congressional elections." American Political Science Review 71: 166–176.

FIORINA, M. P. (1977) "The case of the vanishing marginals: The bureaucracy did it." American Political Science Review 71: 177–181.

JACOBSON, G. C. (1980) Money in Congressional Elections. New Haven, CT: Yale University Press.

______ (1979) "On adding contextual variables to national election surveys: Some examples from the 1972 and 1974 National Election Studies." Presented at the annual meeting of the Midwest Political Science Association, Chicago, April 19–21.

______ (1978) "The effects of campaign spending in congressional elections." American Political Science Review 72: 469–491.

MANN, T. E. (1978) Unsafe at Any Margin: Interpreting Congressional Elections. Washington, DC: American Enterprise Institute for Public Policy Research.

MAYHEW, D. R. (1974a) Congress: The Electoral Connection. New Haven, CT: Yale University Press.

______ (1974b) "Congressional elections: The case of the vanishing marginals." Polity 6: 295–317.

NELSON, C. J. (1976) "The effects of incumbency on voting in congressional elections, 1964–1974." Presented at the 1976 annual meeting of the American Political Science Association, Chicago, September 2–5.

STOKES, D. E. and W. E. MILLER (1966) "Party government and the saliency of Congress," in A. Campbell et al. (eds.) Elections and the Political Order. New York: Wiley.

TUFTE, E. R. (1978) Political Control of the Economy. Princeton, NJ: Princeton University Press.

——— (1975) "Determinants of the outcomes of midterm congressional elections." American Political Science Review 69: 812–826.

6

INCUMBENT POPULARITY AND ELECTORAL SUCCESS

GLENN R. PARKER

One of the most salient features of congressional elections is the electoral safety of incumbents. Although there are many electoral advantages to incumbency, such as the availability of campaign funding and the perquisites of office (Mayhew, 1974; Cover, 1977; Parker, forthcoming b), the ability of an incumbent to maintain a favorable image among constituents may be a central component in electoral success. Evaluations of House incumbents are remarkably favorable, and this popularity may explain the relative invincibility of incumbents at the polls. Not only are popular incumbents better able to retain electoral support but also their standing within their districts may actually deter serious electoral challenges. Qualified and potentially strong challengers may avoid entering contests with popular incumbents, especially in light of the incumbent's arsenal of perquisites and ability to cultivate a favorable image among constituents. This difficulty in recruiting viable challengers may allow incumbents

AUTHOR'S NOTE: The ideas expressed in this article were initially formulated in a memorandum to the Board of Overseers of the National Election Studies in 1977. Subsequent conversations with Richard Fenno, Morris Fiorina, and Barbara Hinckley helped in the further development of the themes presented in this article. The data used here were made available by the Inter-university Consortium for Political and Social Research. These data were originally collected by the Center for Political Studies of the Institute for Social Research, the University of Michigan, under a grant from the National Science Foundation. Neither the original collectors of the data nor the consortium bears any responsibility for the analyses or interpretations presented in this article. An earlier version of this article was presented at the 1979 annual meeting of the American Political Science Association, Washington, D.C., August 31–September 3.

to confront relatively weak electoral competition in their reelection campaigns.

Incumbent popularity appears to be the mediating mechanism through which the characteristics and behavior of incumbents are translated into electoral support. The criteria that constituents employ in their evaluations may help foster the favorable image they have of their representative. Ironically, the incumbent may be indirectly (or even directly) responsible for the criteria that constituents employ in their evaluations. Since constituents are normally uninformed about the behavior of their representative, House incumbents are able to "control" the information that constituents use in forming evaluative judgments of their performance. This "control" is exercised by focusing constituent attention on activities and attributes that will enhance the incumbent's popularity within the district. As a consequence, the criteria that constituents use to evaluate their representative tend to place incumbents in a favorable light (Parker and Davidson, 1979).

Implicit in this argument is the assumption that incumbents display distinct and characteristic behavior patterns in relating to their districts. Evidence to support this assumption is provided by Fenno's (1978) study of House members during their district visits. Fenno describes the district-oriented behavior of incumbents in terms of three characteristics: "allocation of resources," "presentation of self," and "explanations of Washington activity." These behaviors are classified under the rubric of home-style behaviors—the ways in which House members cultivate their constituencies (Fenno, 1978: 31); each of these behaviors plays a role in enhancing the incumbent's popularity. The allocation of the incumbent's resources to district services (e.g., helping constituents with their problems, informing constituents about governmental activity) reflects the amount of attention an incumbent pays to the district and demonstrates his/her concern for the district and the plight of the constituents. Further, incumbents use their district visits as a means of generating constituent trust which in turn helps to boost their popularity. They create this trust by emphasizing their qualifications for office and by exhibiting a sense of identification and empathy with the interests of their constituents (Fenno, 1978: 57). Finally, incumbents develop explanations to rationalize their voting records as well as their quests for power (Fenno, 1978: Ch. 5); these explanations are formulated to enhance constituent trust and the legitimacy of their actions in Washington.

The incumbent thus generates a positive image of his/her performance in office. It is clear, therefore, that home-style behaviors are developed with the aim of placing the incumbent in a favorable light among constituents. Consequently, the popular standing of the incumbent can be expected to be influenced by home-style behavior, especially since constituents are dependent upon the information that incumbents supply about themselves and their activities.

This approach to the electoral advantage of incumbency integrates the ideas of Fenno (1978), Fiorina (1977), and Mayhew (1974). It incorporates the notion of home style which Fenno uses to describe the ways in which incumbents cultivate their districts and electoral support. The importance of district service to electoral support is introduced by Fiorina who suggests that constituent service is a key electoral advantage of incumbency. Finally, the method of translating this service into support is suggested by Mayhew, when he points out that House incumbents use the perquisites of office to "advertise" and "claim credit" for helping the district and its constituents. According to Mayhew, such publicity helps incumbents to stave off electoral defeat. These behaviors can be viewed as direct and indirect causes of incumbent popularity. Incumbent popularity is defined in this article as constituent evaluations (ratings) of the job performance of the incumbent representative.

In this analysis, incumbent popularity is conceptualized as the mediating mechanism through which advertising, credit claiming, constituency service, and home-style behaviors are translated into electoral support. Home-style behavior serves to generate electoral support by placing the performance of the incumbent in a favorable light. Since district service is one incumbent activity that constituents view favorably, it results in positive impressions of the incumbent's overall performance. Finally, as incumbents advertise and claim credit for their achievements, they once again focus constituent attention on those activities that place them in a favorable light.[1] That is, the member's ability to advertise service to the district and to claim credit for helping constituents and channeling federal benefits to the district enhances the saliency of these popularity-generating achievements. The incumbents' emphasis on popularity-generating activities and their ability to enhance the saliency of such activity within the district provide them with an electoral edge. In sum, the popularity of incumbents results from the emphasis that House members place upon those activities that generate positive images of their performance. The purpose of this analysis is to examine the accuracy and validity of this proposition.

Since we are interested in the electoral impact of incumbent popularity, the analysis will focus on two-party contested elections (multicandidate races are excluded from the analysis), which are the most frequent type of congressional race. The data for this analysis are derived from the Center for Political Studies' 1978 National Election Study; the study will also use the Obey Commission's survey of House members (Commission on Administrative Review, 1977) to link the behavior of incumbents to constituent evaluations and electoral support. The analysis will examine, first, the sources of incumbent popularity and, then, the relevance of incumbent popularity to electoral support.

I
SOURCES OF INCUMBENT POPULARITY

There are a number of reasons for incumbent popularity within the district. The personal characteristics and home-style behavior of incumbents place them in a favorable light and tend to produce overall positive evaluations of incumbent performance. Mass mailings and media coverage regarding the activities of House members may also enhance the incumbent's image by expanding constituent awareness of their representative's accomplishments and district service. Finally, attitudes toward political institutions, like Congress, and the major political parties can color constituent perceptions of the performance of their representative. In the following sections, each of these sources of incumbent popularity will be examined: incumbent characteristics and behavior, institutional evaluations, and partisan attitudes.

DISTRICT ATTENTION

One category of incumbent activity that effectively generates favorable images of the representative's performance is district attentiveness. This complex concept entails behaviors on the part of incumbents that are designed to demonstrate the members' concern for the district and its constituents. Constituency service is only one aspect of attentiveness, but it is a behavior that constituents appreciate and reward. The effectiveness of incumbents in responding to the complaints and inquiries of their constituents[2] generates favorable impressions of the incumbent's performance (Democratic incumbent, gamma = .32; Republican incumbent, gamma = .41) and results in a greater awareness of the attentiveness of the incumbent[3] (Democratic incumbent, gamma = .72; Republican incumbent, gamma = .70).

Aside from personal assistance to constituents, district attentiveness also embodies a representational component: a feeling on the part of constituents that the incumbent is listening to them and expressing their views in Congress. In fact, some of the major topics addressed by members in their explanations of Washington activity are their policy positions and voting behavior. This explanatory activity is the means by which "some constituents come to have a 'sense' or 'impression' or 'idea' about a member's 'overall voting record' or 'voting pattern,' or 'policy positions'" (Fenno, 1978: 145). As Table 1 illustrates, the popularity of incumbents is closely tied to constituent perceptions of the extent to which they agree or disagree with the incumbent's voting record. Perceptions of vote agreement, however, are not necessarily based upon a broad or precise awareness of the incumbent's actual voting behavior (Table 2). Even among those who disagree with the incumbent's voting record, close to three of every five respondents are unaware of their representative's vote on a single issue. In addition, perceptions of vote agreement are not strongly related to constituent perceptions of the ideological differences between themselves and the incumbent[4] (Democratic incumbent, gamma = .10; Republican incumbent, gamma = −.17). Not only are constituents generally ignorant of their representative's voting record (Stokes and Miller, 1962) but incumbents are also quite adept at preventing their votes from becoming salient considerations to their constituents. Incumbents have a number of strategies for tempering the impact of their voting behavior on citizen perceptions of their performance. House members may sense that they can avoid accusa-

TABLE 1 Perceived Voting Agreement and Incumbent Popularity

	Extent of Agreement with Incumbent's Voting[b]			
Evaluation of Incumbent[a]	*Agree*	*Agree Somewhat*	*Neither Agree nor Disagree*	*Disagree*[c]
DEMOCRATIC INCUMBENT:				
Very good	71.4%	20.3%	3.2%	—
Good	25.5	59.9	41.9	14.4
Fair	2.0	18.6	48.4	38.1
Poor	1.0	1.2	6.5	38.1
N =	98	172	62	42
		gamma = .82		
REPUBLICAN INCUMBENT:				
Very good	57.1%	19.8%	5.1%	6.1%
Good	42.9	62.6	38.5	24.2
Fair	—	16.8	46.2	42.4
Poor	—	.8	10.3	27.3
N =	56	131	39	33
		gamma = .74		

[a]Question: "In general, how would you rate the job that your U.S. Representative (name) has been doing?"; the initial coding categories of "poor" and "very poor" have been combined because of the small number of cases contained within these two categories.
[b]Question: "Now we would like to know how much you generally agree or disagree with the way (name of incumbent) has voted on bills that have come up in the U.S. House of Representatives in Washington?"
[c]Combines the initial coding categories of "disagree somewhat" and "disagree" because of the small number of cases residing in these two categories.

TABLE 2 Perceived Voting Agreement and Awareness of Incumbent's Votes

	Extent of Agreement with Incumbent's Voting[a]			
Awareness of Any Vote Cast by Incumbent	*Agree*	*Agree Somewhat*	*Neither Agree nor Disagree*	*Disagree*[b]
DEMOCRATIC INCUMBENT:				
Aware of vote	37.8%	18.5%	5.3%	40.9%
Not aware of vote	62.2	81.5	94.7	59.1
N =	98	173	75	44
		gamma = .22		
REPUBLICAN INCUMBENT:				
Aware of vote	32.1%	29.8%	8.9%	42.4%
Not aware of vote	67.9	70.2	91.1	57.6
N =	56	131	45	33
		gamma = .08		

[a]Question: "Now we would like to know how much you generally agree or disagree with the way (name of incumbent) has voted on bills that have come up in the U.S. House of Representatives in Washington."
[b]Combines the initial coding categories of "disagree somewhat" and "disagree" because of the small number of cases contained within these two categories.

tions of misrepresentation by merely refraining from casting a "string" of wrong votes; they may also emphasize their attention to district matters as compensation for their votes in Congress; or they may simply avoid calling attention to votes that may be at odds with district sentiment. In some instances, incumbents may be able to gracefully explain an unpopular vote. The fact that only 15% of the public express any disagreement with their representative's voting record is testimony to the ability of incumbents to effectively generate constituent trust and explain their votes and/or the lack of constituent awareness of their representative's votes.

The saliency of an incumbent's district attentiveness appears to be a potent influence on his or her popularity. For instance, those respondents who mention the district attentiveness of their representative are more positive in their overall evaluations of the incumbent's performance (Table 3). Further, district attentiveness is extremely salient to constituents; as Figure 1 reveals, constituents frequently mention district attentiveness as something they like or dislike about their representative. The positive valence attached to such district attention is evident in the fact that attentiveness is *infrequently* mentioned as something that constituents dislike about the incumbent. In

TABLE 3 Saliency of Incumbent's District Attentiveness and Incumbent Popularity

	Democratic Incumbent		*Republican Incumbent*	
Evaluation of Incumbent[a]	*No Mention of Attentiveness*[b]	*Mention of Attentiveness*	*No Mention of Attentiveness*	*Mention of Attentiveness*
Very good	17.5%	35.1%	14.0%	27.9%
Good	42.6	48.8	46.5	52.3
Fair	34.4	13.1	35.0	15.1
Poor	5.6	3.0	4.5	4.7
N =	486	168	400	86
	Gamma = −.44		Gamma = −.37	

[a] Question: "In general, how would you rate the job that your U.S. Representative (name) has been doing?"; the initial coding categories of "poor" and "very poor" have been combined because of the small number of cases contained within these two categories.

[b] Mention of some aspect of the incumbent's district attentiveness as something "liked" or "disliked" about the incumbent.

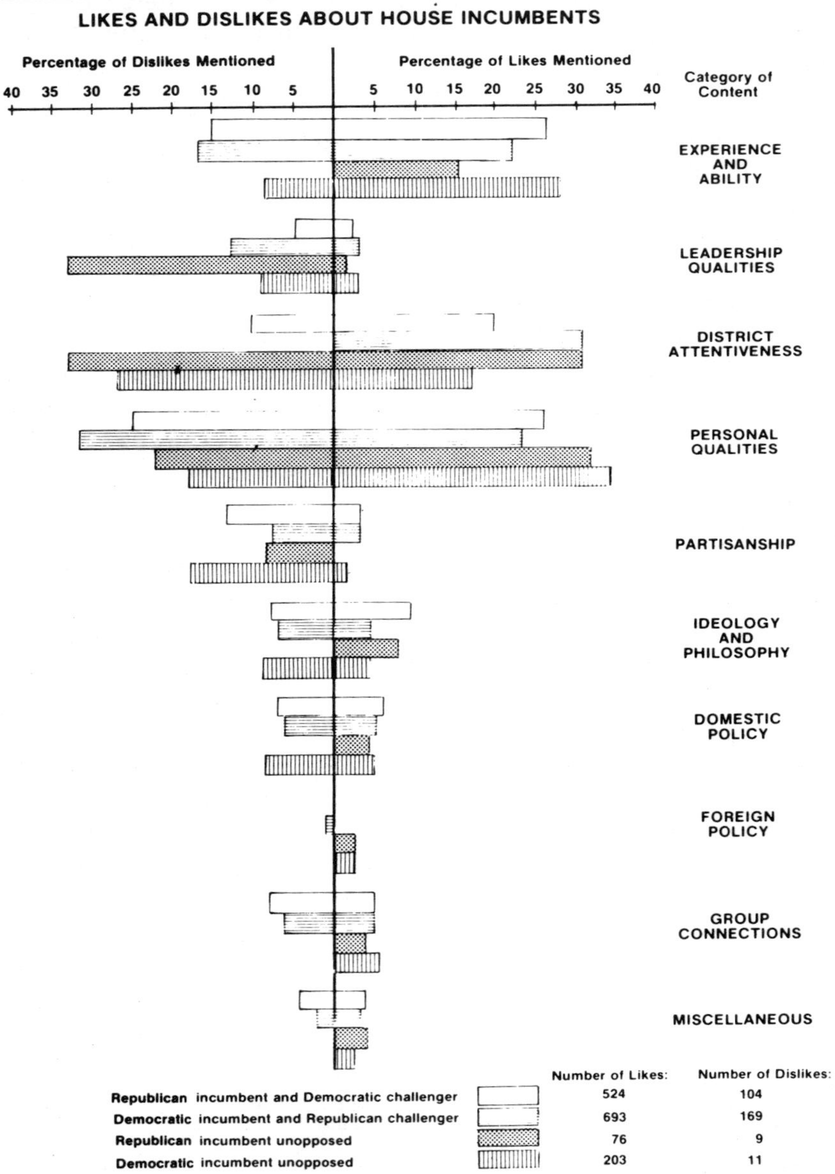

LIKES AND DISLIKES ABOUT HOUSE INCUMBENTS
Percentage of Dislikes Mentioned
Percentage of Likes Mentioned
40 35 30 25 20 15 10 5
5 10 15 20 25 30 35 40
Category of Content
EXPERIENCE AND ABILITY
LEADERSHIP QUALITIES
DISTRICT ATTENTIVENESS
PERSONAL QUALITIES
PARTISANSHIP
IDEOLOGY AND PHILOSOPHY
DOMESTIC POLICY
FOREIGN POLICY
GROUP CONNECTIONS
MISCELLANEOUS
Number of Likes:
Number of Dislikes:
Republican incumbent and Democratic challenger 524 104
Democratic incumbent and Republican challenger 693 169
Republican incumbent unopposed 76 9
Democratic incumbent unopposed 203 11

Figure 1

contrast, rarely is any mention of attentiveness associated with what constituents like about challengers (Table 4). The salience of the representative's attentiveness may reflect a conscious decision on the part of the incumbent to emphasize attention to district affairs in his or her behavior—a resource allocation decision.

The saliency of attentiveness may be due to the effectiveness of the advertising and credit-claiming activities of House members. There are various channels for the representative to disseminate this information to the district, such as radio, television, newspapers, and franked mass mailings; as Tables 5 and 6 demonstrate, the saliency of an incumbent's district attentiveness is related to media recognition and mass mailings.[5] Further, constituents who receive mass mailings from their representatives are better informed about the incumbent's service to the district[6] (Democratic incumbent, gamma = .27; Republican incumbent, gamma = .33). This awareness increases the

TABLE 4 Likes and Dislikes about the Democratic Incumbent

	Democratic Incumbent				*Republican Challenger*			
	Likes	*N*	*Dislikes*	*N*	*Likes*	*N*	*Dislikes*	*N*
Experience/ Ability	21.5%	149	17.2%	29	12.8%	11	6.3%	5
Leadership Qualities	2.5	17	13.0	22	8.1	7	10.1	8
District Attention	29.7	206	7.7	13	2.3	2	0	0
Personal Qualities	23.2	161	32.5	55	40.7	35	30.4	24
Party	2.9	20	7.7	13	7.0	6	36.7	29
Ideology/ Philosophy	4.3	30	7.1	12	11.6	10	11.4	9
Domestic Policy	4.5	31	5.9	10	9.3	8	0	0
Foreign Policy	.6	4	1.2	2	1.2	1	0	0
Group Identification	5.2	36	5.9	10	3.5	3	1.3	1
Miscellaneous	5.6	39	1.8	3	3.5	3	3.8	3
Number of Cases		693		169		86		79

TABLE 4 (cont.) Likes and Dislikes about the Republican Incumbent

	Republican Incumbent				*Democratic Challenger*			
	Likes	*N*	*Dislikes*	*N*	*Likes*	*N*	*Dislikes*	*N*
Experience/ Ability	25.4%	133	15.4%	16	14.1%	14	22.9%	16
Leadership Qualities	2.1	11	4.8	5	4.0	4	4.3	3
District Attention	18.7	98	10.6	11	6.1	6	2.9	2
Personal Qualities	26.3	138	25.0	26	38.4	38	22.9	16
Party	2.7	14	13.5	14	9.1	9	24.3	17
Ideology/ Philosophy	8.8	46	10.6	11	12.1	12	11.4	8
Domestic Policy	6.1	32	6.7	7	9.1	9	1.4	1
Foreign Policy	.4	2	.1	1	0	0	0	0
Group Identification	5.3	28	7.7	8	3.0	3	1.4	1
Miscellaneous	4.2	22	4.8	5	4.0	4	8.6	6
Number of Cases		524		104		99		70

TABLE 5 Media Recognition and the Saliency of Incumbent's District Attentiveness

Mention of Incumbent's[a]	*Extent of Media Recognition of Incumbent*[b]			
District Attentiveness	*0*	*1*	*2*	*3*
DEMOCRATIC INCUMBENTS:				
No mention of attentiveness	95.6%	77.3%	72.0%	66.9%
Mention of attentiveness	4.4	22.7	28.0	33.1
N =	318	225	200	157
		gamma = .51		
REPUBLICAN INCUMBENTS:				
No mention of attentiveness	96.1%	85.3%	81.0%	79.4%
Mention of attentiveness	3.9	14.7	19.0	20.6
N =	155	197	163	107
		gamma = .36		

[a]Mention of some aspect of the incumbent's district attentiveness as something "liked" or "disliked" about the incumbent.
[b]This variable is an index based upon the extent to which the respondent has read about the incumbent in a newspaper or magazine, has heard the incumbent on the radio, or has seen him/her on the television.

likelihood that attentiveness will be mentioned in constituent evaluations of the incumbent (Democratic incumbents, gamma = .66; Republican incumbents, gamma = .57).

EXPERIENCE AND ABILITY

Another frequently mentioned constituent concern is the experience and ability of the representative. These characteristics can be extremely beneficial for the district; capable and experienced mem-

TABLE 6 Mass Mailings and the Saliency of Incumbent's District Attentiveness

	Democratic Incumbent		*Republican Incumbent*	
Mention of Incumbent's District Attentiveness[a]	*Received Mail*[b]	*No Mail Received*	*Received Mail*	*No Mail Received*
No mention of attentiveness	69.8%	88.8%	78.1%	94.5%
Mention of attentiveness	30.2	11.2	21.9	5.5
N=	493	197	356	163
	gamma = −.55		gamma = −.66	

[a]Mention of some aspect of the incumbent's district attentiveness as something "liked" or "disliked" about the incumbent.
[b]Question: "Have you come into contact with or learned anything about (him/her—incumbent) through any of these ways? Received something in the mail from him/her?

TABLE 7 Saliency of Incumbent's Experience and Incumbent Popularity

	Democratic Incumbent		*Republican Incumbent*	
Evaluation of Incumbent[a]	*No Mention of Experience*	*Mention of Experience*[b]	*No Mention of Experience*	*Mention of Experience*
Very good	19.3%	30.6%	13.4%	24.3%
Good	42.1	51.0	45.7	52.2
Fair	34.2	12.1	36.0	19.9
Poor	4.4	6.4	4.9	3.7
N=	497	157	350	136
	gamma = −.32		gamma = −.32	

[a]Question: "In general, how would you rate the job that your U.S. Representative (name) has been doing?"; the initial coding categories of "poor" and "very poor" have been combined because of the small number of cases contained within these two categories.
[b]Mention of some aspect of the incumbent's experience as something "liked" or "disliked" about the incumbent.

bers may be better able to expedite constituent inquiries and complaints, to advance district interests, to expouse district views, and to secure federal funds for the district. As a consequence, experience and ability are characteristics that incumbents emphasize in their interactions with their constituents (Fenno, 1978: 57). It is not surprising, therefore, to find that the incumbent's experience and abilities are frequently mentioned in constituent evaluations of their representatives (Figure 1) and that these attributes tend to generate overall positive impressions of the incumbent's performance (Table 7). The saliency of the incumbent's experience and abilities provides members with another source of popularity and an electoral edge for, as Fenno points out, "Indeed, the opportunity to make a presentation of a qualified self is a potent incumbent advantage" (1978: 137).

PERSONAL CHARACTERISTICS

The most frequently mentioned reason for liking or disliking the incumbent is his/her personal characteristics. Figure 1 demonstrates that personal characteristics are far more apt to be mentioned as something constituents like, rather than dislike, about their representative. While House members tend to occupy the highest education and occupation levels of society, citizens do not appear to perceive their representatives in these social, demographic, or occupational terms. The personal attributes that are most salient to constituents pertain to socially prescribed ethics, norms, and mores; for instance, the honesty, sincerity, fairness, and dedication of the representatives are characteristics that attract constituent attention. However, these attributes do not appear to enhance the popularity of Democrats and Republicans uniformly: Only the popularity of Republican incumbents appears to be influenced by the saliency of personal characteristics (Democratic incumbent, gamma = .08; Republican incumbent, gamma = .29).

PERSONAL CONTACT

Personal contact appears to be an extremely potent influence on the popularity of incumbents in that it tends to reflect favorably on incumbents and to encourage positive impressions of their performance. The more extensive the amount of personal contact, the more positive the evaluations of the incumbent's performance tend to be (Table 8). Personal contact with constituents is also an element of an incumbent's home style and reflects the member's decision to allocate a scarce resource (personal attention) to constituent matters.

By serving as a direct example of the incumbent's concern for the district and constituents, personal contact may help to shape constituent perceptions of the attentiveness of the representative (Democratic incumbent gamma = .56; Republican incumbent, gamma = .50).[7] It may also provide members with a channel through which they can convey a sense of empathy or identification with their constituents' concerns—"I understand your situation and I care about it" or "I think the way you do and I care about the same things you do" (Fenno, 1978: 58–59). Further, personal contact is an effective means for structuring constituent perceptions of the incumbent's *qualifications*—experience and abilities (Democratic incumbent, gamma = .47; Republican incumbent, gamma = .51). Hence, like the attentiveness, qualifications, and characteristics of incumbents, personal contact tends to place House members in a favorable light and to generate positive over all images of the incumbent's performance.

TABLE 8 Personal Contact and Incumbent Popularity

	Extent of Personal Contact with Incumbent[b]					
	Democratic Incumbent			*Republican Incumbent*		
Evaluation of Incumbent[a]	*0*	*1*	*2–3*	*0*	*1*	*2–3*
Very good	16.3%	24.8%	45.2%	12.1%	23.1%	35.8%
Good	44.0	48.8	38.7	44.2	56.4	56.6
Fair	34.6	24.0	8.6	38.3	17.9	5.7
Poor	5.0	2.4	7.5	5.4	2.6	1.9
N=	436	125	93	355	78	53.
	gamma = −.35			gamma = −.50		

[a] Question: "In general, how would you rate the job that your U.S. Representative (name) has been doing?" The initial coding categories of "poor" and "very poor" have been combined because of the small number of cases contained within these two categories.

[b] This variable is an index based upon the total number of ways in which the respondent has had some personal contact with the incumbent—meeting him/her personally, attending a meeting or gathering where he/she spoke, talking to the incumbent or someone in his/her office.

CONGRESS, THE PRESIDENT, AND THE POLITICAL PARTIES

A predictable feature of most congressional contests is the tendency for incumbents to run against Congress as well as their electoral challengers (Fenno, 1975). This posturing is easy to do because it is relatively cost-free for the incumbent:

> It is easy for each congressman to explain to his own supporters why he cannot be blamed for the performance of the collectivity. It is doubly easy to do because the internal diversity and decentralization of the institution provide such a variety of collegial villains to flay before one's supporters at home [Fenno, 1979: 167].

Since the public is easily disillusioned with Congress' inability to resolve societal problems, the congressional environment is rarely viewed in positive terms (Parker and Davidson, 1979), and few constituents harbor favorable impressions of Congress (Davidson and Parker, 1972). It might be suggested that attacks on Congress may be one means by which incumbents attempt to diffuse the impact that persistently low levels of congressional popularity may have on the incumbent's popularity. The question to be asked is: Do House incumbents need to denigrate Congress if the criteria utilized in evaluating the institution are different from, and less demanding than, the criteria cited in constituent evaluations of their representative? There seems to be at least some rationale for attacks on Congress because congressional popularity does exercise a significant influence on incumbent popularity: The more negative the evaluation of Congress, the lower the incumbent's popularity (Democratic incumbent, gamma = .27).[8] Even the relatively weak relationship between congressional popularity and the popularity of Republican incumbents (gamma = .12) becomes significant when the confounding influences of other variables are partialed out (Table 9). It appears, therefore, that neither Democratic nor Republican incumbents are immune from the effects of congressional popularity; yet, these relationships are not strong.

Republican incumbents seem to fare better when the effects of presidential popularity are considered. Evaluations of President Carter's performance in office are positively related to the popularity of

Democratic incumbents (gamma = .22), but not Republican incumbents (gamma = .00). As the party in control of both the White House and Congress, the popularity of Democratic incumbents appears to be influenced by popular evaluations of the performance of the institutions they control. Fortunately for Democratic incumbents, these relationships are modest.

A stronger, and more symmetrical, relationship exists between incumbent popularity and party identification. Favorable attitudes toward one party or the other can shape perceptions of candidates. Not surprisingly, Democrats and Republicans tend to view incumbents from their own party in a more favorable light than incumbents from the opposition party (Democratic incumbents, gamma = .28; Republican incumbents, gamma = −.26). Partisanship is, therefore, another influence on the popularity of incumbents.

II
IMPORTANT PREDICTORS OF INCUMBENT POPULARITY

When incumbent popularity is regressed upon the most significant predictors,[9] one similarity emerges: The popularity of both Democratic and Republican incumbents is strongly influenced by the perceived vote agreement between the respondent and the representative (Table 9). In fact, perception of vote agreement is the most important predictor of incumbent popularity. This suggests that members' explanations of their policy activities in Washington and their ability to generate constituent trust are important influences on their popularity among constituents. This is the one point of similarity between Democratic and Republican incumbents.

Aside from the impact of perceived vote agreement, the popularity of Democratic incumbents is largely influenced by the saliency of the incumbent's attentiveness to district concerns and the popularity of President Carter. Tufte (1975) has shown that presidential popularity influences the electoral fortunes of members of the president's congressional party, and this analysis clarifies this relationship, at least at the level of the individual. Presidential popularity influences the popularity of members of the president's political party, *but* has no direct impact on the strength of electoral preferences for the incumbent. That is, declining presidential popularity influences the electoral fortunes of incumbents from the president's party by diminishing their popularity in the district.

In contrast, the degree of personal contact a respondent has had with the incumbent and the popularity of Congress have the strongest relationships to the popularity of Republican incumbents. Congressional popularity appears to be a more significant influence on the popularity of Republican incumbents than on Democratic incumbents. Democratic House members, however, do not totally escape their association with Congress since congressional popularity is positively related to the strength of the respondent's electoral preference for the Democratic incumbent—a point explored in the next section (Table 11). Partisanship also appears to have a greater impact on the popularity of Republican incumbents.[10] The importance of party identification in the popularity of Republican incumbents is understandable as most congressional districts contain large numbers of Democratic identifiers.[11] Hence, Republican incumbents are easy targets for partisan attacks and appeals.

Media recognition is also a significant factor in the popularity of both Democratic and Republican incumbents, but the effects of this variable are modest and changeable. Media recognition enhances the image of Democratic incumbents while it diminishes the popularity of Republican incumbents (Table 9). The contrasting effects of media recognition are difficult to explain because such recognition has normally been assumed to be an asset in election campaigns—"to be perceived at all is to be perceived favorably" (Stokes and Miller, 1962: 541). It might be speculated that media recognition may be a symptom of the declining electoral fortunes of an incumbent: Extensive media recognition of the incumbent may indicate that the incumbent's behavior or performance has become a critical issue in the campaign. Similarly, extensive media coverage may suggest that the incumbent is in electoral trouble and needs to boost his/her image by counteracting bad publicity with a pervasive media assault. In short, media recognition of an incumbent may mean that the incumbent's

TABLE 9 Important Predictors of Incumbent Popularity (regression coefficients)

Predictor[a]	Democratic Incumbent Standardized	Democratic Incumbent Unstandardized	Republican Incumbent Standardized	Republican Incumbent Unstandardized
Perceived vote agreement	.604*	.564*	.534*	.475*
Media recognition	−.074*	−.064*	.114*	.099*
Saliency of district attentiveness	−.140*	−.257*	.008	.016
Presidential popularity	.099*	.091*	−.067	−.063
Congressional popularity	.054	.054	.152*	.143*
Personal contact with incumbent	−.049	−.053	−.202*	−.225*
Party identification	.069	.030	−.119*	−.049*
Saliency of incumbent's experience & abilities	−.026	−.051	−.119*	−.202*
Multiple correlation coefficient[b]	.72		.67	
Coefficient of multiple determination	.51		.46	
Standard error	.62		.62	
N=	335		235	

*Statistically significant at .01 level

[a]Descriptions of the variable codes can be found in Appendix II.

[b]The multiple correlation coefficients for explanatory equations that include only the statistically significant variables are .70 (Democratic incumbents) and .67 (Republican incumbents).

Source: American National Election Study, 1978, Center for Political Studies, University of Michigan.

image is suffering. In any event, the effects of media recognition warrant further conceptual clarification and empirical examination.

Perhaps the most interesting difference between Democratic and Republican incumbents relates to the saliency of district attentiveness and personal contact on incumbent popularity. In the case of Democrats, the greater the saliency of the incumbent's attentiveness, the greater the popularity of Democratic incumbents. The popularity of Republican incumbents, in contrast, benefits from personal contact with constituents. This as well as other differences suggest that there may be some partisan variation in how Democratic and Republican House members relate to their constituencies. It has been suggested that the saliency of district attentiveness in constituent evaluations may be a consequence of the emphasis that House members place on district-related activities, rather than the importance of such activity to their constituents (Parker, forthcoming c). Therefore, the saliency of district attentiveness and personal contact in the popularity of Democratic and Republican incumbents may be the result of the *emphasis* that members of the two parties place upon these activities.

The Obey Commission's survey of House incumbents (Commission on Administrative Review, 1977) provides some evidence of this hypothesized, behavioral difference between Democratic and Republican House members. Specifically, Democratic incumbents are more likely than Republican incumbents to cite ombudsman activities, such as helping constituents with problems, as an important function for the House to perform (gamma = .24);[12] Democrats also place greater emphasis on channeling federal funds to the district (gamma = .38).[13] Republican incumbents spend a greater proportion of their time meeting personally with constituents (gamma = −.25), giving speeches and making personal appearances (gamma = −.26), and spending time within the district (gamma = −.31). These differences in Democratic and Republican allocations of time and attention reflect priorities. Democrats feel that legislative responsibilities, such as mobilizing support for legislation (gamma = .29), are important activities, while Republicans attach a similar importance to those activities that provide opportunities for personal contact between the member and constituents.[14]

In sum, the differing impact of various influences on the popularity of Democratic and Republican incumbents may result from the contrasting emphasis that Democratic and Republican members place upon district-related activities. In terms of home styles, we might speculate that Republican incumbents emphasize personal contact because they are members of the minority party and, as such, they are constantly attempting to expand their number of supporters. Republican incumbents may view personal contact as the most effective way of expanding their electoral base. Republican members may reason that "as a result of their direct contact with as many supportive constituents as they can reach, they will also reach a great many more people indirectly" (Fenno, 1978: 237). As members of the majority party, Democratic incumbents confront a different situation; they must protect their existing edge in party loyalties. They may feel that they can accomplish this by promoting constituent awareness of their attention to district matters. Thus, the differences in behavior of Democratic and Republican House members may reflect differing electoral needs and priorities.

THE RELEVANCE OF INCUMBENT POPULARITY TO ELECTORAL SUPPORT

It is my contention here that incumbent popularity is the major factor in electoral support; the data in Table 10 appear to support this proposition. Clearly, the greater the incumbent's popularity, the greater the strength of the electoral preference for the incumbent. There is, however, another explanation for the relationship between incumbent popularity and electoral choice that must be explored: The same forces that influence incumbent popularity may exercise a similar influence on vote choice. That is, the relationship between incumbent popularity and electoral choice may actually be spurious. This analysis reveals that this is not the case; incumbent popularity retains its substantive and statistical significance to electoral choice when entered into a regression equation that includes all variables that influence constituent evaluations of the representative. Even when

TABLE 10 Incumbent Popularity and Strength of Vote Preference

	Evaluation of Incumbent[b]			
Strength of Vote Preference[a]	*Very Good*	*Good*	*Fair*	*Poor*
Democratic Incumbent:				
Strong preference for incumbent	96.5%	65.2%	30.1%	—
Not strong preference for incumbent	2.4	23.2	31.3	29.4
Not strong preference for challenger	—	7.9	25.3	11.8
Strong preference for challenger	1.2	3.7	13.3	58.8
N=	85	164	83	18
		gamma = .77		
Republican Incumbent:				
Strong preference for incumbent	94.2%	66.0%	26.2%	—
Not strong preference for incumbent	3.8	20.6	29.5	7.7
Not strong preference for challenger	—	9.9	31.1	46.2
Strong preference for challenger	1.9	3.5	13.1	46.2
N=	52	141	61	13
		gamma = .76		

[a] This variable combines the individual's preference for the incumbent or challenger with the strength of that preference. Questions: "Who did you vote for? Would you say that your preference for this candidate was strong or not strong?"

[b] Question: "In general, how would you rate the job that your U.S. Representative (name) has been doing?"; the initial coding categories of "poor" and "very poor" have been combined because of the small number of cases contained within these two categories.

statistically insignificant predictors of vote choice are removed from the equation, incumbent popularity continues to be the most important predictor of vote choice (Table 11). Therefore, incumbent popularity appears to be a major force in the electoral success of incumbents running in contested elections.

This argument is not intended to suggest that incumbents are invulnerable. Both Democratic and Republican incumbents appear to have areas of weakness that could be exposed and exploited by challengers. As Table 11 illustrates, Republicans are disadvantaged by their party affiliation, and Democratic incumbents are handicapped by constituent perceptions of their voting records and ideology. These perceptions could be a major worry for Democratic incumbents since they are generally more liberal than their constituents. As Table 12 demonstrates, most constituents are in closer agreement with Republican than with Democratic candidates on a variety of issues.[15] This may help to explain why media recognition of Democratic incumbents is negatively related to vote support: Media cov-

TABLE 11 Important Predictors of Incumbent Electoral Support (regression coefficients)

Predictor	Democratic Incumbent Standardized	Democratic Incumbent Unstandardized	Republican Incumbent Standardized	Republican Incumbent Unstandardized
Incumbent popularity	.420*	.514*	.461*	.519*
Party identification	.110*	.054*	−.228	−.109*
Ideological proximity[a]	.160*	.210*	−.059	−.069
Media recognition	.115*	.127*	−.046	−.046
Congressional popularity	.129*	.147*	.063	.071
Contacted incumbent[b]	−.079	−.046	.122*	.059*
Perceived vote agreement	.214*	.244*	.105	.108
Multiple correlation coefficient[c]	.76		.70	
Coefficient of multiple determination	.58		.49	
Standard error	.70		.69	
N=	163		129	

*Statistically significant at .01 level

[a] This variable is calculated by the following manner:

respondent's ideological placement − respondent's ideological placement of incumbent

[b] Question: "Have you (or anyone in your family living here) ever contacted Representative (name) or anyone in his/her office?"

[c] The multiple correlation coefficients for explanatory equations that include only the statistically significant variables are .75 (Democratic incumbents) and .64 (Republican incumbents).

erage can shed light on the incumbent's voting behavior as well as his or her performance in office. As a result, constituents may become more sensitive to the ideological liberalism of their representative. When the ideological divergence between the Democratic incumbent and constituents is great, electoral support within the district may decline.

IV
SUMMARY

The general lack of constituency awareness of the activities and behavior of their representative enables incumbents to fill this void by disseminating information that places their behavior in a favorable

TABLE 12 Perceived Attitudinal Proximity Between Constituents and Their Representative[a]

Scale:	*Democratic Incumbent*			*Republican Incumbent*		
	Respondent:	*D*[b]	*R*	*Respondent:*	*D*	*R*
Government guarantees that each person has a job	4.6 (723)	3.7 (431)	4.3 (150)	4.8 (494)	3.6 (142)	4.3 (328)
Legal rights of the accused	4.6 (786)	3.8 (409)	4.1 (157)	4.6 (526)	3.7 (133)	4.2 (273)
Improve social and economic position of minorities	4.4 (823)	3.5 (467)	4.1 (173)	4.4 (551)	3.7 (139)	4.0 (293)
Government medical insurance plan	3.7 (740)	3.6 (344)	4.4 (140)	4.0 (515)	3.6 (113)	4.4 (224)
Equal rights for women	2.9 (848)	2.8 (409)	3.3 (164)	3.0 (586)	3.2 (160)	3.4 (279)
Ideology	4.1 (662)	3.6 (419)	4.6 (155)	4.2 (464)	3.6 (149)	4.5 (314)

[a]The figures contained within the table are the mean positions of the respondent on the issue and the respondent's placement of the incumbent and his/her challenger on that issue; the numbers in parentheses are the number of cases upon which the means are based.
[b]Placement of Democratic and Republican congressional candidates on various issues scales.

light. Simply put, constituents are captives to the information they receive regarding the activities and behavior of their representative; further, constituents use this information in evaluating the performance of their congressman. Since the major supplier of information about the representative's performance is the incumbent, the disseminated information directs constituent attention to those aspects of the incumbent's performance that place the House member in a favorable light. As a consequence, what constituents learn about their representatives tends to enhance the incumbent's district popularity and, therefore, his or her electoral support.

This argument tends to be supported by this analysis. The important predictors of incumbent popularity (perceived vote agreement, district attention, personal contact) are theoretically and empirically linked to the home-style behaviors of House members. In addition, differences in the sources of Democratic and Republican popularity

TABLE 13 Importance Representatives Should Assign to Various Activities

Activity	*Mentioned As "Most Important"* *Percent*	*N*
Helping people in the district who have personal problems with the government	12%	254
Making sure the district gets its fair share of government money and projects	17	355
Keeping track of the way government agencies are carrying out laws passed by Congress	17	350
Keeping in touch with the people about what the government is doing	33	683
Working in Congress on bills concerning national issues	21	440
Number of Cases		2082

appear to reflect differences in the district-oriented behavior of these partisans. We have speculated that the partisan differences stem from electoral conditions and legislative orientations. Finally, incumbent popularity is the best predictor of congressional election preferences.[16] Thus, House incumbents are continuously able to withstand electoral challenges because their district-oriented behavior serves as the major channel through which constituents learn about the performance of their representative. As a result, constituents develop favorable assessments of the representative's performance in office, and these serve as an important component in their electoral decisions. Perhaps the Miller-Stokes proposition (1962: 541)—"to be perceived at all is to be perceived favorably"—still contains some truth since what citizens are likely to learn about their representative is apt to be positively toned. It appears, therefore, that the incumbency advantage results from the incumbent's ability to control those aspects of his or her performance that emerge on the consciousness of constituents. Clearly, incumbency is "a resource to be employed, an opportunity to be exploited" (Fenno, 1978: 211) rather than an automatic entitlement to a comfortable election margin.

V
SOME INSTITUTIONAL CONSEQUENCES OF STYLISTIC CHANGES IN DISTRICT BEHAVIOR

The analysis suggests that stylistic change in home styles may have a significant impact on the behavior of House incumbents and the operations of Congress. For instance, House members can be expected to continue their emphasis on constituent contact and communication because there is a widespread popular demand for more information about congressional activity—60% of the public "would like to see more reports about the legislation being considered by, and other activities of Congress" (Commission on Administrative Review, 1977: 853). In addition, constituents believe that "keeping in touch with people about what government is doing" is the most important responsibility of their representative (Table 13). The increased importance of legislator-constituent communication is evident in the fact that mention of this role orientation has more than doubled during the last decade (Table 14).

TABLE 14 Public Prescriptions for the Job of the Congressman

	1968[a]		*1977*	
Role Prescription	*Percent*	*N*	*Percent*	*N*
Tribune	3.9	49	11.8	161
Ritualist	45.5	570	13	176
Inventor	25	313	33	448
Broker	4	50	1.7	23
Mentor-Communicator	9.2	115	24.7	225
Good Person	12.5	156	15.9	216
Number of Responses	1253		1359	

[a]Now, we are interested in what people think about the job of being a Member of the House of Representatives in Washington. As a citizen, how would you describe the job of being a Congressman—what are the most important things you think he should do in Washington?
Source: Louis Harris and Associates, Study #1900, contracted by Roger H. Davidson.

[b]Now, I'd like to ask you what kinds of things you feel it is most important for an individual Congressman to do, not what positions he takes on issues, but what he does in his job. What kinds of jobs, duties, or functions do you expect a good Congressman to perform?
Source: Louis Harris and Associates, contracted by the Commission on Administrative Review, U.S. House of Representatives.

Incumbents seem both well-prepared (in terms of allowances and other office perquisites) and highly motivated to provide their constituents with such information. Constituents are able, therefore, to shift the costs associated with becoming informed about the activities of their representative—the procurement, analysis, and evaluation of information (Downs, 1975: 12), but do so only by sacrificing control over the principles that are used in selecting information for dissemination throughout the districts. As a result, constituents tend to receive and absorb primarily information that enhances the popular image of the incumbent. We can expect, therefore, that House members will continue to shower their constituents with information that focuses constituent attention on activities that place them in a favorable light.

The importance of maintaining a popular image among constituents seems certain to increase the emphasis that members place on district services. The electoral benefits that are derived from attention to district matters provides incumbents with an incentive for concentrating his/her energies on these concerns. The increased amount of time that incumbents are spending in their districts is ample evidence of the importance that House members attach to constituent affairs. Since there are finite limits to the time and energies of members, time spent attending to district matters results in less time being devoted to other legislative responsibilities (Fenno, 1978: Ch. 2). In sum, increased emphasis on district affairs may detract from the attention that incumbents focus on strictly legislative matters.

Finally, incumbents may be able to enjoy some policy maneuverability in Washington as a consequence of drawing constituent attention away from the member's votes and focusing it on the incumbent's attention to the district. We generally think of the policy leeway that constituents grant their representatives in terms of the size of the incumbent's electoral margin. House members who narrowly defeat their opponents in the general election are expected to stay close to district sentiment in their voting behavior; incumbents who sweep through their electoral contests with little trouble, while mounting a large majority, can absorb defections in support that might be generated by voting one's conscience rather than district opinion. Even

TABLE 15 Style of Representation Among the Mass Public and House Members

	Mass Public		*House Members*	
	1968[a]	*1977[b]*	*1963*	*1977*
Style of Representation	*Percent*	*Percent*	*Percent*	*Percent*
Follow Conscience	30.5	22	28	65
Follow District	43.2	46	23	5
Depends On Issue	22.8	27	46	25
Not Sure	3.5	5	3	3
Number of Cases	1534	1531	87	142

[a] When there is a conflict between what a U.S. Representative feels is best and what the people in his district want, do you think he should follow his own conscience or follow what the people in the district want?

[b] When there is a conflict between what your Congressman feels is best and what he thinks the people in the district want, do you think he should follow his own conscience or follow what the people in the district want?

Sources: Commission on Administrative Review, U.S. House of Representatives (1977 data). Louis Harris and Associates, Study #1900, contracted by Roger H. Davidson (1968 data). Roger H. Davidson, *The Role of the Congressman,* p. 117 (1963 data).

congressional leaders consider a member's level of electoral support in assigning members to committees that make controversial decisions on major policy issues. Attention to district affairs may enhance constituent trust; the greater the level of trust, the less likely constituents are to require incumbents to explain their votes, and the more willing they may be to accept their representative's explanations when they are given. The ability of incumbents to have their vote explanations accepted within the district strengthens the member's voting leeway in Washington (Fenno, 1978: 151). Perhaps this explains the increased willingness of incumbents to adhere to their own convictions when they disagree with constituent opinion (Table 15). It appears that "policy responsiveness" (Eulau and Karp, 1977) is a component of representation that most incumbents may be able to safely ignore as a result of their attention to district affairs and their control over the information reaching their constituents.

APPENDIX 1

Indicators of Personal Contact and District Attentiveness	*Factor Loadings*[a] *Contact Dimension*	*Awareness of Attention*	*h2*
Met Representative	.76	.02	.58
Attended a meeting or gathering where Representative spoke	.79	−.05	.62
Talked to a member of the Representative's office staff	.56	.24	.37
Knowledge of people having some contact with Representative	.61	.32	.48
Awareness of Representative's attention to district matters	−.39	−.29	.24
Helpfulness of the Representative in doing something about respondent's problem	.28	.24	.13
Respondent contact with Representative or his/her office	.39	.56	.47
Mention of district attention	−.13	−.70	.51
Received mailing from Representative	−.02	.68	.46
Number of cases: 1002			

[a]Varimax rotation of principal-component analysis.

APPENDIX 2
VARIABLE CATEGORY CODES

1. Incumbent popularity (V245)[a]
   very good (1) good (2) fair (3) poor or very poor (4)
2. Perceived voting agreement (V240)
   agree (1) agree somewhat (2) neither agree or disagree (3) disagree (4)
3. Awareness of any vote cast by incumbent (V241)
   aware of vote (1) not aware of vote (5)
4. Saliency of incumbent's district attentiveness
   mention of attentiveness (1) no mention of attentiveness (0)
5. Mass mailing (V190)
   received mail (1) no mail received (5)
6. Saliency of incumbent's experience
   mention of experience (1) no mention of experience (0)
7. Presidential popularity (V80)
   very good (1) good (2) fair (3) poor (4) very poor (5)
8. Congressional popularity (V85)
   very good (1) good (2) fair (3) poor (4) very poor (5)
9. Party identification (V433)
   SD (0) WD (1) ID (2) I (3) IR (4) WR (5) SR (6)
10. Contacted incumbent (V227)
    yes (1) no (5)
11. Strength of incumbent's electoral support
    strong for incumbent (1) not strong for incumbent (2) not strong for challenger (3) strong preference for challenger (4)

[a]Numbers in parentheses are the variable identification numbers for the 1978 American National Election Study, 1979 edition.

NOTES

1. Incumbents may also attempt to divert constituent attention away from actions that might damage his/her popularity (e.g., recent roll-call votes, policy statements).

2. Question: "Have you (or anyone in your family living here) ever contacted Representative (name) or anyone in (his/her) office?"

3. District attentiveness is a category for classifying respondent "likes" and "dislikes" about the incumbent representative. The category includes mention of personally assisting people in the district, soliciting district opinion, representing those views in Congress, keeping people informed about the operations of government, and helping the district's economy. The codes for this category are 321 to 397.

4. This variable is the difference between a respondent's placement on an ideological scale and his/her perceived placement of the incumbent on an identical scale.

5. Media recognition, itself, may foster positive evaluations of the incumbent's performance (Democratic incumbent, gamma = .17; Republican incumbent, gamma = .25).

6. This is a dichotomous variable that records whether a respondent cited some aspect of the incumbent's attentiveness when asked to recall "anything special that your U.S. Representative (name) has done for this district while (he/she) has been in Congress."

7. In order to insure that the personal contact indicators were not merely another indicator of attentiveness, they were factor analyzed along with the measurement of the saliency of attentiveness, the respondent's ability to recall some aspect of the incumbent's attentiveness, the respondent's perception of the helpfulness of their representative, and whether the respondent had ever contacted his/her representative or received any mass mailing from him or her. A principal-component analysis of these variables, rotated to the varimax criterion, produced two "clean" dimensions (see Appendix 1); the most oblique rotation still produced two dimensions that were modestly correlated (r = .56).

8. This relationship persists when the respondent's knowledge of the majority party in Congress is controlled.

9. The most important predictors were determined on the basis of multiple regression equations that included all of the theoretically identified sources of incumbent popularity. Statistically unreliable influences were then deleted from the equations; generally speaking, variables with regression coefficients that were less than twice their standard errors were removed from the equations.

10. When the sample is *not* partitioned according to whether a Democratic or Republican incumbent is running for reelection in a contested district, party identification appears to have no significant influence (Cain et al., 1979).

11. This pattern is evident in the distributions of party identifiers according to type of race and party affiliation of the incumbent in the Center for Political Studies' National Election Study.

12. Question: "I'd like to begin by asking you a few questions about your views of the role of the House as a whole and its place in our system of government. First, what roles should the House play in the federal government—what do you believe ought to be its one or two most important functions?" House members who mentioned ombudsman activity either first or second in their response to this query were categorized as believing that such activity is an important function of Congress.

13. Question: "Here is a card which lists some of the various activities in which House members have told us that they engage in as part of their jobs. For each of the activities listed, I'd like you to tell me whether you actually spend a great deal of your time on that activity, some of your time, only a little of your time, or hardly any of your time on that activity."

14. Analysis of the actual amount of time that House incumbents spend in their districts reveals that Republicans elected prior to 1970 spend more time in their districts than their Democratic counterparts. Northern Democrats elected *since* 1970 appear to spend as much time in their districts as Republicans elected during the same period.

PARTISAN DIFFERENCES IN ATTENTIVENESS AMONG CONTINUING HOUSE MEMBERS[a]

Congress	*Before 1965*	*1965-1970*	*1971*	*1973*	*1975*
		Republicans			
92nd	28.1 (25)	29.2 (37)	29.1 (9)		
93rd	41.6 (25)	41.4 (37)	38.3 (9)	44.9 (30)	
94th	43.5 (25)	50.1 (37)	47.1 (9)	50.9 (30)	53.0 (16)
		Northern Democrats			
92nd	27.1 (45)	27.6 (22)	33.2 (11)		
93rd	36.6 (45)	36.0 (22)	40.8 (11)	32.0 (12)	
94th	37.6 (45)	43.6 (22)	53.4 (11)	51.8 (12)	50.1 (49)
		Southern Democrats			
92nd	29.0 (35)	32.5 (15)	25.0 (3)		
93rd	34.3 (35)	43.7 (15)	38.7 (3)	40.4 (15)	
94th	39.7 (35)	52.4 (15)	42.0 (3)	50.5 (15)	56.3 (15)

[a]The figures contained within the table represent the mean number of weeks per Congress that House members were present in their congressional districts; the figures in parentheses are the number of cases used in the calculation of the means. For a more elaborate discussion of these data see Parker (forthcoming a).

15. I am indebted to Robert Erikson for bringing this relationship to my attention.

16. The regression results in this article rely on a listwise deletion of cases in determining valid cases for analysis. Similar conclusions emerge when cases are excluded from analysis on a

pairwise basis. A listwise deletion of cases avoids a major problem that occurs in comparing the effects of several variables when cases are eliminated in a pairwise fashion: The resulting statistics may be based upon different sample sizes and, perhaps, different subsets of respondents. This would be a potential problem in this analysis since the number of valid cases for any one explanatory variable ranges from 462 to 812 respondents.

REFERENCES

CAIN, E., J. A. FEREJOHN, and M. P. FIORINA (1979) "What makes legislators in Great Britain and the United States so popular?" Presented at the meeting of the American Political Science Association, Washington D.C.

Commission on Administrative Review, U.S. House of Representatives (1977) Final Report: Survey Materials. H. Doc. 95-272, lst session.

COVER, D. (1977) "One good term deserves another: The advantage of incumbency in congressional elections." American Journal of Political Science 21: 523–542.

DAVIDSON, R. H. (1969) The Role of the Congressman. New York: Pegasus.

______and G. R. PARKER (1972) "Positive support for political institutions: The case of Congress." Western Political Quarterly 25: 600–612.

DOWNS, A. (1957) An Economic Theory of Democracy. New York: Harper & Row.

EULAU, H. and P. D. KARP (1977) "The puzzle of representation: Specifying components of responsiveness." Legislative Studies Quarterly 2: 233–254.

FENNO, R. F., Jr. (1978) Home Style: House Members in Their Districts. Boston: Little, Brown.

______(1975) "If, as Ralph Nader says, Congress is 'the broken branch,' how come we love our Congressmen so much?", pp. 227–287 in N. J. Ornstein (ed.) Congress in Change, New York: Praeger.

FIORINA, M. P. (1977) Congress: Keystone of the Washington Establishment. New Haven, CT: Yale University Press.

MAYHEW, D. (1974) Congress: The Electoral Connection. New Haven, CT: Yale University Press.

PARKER, G. R. (forthcoming a) "Sources of change in congressional district attentiveness." American Journal of Political Science.

______(forthcoming b) "Cycles in congressional district attention." Journal of Politics.

______(forthcoming c) "Can Congress ever be a popular institution?", in J. Cooper and G. C. Mackenzie (eds.) Congress at Work. Austin: University of Texas Press.

______and R. H. DAVIDSON (1979) "Why do Americans love their Congressmen so much more than their Congress?" Legislative Studies Quarterly 4: 53–61.

STOKES, D. E. and W. E. MILLER (1962) "Party government and the saliency of Congress." Public Opinion Quarterly 26: 531–546.

TUFTE, E. R. (1975) "Determinants of the outcomes of midterm congressional elections." American Political Science Review 69: 812–826.

CONTRIBUTORS

ALAN I. ABRAMOWITZ is Assistant Professor of Government at the College of William and Mary. His previous research on congressional elections has been reported in the *Western Political Quarterly* and the *American Political Science Review*. He is currently at work on a study of delegates to state party conventions.

JOSEPH COOPER is Professor of Government and Dean of Faculty of Social Science at Rice University. Coeditor of the series in which this volume appears and of two previous volumes, he has written a number of articles on the Congress and is the author of the monograph *The Origins of the Standing Committees and the Development of the Modern House*.

BARBARA HINCKLEY is Professor of Political Science at the University of Wisconsin—Madison. Her articles on the Congress and congressional elections have been published in a number of scholarly journals, including the *American Political Science Review* and the *British Journal of Politics*. She is author of *The Seniority System In Congress* and *Stability and Change in Congress*.

GARY C. JACOBSON is Associate Professor of Political Science at the University of California, San Diego. He has written a number of articles on various aspects of American elections and is the author of *Money in Congressional Elections* and the coauthor of *American Parties in Decline*.

JOHN P. KATOSH is a Ph.D. candidate in Political Science at the University of Michigan and former assistant study director of the National Election Study. He has published previously in *Public Opinion Quarterly*. His major research interests are American public opinion and electoral behavior.

LOUIS SANDY MAISEL is Associate Professor of Government at Colby College. He has served as Sereis Editor for the Sage Electoral Studies Yearbooks since their inception and has edited and written a number of books and articles on both the Congress and American elections.

THOMAS E. MANN is Executive Director of the American Political Science Association. While working on this article he was codirector of the Congress Project at the American Enterprise Institute. He has written a number of articles on the electoral process and is coeditor of *The New Congress* and author of *Unsafe at Any Margin*.

WARREN E. MILLER is Professor of Government and Director of the Center for Political Studies of the Institute for Social Research at the University of Michigan. Immediate past President of the American Political Science Association, he is author or coauthor of some of the preeminent work in the field of voting behavior including the classic *The American Voter*.

GLENN R. PARKER is Associate Professor of Government at Florida State University. While at work on this article he was a guest scholar at the Brookings Institution. His articles on the Congress and on congressional elections have appeared in many scholarly journals including the *American Journal of Political Science* and the *Journal of Politics*.

RAYMOND E. WOLFINGER is Profesor of Political Science at the University of California, Berkeley. His articles on the Congress and on elections have appeared regularly in scholarly journals including the *American Political Science Review*. He is editor, author, or coauthor of a number of books including *The Politics of Progress* and *Who Votes?*

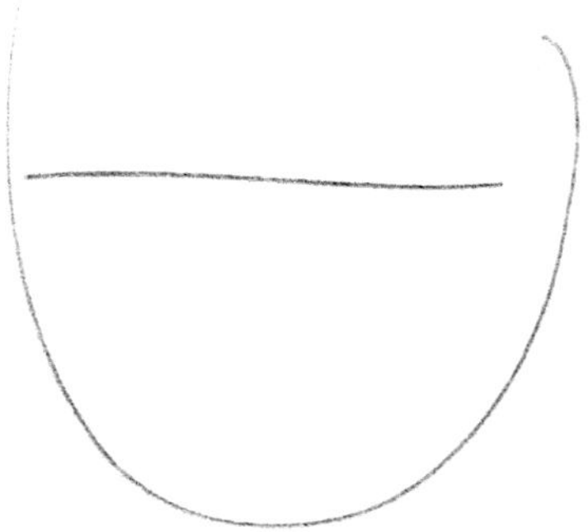